Democracy

Democracy identifies the general processes causing democratization and de-democratization at a national level across the world over the last few hundred years. It singles out integration of trust networks into public politics, insulation of public politics from categorical inequality, and suppression of autonomous coercive power centers as crucial processes. Through analytic narratives and comparisons of multiple regimes, mostly since World War II, this book makes the case for recasting current theories of democracy, democratization, and de-democratization.

Charles Tilly (Ph.D. Harvard, 1958) taught at the University of Delaware, Harvard University, the University of Toronto, the University of Michigan, and the New School for Social Research before becoming Joseph L. Buttenwieser Professor of Social Science at Columbia University. A member of the National Academy of Sciences, the American Philosophical Society, and the American Academy of Arts and Sciences, he has published 50 books and monographs. His recent books from Cambridge University Press include *Dynamics of Contention* (with Doug McAdam and Sidney Tarrow, 2001), *Silence and Voice in the Study of Contentious Politics* (with Ronald Aminzade and others, 2001), *The Politics of Collective Violence* (2003), *Contention and Democracy in Europe, 1650–2000* (2004), and *Trust and Rule* (2005).

Democracy

CHARLES TILLY
Columbia University

CAMBRIDGE
UNIVERSITY PRESS

CAMBRIDGE UNIVERSITY PRESS
Cambridge, New York, Melbourne, Madrid, Cape Town, Singapore,
São Paulo, Delhi, Dubai, Tokyo, Mexico City

Cambridge University Press
32 Avenue of the Americas, New York, NY 10013-2473, USA

www.cambridge.org
Information on this title: www.cambridge.org/9780521701532

First published 2007
8th printing 2009

A catalog record for this publication is available from the British Library.

Library of Congress Cataloging in Publication Data

Tilly, Charles.
Democracy / Charles Tilly.
  p.   cm.
Includes bibliographical references and index.
ISBN-13: 978-0-521-87771-8
ISBN-13: 978-0-521-70153-2 (pbk.)
1. Democracy. I. Title.
JC423.T5 2007
321.8–dc22   2006031969

ISBN 978-0-521-87771-8 Hardback
ISBN 978-0-521-70153-2 Paperback

for Sid Tarrow, intellectual democrat

Contents

Boxes and Figures

Boxes

Figures

Preface

I dared not call this book by its true name: *Democracy, Democratization, De-Democratization, and their Interdependence*. That clunky, cranky title would have driven too many readers away from the book's visibly vital topic. But readers who reach the book's end will, I hope, emerge understanding why it makes no sense simply to describe an ideal political system called democracy and then try to specify conditions under which that system could emerge and survive. Democratization is a dynamic process that always remains incomplete and perpetually runs the risk of reversal – of de-democratization. Closely related processes, moving in opposite directions, produce both democratization and de-democratization. Or so, at least, this book argues at length.

Over long years, the study of democracy, democratization, and de-democratization forced itself on me gradually but inexorably. It grew out of a lifelong effort to explain how the means that ordinary people use to make consequential collective claims – their repertoires of contention – vary and change. Anyone who looks closely at this problem in historical perspective eventually recognizes two facts: first, that undemocratic and democratic regimes feature very different repertoires of contention, indeed that prevailing repertoires help identify a given regime as undemocratic or democratic; second, that as democratization or de-democratization occurs, dramatic alterations of repertoires also occur. Civil wars, for example, concentrate in undemocratic regimes, whereas social movements form almost exclusively in democratic regimes. The correlation is imperfect and contingent, hence more challenging and interesting than would be the case if democracy merely entailed one array of claim-making performances and undemocracy another. Popular struggle affects whether and how democratization comes to pass. This book says how and why.

Perhaps 20 percent of the present text adapts material I have already published in some other form, notably in two previous Cambridge books: *Contention and Democracy in Europe, 1650–2000* (2004), and *Trust and Rule* (2005). Let me defend this wholesale borrowing. In this book the adapted material appears in different contexts that give it substantially new meaning. *Contention and Democracy* used comparative histories of European regimes to demonstrate the interdependence of democratization and popular struggles, whereas *Trust and Rule* analyzed change and variation in connections between interpersonal trust networks and political regimes. Both themes reappear in the present book, now subordinated to a broader question: How, in general, do democratization and de-democratization take place?

This book clarifies and revises some arguments from my earlier publications, especially when it comes to autonomous centers of coercive power and control of public politics over the state as factors in democratization and de-democratization. Although it retains a historical perspective, the book concentrates much more heavily on the recent past and the contemporary world than my previous treatments of democracy. I hope that it will help students of today's struggles over democracy to see the value of historical-comparative analysis in this fraught field. In any case, I regard *Democracy* as the culmination and synthesis of all my work on the subject.

Let me thank five people for their help with this book. I haven't seen my graduate school classmate Raymond Gastil for decades, but he pioneered the Freedom House ratings on which chapter after chapter of the book relies as proxies for the more direct measurement of democratization and de-democratization that my arguments imply. My frequent collaborator Sidney Tarrow did not read the manuscript, but his constant questioning of related ideas in our joint and separate publications has kept me alert to the dangers lurking in concepts such as regime, state capacity, and democracy itself. Viviana Zelizer has once again cast her discerning non-specialist eye over the entire text, drawing my attention forcefully to obscurities and infelicities. Finally, two sympathetic but demanding anonymous readers for Cambridge University Press have required me to clarify and/or defend a number of the book's concepts and arguments, to your benefit and mine.

What Is Democracy?

In 1996, five years after Kazakhstan broke away from the crumbling Soviet Union, Kazakh president Nursultan Nazarbayev had his counselors draft a new constitution. A nationwide referendum for its approval received overwhelming support. The new constitution's very first article declares that:

1. The Republic of Kazakstan [sic] proclaims itself a democratic, secular, legal and social state whose highest values are an individual, his life, rights and freedoms.
2. The fundamental principles of the activity of the Republic are public concord and political stability, economic development for the benefit of all the nation; Kazakstan patriotism and resolution of the most important issues of the affairs of state by democratic methods including voting at an all-nation referendum or in the Parliament. (Kazakh Constitution 2006)

That prominent mention of "public concord and political stability" calls up the image of a vigorously vigilant ruler rather than a standoffish state. Nevertheless, the constitution explicitly calls Kazakhstan a democracy.

Outside observers dispute Kazakhstan's claim. The New York–based democracy-monitoring organization Freedom House annually assigns every recognized country in the world ratings from 1 (high) to 7 (low) on both political rights and civil liberties (Gastil 1991). Box 1-1 sums up the Freedom House criteria. They cover a wide range of citizen's rights and liberties, from institutionalized opposition to personal freedom. In 2005, the Freedom House report gave Kazakhstan a 6 (very low) on political

BOX 1-1. Freedom House Checklist for Political Rights and Civil Liberties (Adapted from Karatnycky 2000: 583–585.)

Political Rights

1. Is the head of state and/or head of government or other chief authority elected through free and fair elections?

2. Are the legislative representatives elected through free and fair elections?

3. Are there fair electoral laws, equal campaigning opportunities, fair polling, and honest tabulations of ballots?

4. Are the voters able to endow their freely elected representatives with real power?

5. Do the people have the right to organize in different political parties or other competitive political groupings of their choice and is the system open to the rise and fall of these competing parties or groupings?

6. Is there a significant opposition vote, de facto opposition power, and a realistic possibility for the opposition to increase its support or gain power through elections?

7. Are the people free from domination by the military, foreign powers, totalitarian parties, religious hierarchies, economic oligarchies, or any other powerful group?

8. Do cultural, ethnic, religious, and other minority groups have reasonable self-determination, self-government, autonomy, or participation through informal consensus in the decision-making process?

9. (Discretionary) In traditional monarchies that have no parties or electoral process, does the system provide for consultation with the people, encourage discussion of policy, and allow the right to petition the ruler?

10. (Discretionary) Is the government or occupying power deliberately changing the ethnic composition of a country or territory so as to destroy a culture or tip the political balance in favor of another group?

Civil Liberties

1. Is there freedom of assembly, demonstration, and open public discussion?

2. Is there freedom of political or quasi-political organization, including political parties, civic organizations, ad hoc issue groups, and so on?

3. Are there free trade unions and peasant organizations or equivalents and is there effective collective bargaining? Are there free professional and other private organizations?

4. Is there an independent judiciary?

5. Does the rule of law prevail in civil and criminal matters? Is the population treated equally under the law? Are police under direct civilian control?

6. Is there protection from political terror, unjustified imprisonment, exile, or torture, whether by groups that support or oppose the system? Is there freedom from war and insurgencies?

7. Is there freedom from extreme government indifference and corruption?

8. Is there open and free private discussion?

9. Is there personal autonomy? Does the state control travel, choice of residence, or choice of employment? Is there freedom from indoctrination and excessive dependency on the state?

10. Are property rights secure? Do citizens have the right to establish private businesses? Is private business activity unduly influenced by government officials, the security forces, or organized crime?

11. Are there personal social freedoms, including gender equality, choice of marriage partners, and size of family?

12. Is there equality of opportunity, including freedom from exploitation by or dependency on landlords, employers, union leaders, bureaucrats, or other types of obstacles to a share of legitimate economic gains?

---

rights and a 5 (almost as low) on civil liberties. It called the country "not free." Here is how the country report began:

Political parties loyal to President Nursultan Nazarbayev continued to dominate parliament following the September 2004 legislative elections, which were criticized by international monitors for failing to meet basic democratic standards. Only one opposition deputy was elected, although he refused to take his seat in protest over the flawed nature of the polls. Meanwhile, the resignations of key senior officials raised questions about internal power struggles and dissension within Nazarbayev's government. (Freedom House Kazakhstan 2005)

Although Kazakhstan's involvement in the international economy and international politics kept Nazarbayev from the sort of blatant public authoritarianism adopted by his Central Asian neighbors (Schatz 2006), it did not keep him from ruthless manipulation of the governmental apparatus to his own advantage. In December 2005, Nazarbayev won a third six-year presidential term with a fantastic 91 percent of the vote. Whenever we see presidential candidates winning election – and especially re-election – by majorities greater than 75 percent, we should entertain the hypothesis that the regime is conducting sham elections.

First secretary of Kazakhstan's Communist Party under Soviet rule, Nazarbayev became Kazakh president as the country moved toward independence in 1991. From that point onward, he consolidated his autocratic power and his family's control over the country's expanding revenues from vast gas and oil deposits. As his clique grew richer, the rest of the country grew poorer (Olcott 2002, chapter 6). Nazarbayev tolerated no serious opposition from the press, civic associations, or political parties. He regularly jailed potential rivals, even among his political and economic collaborators, on charges of corruption, abuse of power, or immorality. Thugs said to work for the state frequently assaulted or murdered dissident politicians and journalists. (We begin to see why Nazarbayev's 1996 referendum did so well.)

All these conditions continued into 2006. In February of that year, a well-organized hit squad murdered Kazakh opposition leader Altynbeck Sarsenbaev and his driver-bodyguard. It soon turned out that five members of an elite unit within the intelligence service KNB (successor to the Soviet KGB) had kidnapped Sarsenbaev, and a former officer of the same unit had killed him. A top Senate administrative official admitted to organizing the abduction and murder, but opposition groups called him a scapegoat for members of even higher levels of the government. Oraz Jandosov, collaborator with Sarsenbaev in the broad opposition front For a Just Kazakhstan (FJK) declared it "impossible" that the Senate official had acted on his own initiative. According to the news magazine *Economist*,

Instead, FJK says it believes the murder was ordered by senior government officials and has called on the interior ministry to broaden its investigation. It wants it to interrogate other public figures, including both the president's eldest daughter, Dariga Nazarbaeva, a member of parliament who had a legal dispute with Mr. Sarsenbaev, and her husband, Rakhat Aliev, who is first deputy foreign minister. Mr. Aliev has called the allegations "vile lies." (*Economist* 2006: 40)

Many Kazakhs see son-in-law and media magnate Aliev as Nazarbayev's hand-picked successor for the presidency. (As of 2006, Nazarbayev was scheduled to end his final presidential term in 2012, at the age of 71.) After the FJK staged a large, illegal demonstration in the Kazakh capital on 26 February to protest the government's inaction on the case, a court sentenced 11 FJK leaders to prison terms. Despite its sonorous self-description, Kazakhstan does not qualify as a democracy in any usual sense of the word.

For a revealing contrast with Kazakhstan, look at Jamaica. Jamaica's legislature adopted a constitution, approved by the United Kingdom's government, shortly before the country became independent in 1962. Unlike the resounding start of Kazakhstan's constitution, the Jamaican document begins with numerous legal definitions, plus details of the transition from colony to independent state. Not until Chapter III – Fundamental Rights and Freedoms – does the constitution begin democracy talk. At that point it stipulates:

Whereas every person in Jamaica is entitled to the fundamental rights and freedoms of the individual, that is to say, has the right, whatever his race, place of origin, political opinions, colour, creed or sex, but subject to respect for the rights and freedoms of others and for the public interest, to each and all of the following, namely a. life, liberty, security of the person, the enjoyment of property and the protection of the law; b. freedom of conscience, of expression and of peaceful assembly and association; and c. respect for his private and family life. (Jamaica Constitution 2006)

Later sections describe familiar features in many of the world's democratic regimes: powerful parliament, executive branch responsible to parliament, competitive elections, and formally independent judiciary. Even as a British colony, Jamaica shone as an example of small-scale democracy (Sheller 2000). Jamaica still stands out from the bulk of parliamentary democracies (but resembles many other former British colonies) by having ultimate executive power formally vested in a governor-general appointed by and representing the British crown. On paper, at least, Jamaica looks more or less democratic.

Freedom House again raises some doubts. True, the 2005 country report (based on performance during the previous year) observed that "Citizens of Jamaica are able to change their government democratically" (Freedom House Jamaica 2005). It gave Jamaica a 2 (quite high) for political rights and a 3 (fairly high) for civil liberties while calling the country "free." But it attached a downward arrow to those ratings and began its description of the previous year's record in these terms:

Jamaica continued to suffer from rampant crime, high levels of unemployment, and a lack of investment in social development in 2004. The government's failure to fully extend the rule of law over its police force was evidenced by a five-year record of failure to successfully prosecute any officers on charges of extrajudicial killings, despite the force's having one of the highest per capita rates of police killings in the world. Meanwhile, a contentious succession struggle wracked the country's main opposition party. (Freedom House Jamaica 2005)

The report went on to describe voter fraud, widespread violence against women, police persecution of homosexuals, politically linked gangs, and criminality fueled by Jamaica's importance as a transit point for cocaine en route to the United States (see also Amnesty International 2001, Human

Rights Watch 2004). Jamaica's businesses suffer widespread protection rackets and property crimes. A 2002 United Nations survey of four hundred Jamaican firms found that two-thirds of all firms reported being victims of at least one property crime during 2001. Smaller firms suffered more from extortion, fraud, robbery, burglary, and arson than large ones (World Bank 2004: 89–90). If Jamaica qualifies as a democracy, it certainly counts as a troubled one.

How *should* we decide whether Kazakhstan, Jamaica, or any other country qualifies as a democracy? The question sounds innocent, but it has serious consequences. At stake is the political standing of regimes across the world, the quality of people's lives within those regimes, and the explanation of democratization.

1. **Political standing:** Far beyond Freedom House, power holders of all sorts must know whether they are dealing with democracies or other sorts of regimes. They must know because two centuries of international political experience tell them that democracies behave differently from the rest. They meet or break their commitments differently, make war differently, respond differently to external interventions, and so on. These differences should and do affect international relations: how alliances form, who wars against whom, which countries receive foreign investment or major loans, and so on.

2. **Quality of life:** Democracy is a good in itself, since to some degree it gives a regime's population collective power to determine its own fate. On the whole, it rescues ordinary people from both the tyranny and the mayhem that have prevailed in most political regimes. Under most circumstances, furthermore, it delivers better living conditions, at least when it comes to such matters as access to education, medical care, and legal protection.

3. **Explanation:** Democratization only occurs under rare social conditions, but has profound effects on the lives of citizens; how can we identify and explain both the development of democracy and its impacts on collective life? If people define democracy and democratization mistakenly, they will botch international relations, baffle explanation, and thereby reduce people's chances for better lives.

The book you are starting to read devotes much more attention to the third problem than to the first two. Although it gives some attention to international relations and treats democracy's substantive effects in passing, it concentrates on description and explanation: How and why do democracies form? Why do they sometimes disappear? More generally, what causes whole countries to democratize or de-democratize? Taking the entire world and a great deal of human history into its scope, this book presents a systematic analysis of the processes that generate democratic regimes. It seeks to explain variation and change in the extent and character of democracy over large blocks of human experience. It asks what difference the extent and character of democracy make to the quality of public life. It takes democracy seriously.

Definitions of Democracy

To take democracy seriously, we must know what we are talking about. Developing a precise definition of democracy is particularly important when trying – as we are here – to describe and explain variation and change in the extent and character of democracy.

Observers of democracy and democratization generally choose, implicitly or explicitly, among four main types of definitions: constitutional, substantive, procedural, and process-oriented (Andrews and Chapman 1995, Collier and Levitsky 1997, Held 1996, Inkeles 1991, O'Donnell 1999, Ortega Ortiz 2001, Schmitter and Karl 1991). A *constitutional approach* concentrates on laws a regime enacts concerning political activity. Thus we can look across history and recognize differences among oligarchies, monarchies, republics, and a number of other types by means of contrasting legal arrangements. Within democracies, furthermore, we can distinguish between constitutional monarchies, presidential systems, and parliament-centered arrangements, not to mention such variations as federal versus unitary structures. For large historical comparisons, constitutional criteria have many advantages, especially the relative visibility of constitutional forms. As the cases of Kazakhstan and Jamaica show, however, large discrepancies between announced principles and daily practices often make constitutions misleading.

Substantive approaches focus on the conditions of life and politics a given regime promotes: Does this regime promote human welfare, individual freedom, security, equity, social equality, public deliberation, and peaceful conflict resolution? If so, we might be inclined to call it democratic regardless of how its constitution reads. Two troubles follow immediately, however, from any such definitional strategy. First, how do we handle tradeoffs among these estimable principles? If a given regime is desperately poor but its citizens enjoy rough equality, should we think of it as more democratic than a fairly prosperous but fiercely unequal regime?

Second, focusing on the possible outcomes of politics undercuts any effort to learn whether some political arrangements – including democracy – promote more desirable substantive outcomes than other political arrangements. What if we actually want to know under what conditions and how regimes promote human welfare, individual freedom, security, equity, social equality, public deliberation, and peaceful conflict resolution? Later we will discuss in depth how whether a regime is democratic affects the quality of public and private life.

Advocates of *procedural definitions* single out a narrow range of governmental practices to determine whether a regime qualifies as democratic. Most procedural observers center their attention on elections, asking whether genuinely competitive elections engaging large numbers of citizens regularly produce changes in governmental personnel and policy. If elections remain a non-competitive sham and an occasion for smashing governmental opponents as in Kazakhstan, procedural analysts reject them as criteria for democracy. But if they actually cause significant governmental changes, they signal the procedural presence of democracy. (In principle one could add or substitute other consultative procedures such as referenda, recall, petition, and even opinion polls, but in practice procedural analysts focus overwhelmingly on elections.)

Freedom House evaluations incorporate some substantive judgments about the extent to which a given country's citizens enjoy political rights and civil liberties. But when it comes to judging whether a country is an "electoral democracy," Freedom House looks for mainly procedural elements:

1. A competitive, multiparty political system
2. Universal adult suffrage for all citizens (with exceptions for restrictions that states may legitimately place on citizens for criminal offenses)
3. Regularly contested elections conducted in conditions of ballot secrecy, reasonable ballot security, and in the absence of massive voter fraud that yields results that are unrepresentative of the public will
4. Significant public access of major political parties to the electorate through the media and through generally open political campaigning (Piano and Puddington 2004: 716)

According to these criteria, in 2004 Kazakhstan failed to qualify procedurally as an electoral democracy, but Jamaica, despite its documented assaults on democratic freedoms, made the grade. Here, then, is the trouble with procedural definitions of democracy, democratization, and de-democratization: despite their crisp convenience, they work with an extremely thin conception of the political processes involved.

Process-oriented approaches to democracy differ significantly from constitutional, substantive, and procedural accounts. They identify some minimum set of processes that must be continuously in motion for a situation to qualify as democratic. In a classic statement, Robert Dahl stipulates five process-oriented criteria for democracy. Speaking first of how they might work in a voluntary association, he proposes:

Effective participation. Before a policy is adopted by the association, all the members must have equal and effective opportunities for making their views known to the other members as to what the policy should be.

Voting equality. When the moment arrives at which the decision about the policy will finally be made, every member must have an equal and effective opportunity to vote, and all votes must be counted as equal.

Enlightened understanding. Within reasonable limits as to time, each member must have equal and effective opportunities for learning about the relevant alternative policies and their likely consequences.

Control of the agenda. The members must have the exclusive opportunity to decide how and, if they choose, what matters are to be placed on the agenda. Thus the democratic process required by the three preceding criteria is never closed. The policies of the association are always open to change by the members, if they so choose.

Inclusion of adults. All, or at any rate most, adult permanent residents should have the full rights of citizens that are implied by the first four criteria. Before the twentieth century this criterion was unacceptable to most advocates of democracy. (Dahl 1998: 37–38)

The final standard – inclusion of adults – ironically rules out many cases that political philosophers have regularly taken as great historical models for democracy: Greek and Roman polities, Viking crews, village assemblies, and some city-states. All of them built their political deliberations by means of massive exclusion, most notably of women, slaves, and paupers. Inclusion of all (or almost all) adults basically restricts political democracy to the last few centuries.

Notice how Dahl's criteria differ from constitutional, substantive, and procedural standards for democracy. Although those of us who have attended endless meetings of voluntary associations can easily imagine the bylaws of such an association, Dahl himself specifies no constitutional forms or provisions. He carefully avoids building social prerequisites or consequences into the definition; even "enlightened understanding" refers to experience within the organization rather than prerequisites or consequences. Finally, Dahl's criteria do include the procedure of equal voting with equal counts, but the list as a whole describes how the association works, not what techniques it adopts to accomplish its goals. It describes an interlocking set of political processes.

When Dahl moves from local associations to national regimes, he holds on to his process-oriented insights, but shifts to talk of institutions. Institutions, for Dahl, consist of practices that endure. The sort of regime that Dahl calls a "polyarchal democracy" installs six distinctive institutions: elected officials; free, fair, and frequent elections; freedom of expression; alternative sources of information; associational autonomy; and inclusive citizenship (Dahl 1998: 85, Dahl 2005: 188–189). Once again, the procedure of voting appears on the list. But taken together Dahl's criteria for polyarchal democracy describe a working process, a series of regularized interactions among citizens and officials. These go far beyond the usual procedural standards.

Yet there is a catch. Basically, Dahl provides us with a static yes-no checklist: if a regime operates all six institutions, it counts as a democracy. If it lacks any of them, or some of them aren't really working, it doesn't count as a democracy. For an annual count of which regimes are in or out, such an approach can do the job even if critics raise questions about whether elections in such places as Jamaica are free and fair. Suppose, however, that we want to use process-oriented standards more ambitiously. We do not want merely to count the democratic house at a single point in time. Instead, we want to do two more demanding things: first, to compare regimes with regard to how democratic they are; second, to follow individual regimes through time, observing when and how they become more or less democratic.

Like Freedom House raters of relative political rights and civil liberties, we can reasonably ask whether some regimes rank higher or lower than others, if only to see whether those rankings correlate with other factors such as national wealth, population size, recency of independence, or geographic location. If we want insight into causes and effects of democratization or de-democratization, we have no choice but to recognize them as continuous processes rather than simple steps across a threshold in one direction or the other. In short, for purposes of comparison and explanation, we must move from a yes-no checklist to a list of crucial variables.

Most of Dahl's standard democratic institutions – elected officials; free, fair, and frequent elections; freedom of expression; alternative sources of information; associational autonomy; and inclusive citizenship – lend themselves awkwardly to comparison and explanation. We might, of course, ask *how* free, fair, and frequent elections are, and so on down the list. But the more we do so, the more we will recognize two draw-backs of Dahl's criteria when it comes to the work at hand:

1. Together, they describe a minimum package of democratic institutions, not a set of continuous variables; they do not help much if we are asking whether Canada is more democratic than the United States, or whether the United States became less democratic last year.

2. Each of them operates within significant limits, beyond which some of them conflict with each other; working democracies often have to adjudicate deep conflicts, for example, between freedom of expression and associational autonomy. Should a democracy muzzle animal rights organizations because they advocate attacks on associations that hold dog shows or support animal experimentation?

Furthermore, the autonomy of powerful elitist, racist, sexist, or hate-mongering associations regularly undermines the inclusiveness of citizenship. Should a democracy let well-financed pressure groups drive punitive anti-immigrant legislation through the legislature? To enter fully into comparison and explanation, we will have to improve on Dahl's criteria while remaining faithful to their process-oriented spirit.

Elements of Democracy, Democratization, and De-Democratization

How can we move ahead? Before identifying process-oriented criteria for democracy, democratization, and de-democratization, let us clarify what we have to explain. In order to do so, it will help to simplify radically. Later we can return to complications that our first take on the problem ignores. Let us adopt three simple ideas.

First, we start with a state, an organization that controls the major concentration of coercive means within a substantial territory, exercises priority in some regards over all other organizations operating within the same territory, and receives acknowledgment of that priority from other organizations, including states, outside the territory. You begin to see the complications: what about federal systems, civil wars, warlord-dominated enclaves, and rival factions within the state? For the time being, nevertheless, we can pose the problem of democracy more clearly by assuming a single, fairly unitary state.

Second, we lump everyone who lives under that state's jurisdiction into a catchall category: citizens. Again complications immediately come to mind: what about tourists, transnational corporations, members of the underground economy, and expatriates? Soon I will point out that most historical regimes have lacked full-fledged citizenship, which plays a crucial part in democracy. But for a start, calling everyone who lives under a given state's jurisdiction a citizen of that state will clarify what we have to explain. Democracy will then turn out to be a certain class of relations between states and citizens, and democratization and de-democratization will consist of changes in those sorts of relations.

Dahl's principles already imply such a step; even associational autonomy, for example, depends on state backing of associations' right to exist rather than the sheer presence of many, many associations. For the moment, let us call a set of relations between states and citizens a *regime*, with the understanding that later on we will complicate that idea by including relations among major political actors (parties, corporations, labor unions, organized ethnic groups, patron-client networks, warlords, and more) in regimes as well.

In the meantime, notice that the second step breaks sharply with a common (and at first glance appealing) notion. It rejects the widespread idea that if only existing holders of power agree on how they want a regime to operate they can decide on democracy as a more attractive – or less disagreeable – alternative to existing political arrangements. In this view, workers, peasants, minorities, and other citizens might cause enough trouble to make some concessions to representation and inclusion less costly to elites than continuing repression, but the citizenry at large plays only a marginal role in the actual fashioning of democratic politics. Such a view underlies the policy of exporting democracy from the United States or the European Union by making attractive deals with national leaders – or, for that matter, by coercing leaders to adopt democratic institutions. On the contrary, this book's explanations of democratization (and of de-democratization as well) center on the state-citizen struggle. Even a conquering military power such as the western Allies in Japan and Germany after World War II must bargain extensively with citizens to create a new democratic regime where authoritarians previously ruled.

Third, let us narrow our analytic range to public politics, not including all transactions, however personal or impersonal, between states and citizens but only those that visibly engage state power and performance. Public politics includes elections, voter registration, legislative activity, patenting, tax collection, military conscription, group application for pensions, and many other transactions to which states are parties. It also includes collective contention in the form of coups d'état, revolutions, social movements, and civil wars. It excludes, however, most personal interactions among citizens, among state officials, or between state officials and citizens.

Some of public politics consists of *consulting* citizens about their opinions, needs, and demands. Consultation includes any public means by which citizens voice their collective preferences concerning state personnel and policies. In relatively democratic regimes, competitive elections certainly give citizens a voice, but so do lobbying, petitioning, referenda, social movements, and opinion polling. This time the missing complications are obvious: bribes, patron-client chains, favors to constituents and followers, kinship connections among officials, and similar phenomena blur the boundary between public and private politics. What is more, we will soon discover that we can't make sense of public politics by focusing on citizen-state interactions alone, but must examine coalitions, rivalries, and confrontations among major political actors outside of the state as well. Later I will insist that prevailing non-state forms of power strongly affect the possibility of democratization. Again we can pay attention to the complications once we have the problem under control. For the moment, we scrutinize public political interactions between states and citizens for signs of democracy, democratization, and de-democratization.

What do we look for in these interactions? One more simplification can guide us. Judging the degree of democracy, we assess the extent to which the state behaves in conformity to the expressed demands of its citizens. Gauging democratization and de-democratization, we assess the extent to which that conformity is increasing or decreasing. So doing, we set aside venerable alternatives in democratic theory. We do not ask whether the state is enhancing its citizens' welfare, whether it behaves in accordance with its own laws, or even whether ordinary people control the levers of political power. (Later, we can of course ask whether democratization thus understood enhances popular welfare, entails the rule of law, or depends on citizens' direct empowerment.)

Judging conformity of a state's behavior to its citizens' expressed demands necessarily involves four further judgments: how wide a range of citizens' expressed demands come into play; how equally different groups of citizens experience a translation of their demands into state behavior; to what extent the expression of demands itself receives the state's political protection; and how much the process of translation commits both sides, citizens and state. Call these elements breadth, equality, protection, and mutually binding consultation.

In this simplified perspective, *a regime is democratic to the degree that political relations between the state and its citizens feature broad, equal, protected and mutually binding consultation.* Democratization means net movement toward broader, more equal, more protected, and more binding consultation. De-democratization, obviously, then means net movement toward narrower, more unequal, less protected, and less binding consultation. In Germany, we can reasonably say that the formation of the Weimar Republic in the German Empire's ruins after World War I introduced a measure of democratization, whereas Hitler's seizure of power in 1933 pushed the country brutally back into de-democratization. In Japan, we can reasonably treat the buildup of militarized state power during the 1930s as a time of de-democratization while treating the period of Allied conquest, occupation, and reconstruction as the start of democratization.

The terms *broad, equal, protected,* and *mutually binding* identify four partly independent dimensions of variation among regimes. Here are rough descriptions of the four dimensions:

1. **Breadth:** From only a small segment of the population enjoying extensive rights, the rest being largely excluded from public politics, to very wide political inclusion of people under the state's jurisdiction (at one extreme, every household has its own distinctive relation to the state, but only a few households have full rights of citizenship; at the other, all adult citizens belong to the same homogeneous category of citizenship)
2. **Equality:** From great inequality among and within categories of citizens to extensive equality in both regards (at one extreme, ethnic categories fall into a well-defined rank order with very unequal rights and obligations; at the other, ethnicity has no significant connection with political rights or obligations and largely equal rights prevail between native-born and naturalized citizens)

Together, high levels of breadth and equality comprise the crucial aspects of citizenship: instead of a mosaic of variable relations to the state depending on particular group memberships, all citizens fall into a limited number of categories – at the limit, just one – whose members maintain similar rights and obligations in their interactions with the state. By themselves, breadth and equality do not constitute democracy. Authoritarian regimes have often imposed undemocratic forms of citizenship from the top down. But in the company of protection and mutually binding consultation, breadth and equality qualify as essential components of democracy.

3. **Protection:** From little to much protection against the state's arbitrary action (at one extreme, state agents constantly use their power to punish personal enemies and reward their friends; at the other, all citizens enjoy publicly visible due process)
4. **Mutually binding consultation:** From non-binding and/or extremely asymmetrical to mutually binding (at one extreme, seekers of state benefits must bribe, cajole, threaten, or use third-party influence to get anything at all; at the other, state agents have clear, enforceable obligations to deliver benefits by category of recipient)

Net movement of a regime toward the higher ends of the four dimensions qualifies as democratization. Net movement toward the lower ends qualifies as de-democratization. When Freedom House put downward arrows on Jamaica's political rights and civil liberties ratings for 2004, it was warning that Jamaica ran the risk of de-democratizing. In terms of our four dimensions, it called special attention to Jamaica's increases of inequality and decreases of protection.

In later discussions, we will sometimes focus on breadth, equality, protection, or mutually binding consultation separately. Analyses of citizenship, for example, will naturally focus on breadth and equality. Most of the time, however, we will sum up average location on the four dimensions as a single variable: degree of democracy. Likewise, we will treat democratization as an average movement upward on the four dimensions, de-democratization as an average movement downward on the four dimensions. That strategy simplifies the analysis greatly. It takes advantage of the fact that locations on one dimension correlate roughly with locations on another dimension; regimes that offer extensive protection, in general, also establish broad categories of citizenship rather than treating each person or small group of citizens differently.

State Capacity and Regime Variation

So far I have purposely omitted an important feature of regimes: the state's capacity to enforce its political decisions. No democracy can work if the state lacks the capacity to supervise democratic decision making and put its results into practice. This is most obvious for protection. A very weak state may proclaim the principle of shielding citizens from harassment by state agents, but can do little about harassment when it occurs. Very high-capacity states run the opposite risk: that decision making by state agents acquires enough weight to overwhelm mutually binding consultation between government and citizens.

State capacity has already entered our discussion indirectly. Some of the Freedom House political rights and civil liberties, for example, would mean nothing without substantial state backing. Note the following:

PR # 3: Are there fair electoral laws, equal campaigning opportunities, fair polling, and honest tabulations of ballots?

PR # 4: Are the voters able to endow their freely elected representatives with real power?

CL # 5: Does the rule of law prevail in civil and criminal matters? Is the population treated equally under the law? Are police under direct civilian control?

CL # 10: Are property rights secure? Do citizens have the right to establish private businesses? Is private business activity unduly influenced by government officials, the security forces, or organized crime? (Karatnycky 2000: 583–585)

We see Freedom House evaluators trying to find a middle ground between too little and too much state capacity, on the implicit assumption that either one hinders political rights and civil liberties. This assumption generalizes that extremely high and extremely low state capacity both inhibit democracy.

State capacity means *the extent to which interventions of state agents in existing non-state resources, activities, and interpersonal connections alter existing distributions of those resources, activities, and interpersonal connections as well as relations among those distributions.* (State-directed redistribution of wealth, for example, almost inevitably involves not only a redistribution of resources across the population but also a change in the connection between the geographic distributions of wealth and population.) In a high-capacity regime, by this standard, whenever state agents act, their actions affect citizens' resources, activities, and interpersonal connections significantly. In a low-capacity regime, state agents have much narrower effects no matter how hard they try to change things.

We have already glimpsed the variability of state capacity in Kazakhstan and Jamaica. In Kazakhstan, as elsewhere in the disintegrating Soviet Union, state capacity diminished sharply during the turmoil of 1986 to 1991. But soon after Kazakhstan's independence (1991), Nazarbayev began related campaigns to expand the state's power and his personal power within the state. Non-state enterprises, the independent press, and private associations soon felt the weight of an increasingly demanding and interventionist state. Jamaica moved in the opposite direction. Human Rights observers worried openly that the Jamaican state had lost control over its own police, not to mention armed gangs and drug runners.

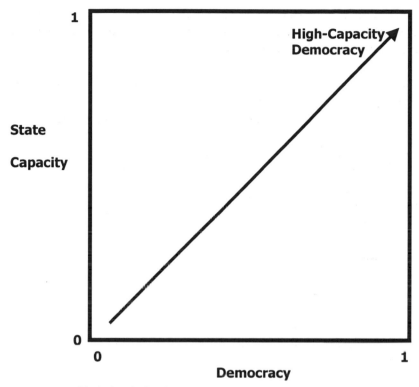

FIGURE 1-1. Variation in Regimes

Neither case marks the extreme. At the high-capacity end, Nazarbayev's Kazakhstan deploys nothing like the power to shift resources, activities, and interpersonal connections exercised by today's Chinese state. At the low-capacity end, shattered Somalia makes the Jamaican state look like a behemoth.

We begin to see the value of distinguishing capacity from democracy before relating them analytically. Clearly capacity can range from extremely high to extremely low independently of how democratic a regime is, and democracy can appear in regimes that vary markedly with regard to state capacity. Figure 1-1 schematizes the field of variation. It identifies some distinctly different zones of political life marked by varying combinations of capacity and democracy.

On the vertical axis, state capacity varies from 0 (minimum) to 1 (maximum). Although we could think of capacity in absolute terms, for comparative purposes it helps more to scale it against the histories of all states that have actually existed within a given era. Over the period since 1900, for example, the dimension might run from Somalia or Congo-Kinshasa in 2006 (minimum) to colossal Nazi Germany on the eve of World War II (maximum). On the horizontal axis, we find the familiar range from minimum democracy at 0 (for which the authoritarian rule of Stalin's Russia might be a candidate) to maximum democracy at 1 (for which today's Norway would certainly be in the running).

For many purposes, another radical simplification will aid our attempt to describe and explain variation in regimes. Figure 1-2 identifies the four crude regime types implied by our more general map of regimes. It reduces the space to four types of regime: low-capacity undemocratic, high-capacity undemocratic, high-capacity democratic, and low-capacity democratic. Examples of each type in the diagram include:

High-capacity undemocratic: Kazakhstan, Iran
Low-capacity undemocratic: Somalia, Congo-Kinshasa
High-capacity democratic: Norway, Japan
Low-capacity democratic: Jamaica, Belgium

Over human history regimes have distributed very unevenly across the types. The great bulk of historical regimes have fallen into the low-capacity undemocratic sector. Many of the biggest and most powerful, however, have dwelt in the high-capacity undemocratic sector. High-capacity democratic regimes have been rare and mostly recent. Low-capacity democratic regimes have remained few and far between.

Over the long run of human history, then, the vast majority of regimes have been undemocratic; democratic regimes are rare, contingent, recent creations. Partial democracies have, it is true, formed intermittently at a local scale, for example in villages ruled by councils incorporating most heads of household. At the scale of a city-state, a warlord's domain, or a regional federation, forms of government have run from dynastic hegemony to oligarchy, with narrow, unequal citizenship or none at all; little or no binding consultation; and uncertain protection from arbitrary governmental action.

Before the 19th century, furthermore, large states and empires generally managed by means of indirect rule: systems in which the central power received tribute, cooperation, and guarantees of compliance on the part of subject populations from regional power holders who enjoyed great autonomy within their own domains. Even in supposedly absolutist France, for example, great nobles only started to lose their regional power during the later 17th century, when Louis XIV undertook a sustained (and ultimately successful) effort to replace them with government-appointed

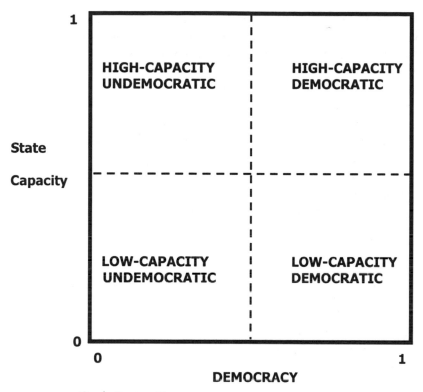

FIGURE 1-2. Crude Regime Types

and removable regional administrators. Before then, great lords ran their domains like princes and often took up arms against the French crown itself.

Seen from the bottom, such systems often imposed tyranny on ordinary people. Seen from the top, however, they lacked capacity; the intermediaries supplied soldiers, goods, and money to rulers, but their autonomous privileges also set stringent limits to rulers' ability to govern or transform the world within their presumed jurisdictions.

Only the 19th century brought widespread adoption of direct rule: creation of structures extending governmental communication and control continuously from central institutions to individual localities or even to households, and back again. Creation of direct rule commonly included such measures as uniform tax codes, large-scale postal services, professional civil services, and national military conscription. Even then, direct rule ranged from the unitary hierarchies of centralized monarchy to the segmentation of federalism. On a large scale, direct rule made substantial citizenship, and therefore democracy, possible. Possible, but not likely, much less inevitable: instruments of direct rule have sustained many oligarchies, some autocracies, a number of party- and army-controlled states, and a few fascist tyrannies. Even in the era of direct rule most regimes have remained far from democratic.

Location in one or another of the four quadrants makes a powerful difference to the character of a regime's public politics (Tilly 2006). For elaboration later in the book, here are some preliminary descriptions of the kinds of politics that prevail in each quadrant:

High-capacity undemocratic: Little public voice except as elicited by the state; extensive involvement of state security forces in any public politics; regime change either through struggle at the top or mass rebellion from the bottom

Low-capacity undemocratic: Warlords, ethnic blocs, and religious mobilization; frequent violent struggle including civil wars; multiple political actors including criminals deploying lethal force

High-capacity democratic: Frequent social movements, interest group activity, and political party mobilizations; formal consultations (including competitive elections) as high points of political activity; widespread state monitoring of public politics combined with relatively low levels of political violence

Low-capacity democratic: As in high-capacity democratic regimes, frequent social movements, interest group activity, and political party mobilizations plus formal consultations (including competitive elections) as high points of political activity, but less effective state monitoring, higher involvement of semi-legal and illegal actors in public politics, and substantially higher levels of lethal violence in public politics

These are, of course, "on average" descriptions. Within the high-capacity undemocratic quadrant, for example, we find some regimes whose states' monitoring and intervention extend throughout the whole territory and population; Iran fits the description. But we also notice others in which the state has nearly the same control as Iran over its central territory but has edges or enclaves that largely escape control; Morocco, with authoritarian rule in its main territory but a long-running civil war with independence-minded Polisario forces in the former Spanish Sahara, belongs to this subset of regimes.

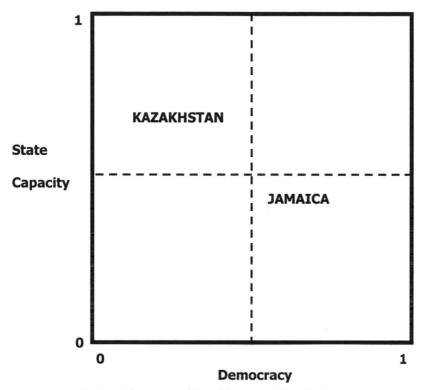

FIGURE 1-3. Regime Placement of Kazahkstan and Jamaica in 2006

Where, then, do our test cases of Kazakhstan and Jamaica fall within regime space? During its few years of exiting from the Soviet Union, Kazakhstan dropped a bit in capacity and edged a bit toward democracy. By the time Nazarbayev had consolidated his family's power in the later 1990s, however, Kazakhstan operated as a high-capacity, low-democracy regime. Jamaica has fluctuated more since its 1962 independence, but the state has never acquired substantial capacity and the regime as a whole has never quite fallen from the ranks of democracy. When considering the recent past, we can place Jamaica high in the opposite quadrant from Kazakhstan: low to middling state capacity combined with precarious democracy. Figure 1-3 places Kazakhstan and Jamaica on the diagram of the four crude regime types.

The placement of two regimes at a single point in time only starts our work. Still, by themselves Kazakhstan and Jamaica in the recent past allow us to identify the sorts of questions that arise in the remainder of this book:

- Considering that competing nomadic hordes, but no centralized state, existed in the territory now occupied by Kazakhstan until the Russian empire started consolidating its rule during the 19th century, by what path and how did the current high-capacity undemocratic regime come into existence?
- Under what conditions and how could Kazakhstan 1) drop into the low-capacity undemocratic quadrant, as several of its Central Asian neighbors have, and 2) move firmly into democratic territory?
- How did the model democratic colony of Jamaica, based on Westminster-style public politics that prevailed before Jamaica's independence, become the troubled sovereign democracy of today?
- What would it take for Jamaica to drop out of democratic ranks entirely, abandon its social movement politics, and thus become even more vulnerable to warlords, ethnic blocs, religious mobilization, frequent violent struggle including civil wars, and multiple actors including criminals deploying lethal force?
- What would it take, on the contrary, for Jamaica to become a high-capacity democracy, with frequent social movements, interest group activity, political party mobilizations, formal consultations (including competitive elections) as high points of political activity, and widespread state monitoring of public politics combined with relatively low levels of political violence?

Imagine asking questions of this sort, not just about Kazakhstan and Jamaica, but about any regime that happens to interest you anywhere, at any point in time. The point is to build a general account of change and variation in regimes on the way to describing paths that lead toward and away from democracy.

When I say "general account," let me state clearly what I do and do not mean. I do mean to identify a set of explanations for democratization and de-democratization that apply equally to Kazakhstan, Jamaica, and a wide variety of other regimes, past and present. I do *not*, however, mean to propose a general law, a unique trajectory, or a single set of necessary and sufficient conditions for democratization and its reversals.

As an alternative, I argue that democratization and de-democratization depend on some recurrent causal mechanisms that compound into a small number of necessary processes. By *mechanisms*, I mean events that produce the same immediate effects over a wide range of circumstances. As we move into concrete cases of democratization, for example, we will frequently encounter the mechanism of coalition formation: creation of a new form of coordination between previously autonomous political actors. A new coalition does not in itself produce democratization, but it often contributes to moves toward democracy by connecting political actors who have interests in democratic outcomes and who had not been coordinating their efforts up until that point.

By *processes*, I mean combinations and sequences of mechanisms that produce some specified outcome. Democratization and de-democratization are themselves very large processes, but within them we will often discern smaller processes such as upward scale shift, in which the level of coordination among different sites or actors rises (Tarrow and McAdam 2005).

In addition to the master processes of democratization and de-democratization, this book looks hard at the processes by which state capacity increases or decreases, generalizing the process by which Kazakhstan recovered from its weakening as the Soviet Union disintegrated and the opposite process by which the Jamaican state lost control over many activities within its purview after independence. It shows how democratization and de-democratization interact with changing state capacity. After putting more preliminaries into place, the book organizes its main explanations of democratization and de-democratization around three central clusters of changes:

1. Increase or decrease of integration between interpersonal networks of trust (e.g., kinship, religious membership, and relationships within trades) and public politics
2. Increase or decrease in the insulation from public politics of the major categorical inequalities (e.g., gender, race, ethnicity, religion, class, caste) around which citizens organize their daily lives
3. Increase or decrease in the autonomy of major power centers (especially those wielding significant coercive means) such as warlords, patron-client chains, armies, and religious institutions with respect to public politics

The fundamental processes promoting democratization in all times and places, the argument runs, consist of increasing integration of trust networks into public politics, increasing insulation of public politics from categorical inequality, and decreasing autonomy of major power centers from public politics.

But detailed explanations come later. This chapter has stuck mainly to description, with only wisps of explanation. Later chapters introduce explanatory elements step by step: relationships between democracy and trust, democracy and inequality, and democracy and autonomous power clusters. We will eventually see how much more contingency, negotiation, struggle, and adjustment go into democratic politics than the simple identification of breadth, equality, protection, and mutually binding consultation, as democratic essentials suggest. We will also see that democratization and de-democratization occur continuously, with no guarantee of an end point in either direction.

First we need to clarify what we have to explain. We will close in slowly on detailed explanations, first looking at the long run of democracy in hope of identifying conditions that commonly accompany its expansion or contraction, then systematically asking what produces such conditions, then moving on to a discussion of the recurrent processes that drive democratization and de-democratization, and finally specifying the causes, effects, and consequences of these recurrent processes in greater detail. Chapter 2 sketches the place of democracy and democratization in the long history of mostly undemocratic regimes. Chapter 3 then proceeds to look more specifically at the processes of democratization and de-democratization. Chapters 4, 5, and 6 take up trust, inequality, and major power configurations separately as phenomena whose changes and intersections with public politics shape the possibility of democratization and de-democratization.

Chapter 7 applies the lessons of Chapters 4–6 to the alternative trajectories (for example, out of high-capacity and out of low-capacity undemocratic regimes) that lead to democracy or its opposite. Chapter 8 draws conclusions from the book as a whole, including speculations concerning the future of democracy. Because working democracies display some of humanity's finest political accomplishments and because democracy remains threatened throughout much of the contemporary world, we are engaged in a search of the greatest urgency.

2

Democracy in History

As I longer told us long ago, violence visibly bathed the lives and imaginations of citizens in classical Greece. My onetime collaborator, the irrepressibly witty political scientist Samuel Finer, phrased it this way: "Competitive, acquisitive, envious, violent, quarrelsome, greedy, quick, intelligent, ingenious – the Greeks had all the defects of their qualities. They were troublesome subjects, fractious citizens, and arrogant and exacting masters" (Finer 1997, I: 326). Among other forms of violence, the region's city-states warred repeatedly against one another.

In 431 BCE, nevertheless, a delegation went from Sparta to Athens in the name of peace. All the Athenians needed to do to avoid war, the Spartan delegates declared, was to stop interfering militarily and economically with Sparta's allies in the region. Athens' citizens held a general assembly to debate their response to Sparta's challenge. Advocates both of immediate war and of peacemaking concessions spoke to the assembly. But Pericles, son of Xanthippus, carried the day. Pericles (rightly thinking that in case of war the Spartans would invade Athenian territory by land) recommended preparation for a naval war and reinforcement of the city's defenses, but no actual military action until and unless the Spartans attacked.

Thucydides, the first great Greek historian to work on contemporary events using contemporary sources, transcribed Pericles' speech. Thucydides concluded the episode with these words:

Such were the words of Pericles. The Athenians, persuaded of the wisdom of his advice, voted as he desired, and answered the Lacedaemonians [Spartans] as he recommended, both on the separate points and in the general; they would do nothing on dictation, but were ready to have the complaints settled in a fair and impartial manner by the legal method, which the terms of the truce prescribed. So the envoys departed home, and did not return again. (Thucydides 1934: 83)

Sparta's ally Thebes soon attacked Athens' tributary territories, and the Second (Great) Peloponnesian War began. Formally, it lasted just ten years, until the Peace of Nicias (421). But counting its sequels the war did not really stop until Sparta and its allies conquered Athens in 404. Remember the comedy Lysistrata? Its plot centers on the campaign of Athenian women to end the long war with Sparta by refusing to have sex with their husbands. The great Athenian dramatist Aristophanes produced his play in 411 BCE.

Western histories of democracy typically start with the extraordinary politics of these same bellicose Greek city-states between about 500 and 300 BCE. Each city-state had its own distinctive history and institutions. Yet broadly speaking all of them balanced power among three elements: a central executive, an oligarchic council, and a general assembly of citizens. Athens in the time of Pericles had long since displaced kings from its central executive in favor of short-term offices filled by lot or (in the rare cases of specialized skills and military emergency) election. Wealthy lineages dominated the great trading city's councils, but all citizens had the right to voice in general assemblies. As in the story of Pericles' great speech, those assemblies decided matters of deep importance to the Athenian state.

Before we rush to identify Greek city-states as the original democracies, however, we should reflect on a fundamental fact: around half of Athens' population consisted of slaves. Slaves had no citizenship rights whatsoever; citizens owned them as chattel, and mediated any connections slaves had with the Athenian state. Nor did resident foreigners or wives and children of citizens qualify as citizens. Only free adult males could hold citizenship. Slaves nevertheless played critical parts in the Athenian polity; their labor freed slave-owning citizens to participate in public politics. Even if Athenians sometimes called their polity a *demokratia* (rule by the people), the massive presence of slaves raises doubts as to whether 21st-century students of democracy ought to include Greek city-states of the fifth and fourth centuries BCE in their subject matter.

Two features of those regimes do argue for placing them among the ancestors of modern democracies. First, they created a model of citizenship that had no known predecessors. Of course old lineages and the rich enjoyed political advantages in these city-states. In the sovereign assembly, however, every citizen however patrician or parvenu, rich or not so rich, had a voice and a roughly equal relationship to the state. Second, these regimes generally rotated civic responsibilities very widely. Athens even filled its magistracies by lot for one-year terms rather than by election or inheritance. Within the citizenry, then, the principle of equal rights and equal obligations prevailed.

The case *against* calling these regimes full-fledged democracies, however, eventually gains overwhelming weight. In these city-states, did relations between the state and its citizens feature broad, equal, protected, mutually binding consultation? If we narrow our attention to the free adult males who then qualified as citizens, the answer is probably yes; this is why so many historians have considered the Greeks to have invented democracy. But if we consider the whole population under the state's jurisdiction – women, children, slaves, the many resident foreigners – the answer becomes emphatically no. After all, inequality pervaded the city-state political system as a whole. Athenian arrangements excluded the great bulk of the population from protected, mutually binding consultation. Nor did republican Rome perform democratically by these standards.

Which regimes did perform democratically, how, and why? As a preface to explanations of democratization and de-democratization in later chapters, this chapter surveys where and when democratic regimes multiplied. It notes some patterns of change and variation in democratic forms for further explanation. It makes the case for Western Europe and North America during the later 18th century as crucial staging areas for democratic regimes at a national scale. But mostly it clarifies what we must explain: how, over the centuries, democracy rose, fell, and varied in character.

Between 300 BCE and the 19th century CE, a number of European regimes adopted variants on the Greek model: privileged minorities of relatively equal citizens dominated their states at the expense of excluded majorities. In their days of republican government (that is, when some tyrant had not seized power), such commercial city-states as Venice, Florence, and Milan all lived on the labor of excluded, subordinate classes. After the turmoil of Florence's politics had excluded him from his previous career as official and diplomat in 1512, Niccolò Machiavelli began to write the great analyses of politics that still make his work required reading today. His *Discourses* ostensibly consider the constitutions of classical Rome, but actually range widely over the Italian politics of his own time.

Gesturing back to a tradition for which the Athenian Aristotle laid some of the foundations, Machiavelli conceded that many authors before

him had distinguished three main types of government: monarchy, aristocracy, and democracy. They had, furthermore, often seen monarchy as
disintegrating into tyranny, aristocracy into oligarchy, and democracy into
"licentiousness" (Machiavelli 1940: 111–112). But, according to Machiavelli, the best constitutions balanced the three elements – prince, aristocracy, and people – under a common constitution. Legendary lawgiver
Lycurgus bestowed just such a constitution on long-surviving Sparta,
while equally legendary Athenian lawgiver Solon made the mistake of
establishing popular government alone.

Nevertheless, following his interpretation of Greek and Roman
regimes, Machiavelli eventually made the case for a choice between just
two models: a principality in which the ruler governs with support of
an aristocracy and pacifies the populace with good works (an idealized
picture of Florence under the more benign of the Medici) and a republic
in which the aristocracy actually rules, but appoints an executive power
and deals judiciously with the common people (an idealized picture of the
republican Florence he had long served before his exile).

What was Machiavelli describing? Italian city-states lacked slaves, but
they strikingly resembled Greek city-states in other regards. Although
the capital cities themselves commonly instituted general assemblies of
property-holding adult males, they rarely consulted them except in emergencies. Small proportions of all adult males qualified as full-fledged citizen members of governing councils, and even fewer could hold major
offices. All city-states governed tributary areas from which they drew revenue but to which they granted no political rights. As a matter of course,
women, children, and servants likewise lacked political standing. Whether
principalities or republics, they fell far short of broad, equal, protected,
mutually binding consultation.

Nor, up to this time, had democratic regimes existed at a national scale
elsewhere in Europe or anywhere else on earth. Europe pioneered democracy in two ways: by creating the distinctive, if restrictive, institutions of
citizenship we can witness in Greek and Italian city-states and eventually
by battling toward broad, equal, protected, mutually binding consultation. But only the 18th century brought significant steps in that direction,
only the 19th century established partial democracies in Western Europe
and its settler colonies, and only the 20th century saw the extension of
something like full citizenship to many European women.

At this point, many readers will no doubt complain that such a position
is Eurocentric, modernist, both, or worse. Well outside of Western Europe,
what about the simple democracies of pastoralists, hunter-gatherers,

subsistence peasants, fisherfolk, and warrior bands? Leaving aside the subordinate position of women in the political lives of almost all such communities, let me declare at once: some elements of democracy existed at small scales across the world well before the 18th century. Taken separately, some forms of broad participation, rough equality, binding consultation, and (more rarely) protection have sometimes governed local and regional politics. On all inhabited continents, councils of lineage heads occasionally met to make momentous collective decisions in rough equality for millennia before glimmers of democracy appeared in Europe. If, under the heading of democracy, all we are looking for is negotiated consent to collective decisions, democracy extends back into the mists of history.

But here I must again insist on the questions this book is pursuing: Under what conditions and how do relations between states and the populations subject to their rule become more – or, for that matter, less – broad, equal, protective, and consultative? At a national scale, how do democratization and de-democratization occur? How do they affect the quality of political life? For those questions, the bulk of the relevant experience comes first from western countries and their settler colonies during the 19th century, spreading across the world during the 20th and 21st centuries. Democracy is a modern phenomenon.

Precursors of Democracy

Within European experience before the 19th century, four main sorts of settings most dramatically assembled elements of broad, equal, protected, mutually binding consultation: 1) merchant oligarchies, 2) peasant communities, 3) religious sects, and 4) revolutionary moments. Italian city-states constituted early examples of an urban genre that flourished until the 18th century. Although (like their counterparts in Italian city-states) Dutch burghers drew their wealth from the labor of disfranchised urbanites as well as peasants and artisans in tributary areas, they commonly formed corps of citizens who rotated offices, manned the night watch, ran the guilds, and met in assemblies to deliberate the city's political decisions. Throughout mercantile Europe, urban oligarchies engaged in simulations of democracy (te Brake 1998, Mauro 1990, Tilly and Blockmans 1994). But they remained oligarchies. In fact, they never became explicit models for national government above the scale of the city-state (Prak 1999).

Some European peasant communities formed what lovers of oxymoron could call *plebeian oligarchies*. They practiced rotation of posts through election or lot, well-defended rights of participation, general assemblies with binding power, and judicial procedures for reviewing wrongs to individuals or the community (Barber 1974; Blickle 1997; Cerutti, Descimon, and Prak 1995; Luebke 1997; Sahlins 2004, Wells 1995). But almost universally the citizens in question consisted of either all adult males or all property-holding adult males within the central community. Once again, furthermore, peasant communities often controlled tributary areas and populations in which no citizenship existed.

Highland Switzerland generally conformed to those patterns. In a book he dares to call *Early Modern Democracy in the Grisons*, Randolph Head describes village practices in the Swiss canton variously known as Graubünden, Grisons, Grigioni, or the Rhaetian Freestate:

> Every viable political entity must reach legitimate decisions – ones accepted by a preponderance of its members – and must distribute benefits and burdens in a predictable way. The village and political communes of the Rhaetian Freestate developed distinctive (though by no means unique) solutions for these tasks: legitimate decisions were those reached by a majority of the assembled male members, and political goods were distributed proportionally among the membership, either by dividing them when possible, or else by rotating access to them among eligible members. These two principles reflected both the social practice and the conceptual principles of late medieval village communes. In practice, the village was a group of cultivators, each of whom worked his own land under collective management. The fact that most material benefits from the commune were divided among the members rather than being held in common reflected this. Conceptually, though, the village commune was an association of equal members. This equality was expressed in the duty of all members to participate in village assemblies and to share in public burdens. (Head 1995: 74)

In these villages, men who owned farms (and, occasionally, their widows) qualified as citizens. Hired hands, servants, and children need not apply. Europe's many rural variants on this pattern fell far short of broad, equal, protected, mutually binding consultation.

Some religious sects, especially those in pietist and primitive Christian traditions, practiced a sort of democracy within their congregations. Whether they pooled property or not, members treated each other as equals, rotated responsibility for parish affairs, subjected their conduct to community discipline, and organized general assemblies to make collective decisions (MacCulloch 2003). In the Nordic countries, religious congregations blossomed with associations that operated more or less democratically and became nuclei for reformist movements long before ordinary people had much right to associate elsewhere in Europe; church-backed associations then became models for secular action as well (Lundqvist 1977; Öhngren 1974; Seip 1974, 1981; Stenius 1987;

Wåhlin 1986). It seems likely that the prevalence of such reformist associations in 18th-century Norway, Denmark, Sweden, and Finland set the
background for the precocious development of social movements and
democratic institutions in the North.

Well before the 18th century, Europe's revolutionary mobilizations
(especially those tinged with pietist and primitive Christian traditions)
sometimes broadcast visions of collective consent and radical egalitari-
anism. In England, although neither Catholics nor Anglicans tended to
warm themselves at democratic fires, a variety of dissenting Protestants,
including Quakers and Congregationalists, pressed for egalitarian programs. Some called for rule by a parliament elected through manhood
suffrage. Quakers went a step beyond by instituting rough equality of
women and men within their congregations.

Inside Oliver Cromwell's revolutionary New Model Army, radicals
established representation by elected men tellingly called Agitators. During the great Putney debates of the army's General Council (October–
November 1647), Cromwell's son-in-law Henry Ireton defended the case
for authoritarian control in the face of emergency. Colonel Thomas Rain-
borough replied to Ireton's challenge in strikingly democratic, if still very
masculine, terms:

Really I think that the poorest he that is in England hath a life to live as the greatest
he; and therefore truly, sir, I think it's clear, that every man that is to live under a
government ought first by his own consent to put himself under that government;
and I do think that the poorest man in England is not at all bound in a strict
sense to that government that he hath not had a voice to put himself under. And
I...doubt whether he was an Englishman or no that should doubt of these things.
(Gentles 1992: 209)

At the same time Levellers in the army and in London were circulating a
radical call for a written constitution, an Agreement of the People. The
Agreement included electoral redistribution of parliamentary seats in proportion to population, biennial parliamentary elections, and supremacy
of the Commons (Gentles 2001: 150). Levellers claimed to speak for the
English people. But, of course, they lost.

A century or so later, democratic revolutionaries were starting to win.
The American Revolution (1765–1783) began with resistance to royal
taxes and commercial controls imposed by the British crown in an attempt
to redress some of its massive financial losses during the Seven Years
War (1756–1763). But, organizing especially around the theme of no taxation without representation, American revolutionaries soon turned to

democratic programs. They not only organized Committees of Correspondence linking resistance to arbitrary British power across the colonies, but they demanded rights of representation from the King and the Parliament. What is more, opponents of arbitrary rule within Great Britain itself, such as Thomas Paine and John Wilkes, joined their cause. They began articulating doctrines of popular sovereignty (Brewer 1980, Morgan 1988, Tilly 1995, chapter 4).

During the later 18th century, we also see the emergence of concerted demands for broad participation in Dutch local and provincial government. R. R. Palmer's influential *Age of the Democratic Revolution* (1959, 1964) bracketed the Dutch Patriot Revolt of the 1780s with the American Revolution as significant representatives of the democratic-revolutionary current. Dutch forces joined indirectly in the wars of the American Revolution, taking a severe beating from superior British naval power. As the disastrous naval engagements continued, a sort of pamphlet war broke out within the Netherlands. Supporters of the Prince of Orange attacked the leaders of Amsterdam and its province Holland as the opposing Patriots (based especially in Holland) replied in kind; each blamed the other for the country's parlous condition.

Drawing explicitly on the American example, Patriots called for a (preferably peaceful) revolution. During the 1780s petition campaigns began in earnest: first demanding recognition of John Adams as a legal representative of that contested entity, the United States of America, then proposing remedies to a whole series of domestic political problems. Citizens' committees (possibly modeled on American committees of correspondence) soon began to form along with citizens' militias across Holland's towns. In a highly segmented political system, their incessant pressure on local and regional authorities actually worked.

Between 1784 and 1787, Patriot factions managed to install new, less aristocratic constitutions in a number of Dutch cities, and even in a whole province, Overijssel. The Prince of Orange and his followers, however, still disposed of two crucial advantages: British financial support and military backing from the Prince's brother-in-law, King Frederick William of Prussia. Late in 1787, a Prussian invasion broke the Dutch Patriot Revolution (te Brake 1989, 1990; Schama 1977).

After France declared war on Britain and the Netherlands in 1793, Francophile Patriots revived their opposition. A French invasion of 1795 installed the so-called Batavian Republic, in which an elected national assembly ruled from 1796 to 1798, until a French army coup drove out the radical democrats. From then to the end of the Napoleonic Wars, the Netherlands operated first as a nominally independent kingdom under

Napoleon's brother Louis, then as an integral region of an undemocratic France. Although American democrats won, Dutch democrats lost. Serious democratization did not begin again in the Netherlands until the 19th century.

French Democratization and De-Democratization, 1600–2006

Dutch experience between the 1780s and the 1830s teaches an important lesson. Even during its recent history, democracy has been a precarious and reversible form of rule. To see the recency, precariousness, and reversibility of democracy, we might inspect the history of France since 1600. Here I can draw on a lifetime's work in French political history (especially Shorter and Tilly 1974; Tilly 1964, 1986, 1993, chapter 5, 2004, chapter 4). France offers a fascinating challenge to common explanations of democratization and de-democratization. It emphatically refutes any notion of democratization as a gradual, deliberated, irreversible process or as a handy set of political inventions a people simply locks into place when it is ready. On the contrary, it displays the crucial importance of struggle and shock for both democracy and its reversals.

Following the North American and Dutch revolutions of the previous two decades, the early French Revolution (1789–1793) established one of history's most influential models of national democratic government. In an Athenian gesture that Machiavelli might well have deplored, the early revolutionaries replaced the sovereign king and his council with a parliament elected by citizens at large. Only through vast experimentation and struggle, including civil wars, did they work their way back to a central executive, with Napoleon's rise to power from 1799 onward its culmination (Woloch 1970, 1994). Under Napoleon's rule, moreover, democracy declined as state capacity rose.

By no means did Napoleon's authoritarian regime bring the end of struggles and reversals. (For compact summaries of French constitutional regimes and elections, see Caramani 2000: 292–373, 2003: 146–148.) During the 19th century, France not only returned to the (more or less constitutional) Restoration and July monarchies from 1815 to 1848, but then underwent another democratic revolution before moving back into an authoritarian regime (1851–1870) under Louis Napoleon Bonaparte. A relatively peaceful and relatively democratic revolution (1870) preceded a year of struggle with and within the Communes of Paris and other major cities.

The Communes bring us only to the halfway point between the great revolution of the 1790s and the French regime we know today. A

long-lived Third Republic (relatively democratic except for the exclusion
of women) took shape during the 1870s and lasted until the Nazi occupation of 1940. Not until the conclusion of major postwar struggles (1944–
1947), however, did contemporary France's more or less continuously
democratic regime lock into place. Finally (1945) women acquired the
rights to vote and hold elective office in France. (Even then we might consider the fierce Algerian civil war of 1954–1962 and Charles de Gaulle's
war-induced return to power in 1958 to count as a democratic reces-
sion, and think of the vast mobilizations against de Gaulle in 1968 as yet
another crisis of democracy.) Depending on how we count lesser reversals,
between 1789 and the present, France underwent at least four substantial
periods of democratization, but also at least three substantial periods of
de-democratization.

Let us return to our capacity-democracy regime space for greater clar-
ity. By *democracy*, we still mean the extent to which the regime features
broad, equal, protected, binding consultation of citizens with respect to
state actions. By *state capacity*, we still mean the extent to which interventions of state agents in existing non-state resources, activities, and
interpersonal connections alter existing distributions of those resources,
activities, and interpersonal connections as well as relations among those
distributions. In these terms, Figure 2-1 traces France's complex trajectory from 1600 to the present. Despite its many turns, the graph actually
simplifies greatly, in ways that bear on the rest of our analysis. Take, for
example, the middle of the 17th century. At 1600 the graph properly por-
trays France at a low point of both democracy and state capacity as it
emerged shattered from the 16th century's titanic Wars of Religion. Precious little breadth, equality, protection, mutually binding consultation,
or state capacity existed in the battered kingdom. Capacity then recovered
somewhat under aggressive kings, with no move toward anything faintly
resembling democracy for the bulk of French people.

The period from 1648 to 1653 brought a France that had partly recovered from anarchy under kings Henry IV and Louis XIII back into the
same anarchic zone of low capacity and minimal democracy. The civil
wars of the Fronde split France repeatedly. The young Louis XIV and his
advisors only started to regain control of vast regions during the mid-
1650s, and managed to subdue large areas of Protestant autonomy within
the self-declared Catholic state beginning in the 1680s.

It will not help us much to follow every squiggle and turn of French
political history from 1600 to the present. Here are the main messages to
draw from the diagram:

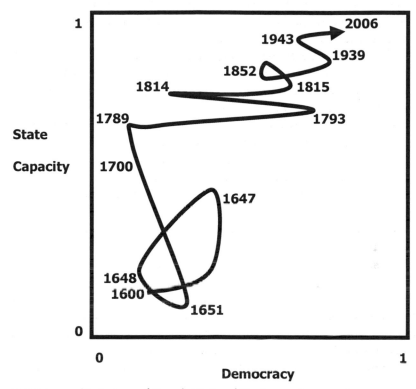

FIGURE 2-1. Trajectory of French National Regimes, 1600–2006

- Over the first half of the 17th century the French regime stayed entirely out of democratic territory but gained and lost capacity at a dizzying pace.
- Only when the king and his close allies were able to subdue or buy off their largely autonomous rivals within the country did state capacity increase significantly; rebellions and demands led by regional magnates repeatedly reversed the growth of capacity.
- During the second half of the same century the consolidating rule of Louis XIV built up capacity enormously, at the expense of an even greater retreat from anything resembling democracy; regional power holders and enclaves lost autonomy massively.
- No major change of direction occurred until the Revolution of 1789, when France began an extraordinary experiment with democratic forms.

- Soon, however, revolutionaries' efforts to combat both domestic and foreign enemies led to a new buildup of capacity at the expense of democracy.
- From the end of the Napoleonic Wars (1814) to the end of World War II, the country veered constantly between spurts of democratization and de-democratization; state capacity usually headed upward in either phase.
- During the postwar period, France built a high-capacity democratic state that (at least so far) does not seem to be reversing its direction significantly.

A high-capacity democratic state? Compared to Jamaica and Kazakhstan, the contemporary French state exercises significantly more control over the people, resources, and activities within its territory. Despite – or rather because of – incessant struggle over rights and obligations, French citizens exercise fairly broad and equal rights vis-à-vis the state. They exercise extensive citizenship. Through elections, polls, the press, social movements, and direct contact with officials, they engage in mutually binding consultation over matters of public politics. Although French citizens often complain about "insecurity," on the whole they receive far more protection from arbitrary state action than their Jamaican and (especially) their Kazakh counterparts. Those institutions only came into being through two centuries of conflict-filled changes in French public politics.

Box 2-1 provides another look at the same set of changes. I have counted as a "revolutionary situation" every juncture in French history from 1648 to the present in which some group bearing arms and receiving support from substantial groups of citizens controlled major national regions and/or significant segments of the state apparatus for a month or more. (A revolutionary *outcome*, in this perspective, involves an actual transfer of power from existing rulers to a new ruling bloc.) The chronology adds an element that was missing in my earlier account: repeated rebellions up to the scale of revolutionary situations arose in reaction to Louis XIV's ultimately successful expansion of state capacity during the latter half of the 17th century.

Much of the royal effort during that half-century went into raising new taxes to support the central administrative apparatus and, especially, its pursuit of war. Major rebellions typically began with scattered resistance to taxation, but then consolidated into much more sustained opposition under the leadership of regional power holders. The fierce Camisard rebellions of 1702 to 1706 marked an exception: they resulted from Louis XIV's

---

BOX 2-1. Revolutionary Situations within Metropolitan France,
1648–2006

1648–1653	The Fronde
1655–1657	Tardanizat Rebellion (Guyenne)
1658	Sabotiers Rebellion (Sologne)
1661–1662	Bénauge Rebellion (Guyenne)
1662	Lustucru Rebellion (Boulonnais)
1663	Audijos Rebellion (Gascony)
1663–1672	Angelets guerrilla warfare (Roussillon)
1675	Papier Timbré, Bonnets Rouges (or Torrében) rebellions (Brittany)
1702–1706	Camisard rebellions of Cévennes and Languedoc
1768–1769	Corsican Rebellion
1789–1799	Multiple French revolutions and counter-revolutions
1815	Hundred Days
1830	July Revolution
1848	French Revolution
1851	Louis Napoleon *coup d'état*, insurrection
1870	State collapse, German occupation, republican revolutions
1870–1871	Multiple Communes
1944–1945	Resistance and Liberation

---

attempt to stamp out Protestant pockets of faith and autonomy. In either case, the king and his increasingly formidable military forces fed state capacity by driving down resistance to central rule. By the 18th century's start, the French crown had become Europe's mightiest.

Nonetheless, fully revolutionary situations continued into the 18th century and accelerated during the 19th. The country did not escape massive, if intermittent, fragmentation of state control over its people, resources, and territory until the end of World War II. If we extend the count of revolutionary situations from Metropolitan France to overseas territories, the Algerian and Vietnamese wars would greatly extend the period of threatened revolutionary disruption. Even more than the capacity-democracy diagram, the chronology shows to what extent French democratization resulted from revolutionary struggle.

What, then, does this turbulent history from 1600 to the present require us to explain? Three main features of French experience with democratization and de-democratization cry out for analysis. First, before 1789 the regime never came close to democratic territory. Yet from that point onward it repeatedly produced relatively democratic forms of government; why the big switch? Second, despite France's revolutionary start, major reversals of democratization occurred multiple times, quite rapidly each time. What accounts for the faster pace of de-democratization than of democratization? Third, political shocks such as the wide-ranging revolution of 1848 and the devastating loss of the Franco-Prussian War played a disproportionate part in accelerations of French democratization. What connects democratization to revolution and other shocks?

The first question directs our attention to how regime-citizen interaction was changing before 1789. As we will see in detail later, increases in state capacity vary wildly from regime to regime in the extent to which they involve bargaining with citizens for state-operating resources that the citizens already control. At one extreme, the people who run mineral-rich states of our own time need bargain very little with their citizens if the state itself dominates the extraction of oil, gold, diamonds, or other precious goods.

At the other extreme, in a fundamentally agrarian economy increases in capacity only occur through direct delivery of agricultural products or their monetary proceeds to the state. Establishing that delivery necessarily engages the state in bargaining with whoever controls the land and in creating institutions that actually deliver agricultural proceeds. In between the two extremes, we find states based on highly commercialized economies – the Netherlands offers a crucial case – in which rulers cannot simply run off with the goods but need not bargain much with peasants and their landlords either. In such economies, bargains with merchants generally produce enough consent to keep the state enterprise going (Adams 2005, Tilly 1992). Hence the crucial importance of merchant oligarchies to Europe's systems of semi-democratic rule.

Extensive bargaining of this sort sets conditions for democratization in two crucial ways: by making rulers depend on widespread compliance from their citizens and by laying down rights and obligations that amount to mutually binding consultation. At the same time, it makes de-democratization possible as well: compliance by one group of citizens regularly harms the interests of elites who have previously maintained themselves by drawing resources and support from those same citizens. Landlords often lose when states win. This insight leads us to look for major shifts in state-citizen bargaining over state-sustaining resources as causes of a regime's entry into democratic struggle – not only in France, but all over the world.

The second question – why de-democratization generally occurs more rapidly than democratization – opens up a whole new perspective. As Figure 2-1 has already shown us, France did make spectacularly rapid moves into democratic territory after 1789, during 1848, and at the end of World War II. In those cases, struggle between rulers and ruled had already been going on for some time: interlocking contests over revenues, rights, and autonomies of semi-representative institutions before 1789; continuous battles between the crown and its opponents during the 1830s and 1840s; and resistance to the German occupation and the Vichy puppet state during the later years of World War II.

In each case, de-democratization occurred much faster than the previous or subsequent democratization. In all of these cases, furthermore, large popular mobilizations preceded democratization's acceleration. In the cases of reversal, major splits in the ruling coalition precipitated drastic action by segments of those coalitions to retain or restore their power. In short, rapid de-democratization resulted not from popular disaffection with democracy but chiefly from elite defection.

Looking at 20th-century reversals of democracy, Nancy Bermeo makes a parallel, if narrower, observation:

Though citizen passivity made the dismantling of democracy easier, it is undeniable that the democracies studied here were brought down by their own political elites. Elite actions followed a range of trajectories. At one extreme, politicians (and sometimes monarchs) chose dictatorship deliberately. They either became dictators themselves, or they knowingly made anti-democratic figures head of government. At another extreme, political elites brought on dictatorship through their own ineptitude: they made a series of errors that produced a coup coalition. Their errors were surprisingly similar, despite the great variation in our cases: they always produced a coup coalition including military elites. (Bermeo 2003: 237)

Except for Iberia, Latin America, and the Balkans, "coup coalitions including military elites" played smaller parts in democracy's reversals before the 20th century than they did between 1900 and the 1980s. As distinguished from merely authoritarian rulers, furthermore, "dictators" did not come into their own until the 20th century. Nevertheless, Bermeo's observation generalizes nicely: from the 19th century onward, holders of power who found democratization threatening disengaged much more readily from semi-democratic and democratic compacts than did ordinary people.

That brings us to the third question: the association of accelerated democratization with revolution and other shocks. Eventually we will see that not only revolution but also domestic confrontations, military conquest, and colonization maintain distinctive connections with democratization, not by any means bringing democracy automatically but often accelerating democratization where some of its elements were already in motion. For later investigation, let us entertain the hypothesis that such shocks matter because all of them undermine self-reproducing systems of control over states and thereby weaken the elites that have the most to lose from democratization. They open up room in which ordinary people can negotiate consent to newly emerging systems of rule. On the whole, ordinary people have something to gain from democratization and a lot to lose from de-democratization. France's ordinary people repeatedly learned that lesson the hard way.

Waves of Democratization

As evidenced by such points as France's revolution of 1848, democratization and de-democratization do not usually occur just one regime at a time. During the middle of the 19th century, Belgium, Hungary, Germany, Bohemia, Austria, Italy, and Switzerland all experienced revolutionary bids for democracy, most of which were quickly reversed. Adjacent and connected regimes influence one another. John Markoff, from whose book *Waves of Democracy* I have adapted this section's heading, puts it this way:

During a democratic wave, the organization of governments is altered – sometimes by peaceful reform, sometimes by dramatic overthrow – in ways that are widely held to be more democratic. During such a democratic wave, there is a great deal of discussion of the virtues of democracy, social movements often demand more democracy, and people in positions of authority proclaim their democratic intentions. During antidemocratic waves, governments are transformed in ways that are widely held to be undemocratic, social movements proclaim their intention to do away with democracy, and government figures proudly express their hostility to democracy. (Markoff 1996b: 1–2)

How can we identify such waves concretely? Whether they follow constitutional, substantive, procedural, or process-oriented definitions of democracy, most people who study multiple cases of democratization and de-democratization simplify their work with a straightforward device. They identify a threshold, placing non-democracy on one side and democracy on the other, then ask when, how, under what conditions, and why regimes cross the threshold in either direction. They adopt a procedural standard. (Even process-oriented Markoff uses presence or absence of different kinds of voting rights as his chief sorting device.) Although from time to time I will flatly call a regime democratic or undemocratic, that device will not serve this book's explanatory purposes well.

Why not? First, because we are not trying to explain yes-no switches between undemocratic and democratic conditions. We are trying to explain degrees and changes of democracy. Second, because to do so we must look at a broad range of processes: from those that would move a country like Kazakhstan toward a more democratic regime to those that would introduce yet another reversal into France's long-term democratization. For our purposes, it will work much better to identify substantial periods and places in which significant movement anywhere along the undemocracy-democracy dimension was occurring and to ask what was going on during those periods.

Pursuing rather different purposes, Tatu Vanhanen has provided us with a first rough handle on the problem. Vanhanen has computed an "index of democratization" by decade from 1850 to 1979 for a large number of countries. The index multiplies 1) the share of the vote that all parties, except the largest party, received in national elections by 2) the proportion of the total population voting. Thus, from 1901 to 1909, when smaller Australian parties took 61.8 percent of the vote and 18.9 percent of the population voted, Australia's index became 61.8% × 18.9% = an index of democratization of 11.7.

By adopting Vanhanen's numbers, I have of course returned to the procedural criterion of voting. The measure tells us nothing about changes in protection, merely gestures at breadth and equality, and only bears on mutually binding consultation indirectly. It neglects lower levels of democratization, those that usually appear before the full-scale national electoral systems on which Vanhanen concentrates. The handle is crude, like knotted string that lifts a fragile appliance. Yet, extended over several decades, it at least indicates where and when major expansions of competitive electoral activity were occurring.

I have divided Vanhanen's data into three panels: 1850 to 1899, 1900 to 1949, and 1950 to 1979. During the period from 1850 to 1899, the United States absents itself from the list; it had already passed through major periods of democratization, by this index, before 1850. Canada, likewise absent, remained a cluster of British colonies until 1867, but

BOX 2-2. Sites of Relatively Rapid Democratization, 1850–1979

1850–1899

Asia-Pacific: None

Europe: Austria, Belgium, Denmark, France, Greece, Italy,
                Netherlands, Norway, Portugal, Spain, Sweden, Switzerland,
                United Kingdom

Americas: Argentina, Bolivia, Chile, Dominican Republic, Ecuador,
                Uruguay

Africa: None

1900–1949

Asia-Pacific: Australia, Japan, New Zealand

Europe: Austria, Denmark, Finland, France, Germany, Greece,
                Hungary, Italy, Netherlands, Norway, Portugal, Romania,
                Russia, Spain, Sweden, Switzerland, United Kingdom

Americas: Argentina, Bolivia, Brazil, Canada, Chile, Colombia, Costa
                Rica, Cuba, Dominican Republic, Ecuador, Honduras,
                Mexico, Panama, Peru, United States, Uruguay

Africa: Egypt

1950–1979

Asia-Pacific: India, Israel, Lebanon, South Korea, Thailand, Turkey

Europe: Greece, Portugal, Spain

Americas: Colombia, Costa Rica, Dominican Republic, El Salvador,
                Guatemala, Nicaragua, Paraguay, Peru, Venezuela

Africa: Egypt, Morocco, Zambia

Source: Vanhanen 1997: 251–271

the newly unified regime then entered dominion status with comparatively democratic institutions, which changed relatively little across the rest of the 19th century. During the same period, in contrast, almost all of Africa lay under colonial rule, and the Asia-Pacific region was divided into colonies and regimes that showed little or no signs of democratization. In short, if we want to look for democratizing processes during the latter half of the 19th century, we should fix our gaze on Western Europe and Latin America.

During the half-century from 1900 to 1949, expansion of suffrage – especially female suffrage – brings a number of older democracies, including the United States and Canada, back onto the list. But increases in Vanhanen's index also register the experimentation with democracy that accelerated in Europe – with many, many reversals – after the devastation of World War I. Europe and the Americas continue to dominate the map of democratization. But we see democracy moving east and south within Europe and expanding in scope within Latin America. We even see glimmers of democratization in Japan and Egypt.

The three decades after 1949 actually feature fewer cases of substantial democratization than the previous half-century. Yet these decades show a significant shift in the geography and character of democratization. Military regimes continued to rise and fall in Latin America, but Latin American countries increasingly moved toward relatively democratic civilian rule. Within Europe, similarly, Greece, Portugal, and Spain provide the main sites of renewed democratization, all of them involving increased subordination of the military to civilian authority. Although Latin American regimes continue to figure prominently, we now also see spurts of democratization in both Asia and Africa. The decline of European and Japanese colonialism opened up new opportunities for democracy outside its long-established homes in the Americas and Europe.

Since 1850, democratization has clearly arrived in waves, with Western Europe leading the first wave, then rejoining the wave from 1900 to 1949. After that, Latin America began a third wave as Asia and Africa began to move toward democracy. Because Vanhanen's statistics terminate in 1979, the chronology stops short of showing how rapidly further democratization proceeded in post-colonial areas after that point (Bratton and van de Walle 1997, Diamond 1999, Geddes 1999, Lafargue 1996, Markoff 2005, Przeworski et al. 2000, Whitehead 2002). A Freedom House inventory of transitions from authoritarian rule since 1979 lists these regimes as having moved into "free" territory (Karatnyky and Ackerman 2005):

Asia-Pacific: Mongolia, Philippines, South Korea, Taiwan, Thailand
Europe: Bulgaria, Croatia, Czech Republic, Estonia, Hungary, Latvia, Lithuania, Poland, Romania, Serbia-Montenegro, Slovakia, Slovenia
Americas: Argentina, Brazil, Chile, El Salvador, Guyana, Mexico, Panama, Peru, Uruguay
Africa: Benin, Cape Verde, Ghana, Mali, Senegal, South Africa

The listing reminds us of Europe's enormous surge of democratization as the region's state socialist regimes collapsed in 1989 and thereafter; more on those changes in a moment. It also calls attention to continuing democratization (now looking more definitive than before) in Latin America. But most notably it identifies Asia and Africa as zones in which significant democratization began to occur after 1979.

The chronology tells us something even more important. Its lessons parallel those we have already drawn from France's long oscillation between democracy and undemocracy. Large clusters of regimes moved from long periods of unavailability for democratic change to volatile movement back and forth between democratization and de-democratization. Take, for example, the European period from 1900 to 1949, during which 17 regimes underwent at least one period of accelerated democratization. Of those 17, 12 – Austria, Finland, France, Germany, Greece, Hungary, Italy, Portugal, Romania, Russia, Spain, and (if we count the Nazi occupation) the Netherlands – also underwent even more rapid de-democratization at least once.

European regimes became much more available for both democratization and de-democratization than they were in the 18th century. Latin American regimes became similarly available for movement in both directions once they declared independence from Spain during the 19th century's first decades. History threw a parallel switch with the decolonization of Asia and Africa after World War II. The Philippines, Thailand, and Senegal, for example, all look like recent democracies that could well move back into de-democratization, because powerful elites feel the threat of further democracy. We will obviously have to look more closely at the timing, location, and operation of such historical switches.

This evidence echoes another conclusion from French experience: once a regime has entered the volatile zone of democratization and de-democratization, on the whole, moves away from democracy occur more rapidly, with less popular participation, and under greater elite influence than moves toward democracy. Indeed, in recent transitions studied by the Freedom House team, mainly nonviolent but massive popular mobilizations against authoritarian regimes have increasingly pushed those regimes toward democracy. In contrast, top-down attempts to reform similar regimes have had much less effect (Karatnycky and Ackerman 2005). Think of Burma, China, Nepal, and Thailand, in all of which challenges to state power brought on massive repression and demobilization (Schock 2005, chapters 4 and 5). Popular mobilizations often fail. In our time, nevertheless, ordinary people are becoming increasingly involved in pressing for democratization.

Post-Socialist Democratization

Many of the most dramatic cases of popular mobilization against authoritarian rulers occurred as democratic regimes emerged from the ruins of the Soviet and Yugoslav socialist states. Consider Ukraine in 2004. The rights-monitoring organization Human Rights Watch sets the scene in December of that year:

> For years, under the leadership of President [Leonid] Kuchma, the government imposed ever stricter controls on media coverage, repeatedly sought to manipulate electoral processes, and ignored widespread popular discontent. By doing so, it has undermined legitimate avenues for people to express their grievances in a meaningful way. The government's blatant attempts to manipulate the presidential vote in favor of Prime Minister Viktor Yanukovich – notwithstanding a clear popular preference for opposition candidate Viktor Yushchenko – served to convince many Ukrainians that mass street protests are their only hope of being heard. (Human Rights Watch 2005: 441)

Kuchma's agents poisoned Yushchenko with dioxin. Activists from nearby states, human rights organizers from across the western world, and masses of Ukrainians converged on the capital, Kiev. Citizens poured into the streets. They sang and chanted through winter nights and blocked entry to government buildings. They staged the Orange Revolution. The Ukrainian protests followed similar episodes in Serbia during 2000 and in Georgia during 2003. They belonged to a wave of popular protest against electoral fraud that spread throughout the former Soviet Union and adjacent regions.

None of those regimes qualified remotely as democratic in 1989. But a great deal has changed since then. Figure 2-2 uses Freedom House ratings on political rights and civil liberties to map the distribution of post-socialist regimes in 2006. (Remember that 1 on political rights or civil liberties is the highest possible score, 7 the lowest.) Roughly speaking, political rights correspond to broad, equal, mutually binding consultation, whereas civil liberties refer especially to protection. The Freedom House ratings thus provide information about the extent and direction of post-socialist democratization since 1989.

As the figure shows, by no means did all post-socialist regimes move significantly away from undemocratic politics. In the lower left-hand corner of the diagram reside Turkmenistan, Uzbekistan, Azerbaijan, Kazakhstan, and Russia, with Armenia and Kyrgyzstan not far away, ranking fifth on political rights and fourth on civil liberties. Yet in the upper right-hand corner – the highest possible rankings in both regards – we find the Czech Republic, Estonia, Hungary, Lithuania, Poland, Slovakia, and Slovenia.

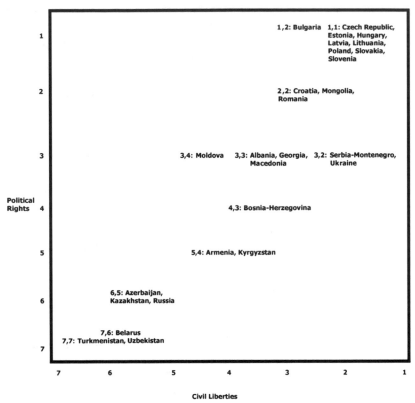

FIGURE 2-2. Freedom House Ratings of Post-Socialist Regimes on Political Rights and Civil Liberties, 2006
Source: Compiled from Freedom House 2006

Within 17 years of 1989, all of them had established recognizably democratic regimes.

However, not all post-socialist regimes headed for democracy (Bunce 2001; Fish 2001, 2005; Khazanov 1995; McFaul 1997; Suny 1993; Tishkov 1997). Again using Freedom House measures, Figure 2-3 displays trajectories of four post-socialist countries from 1991 to 2006. (Freedom House first began treating Belarus, Croatia, Estonia, and Russia separately from their preceding socialist federations in 1991.) According to these ratings, each of the four countries passed through an early decline of political rights and/or civil liberties. But after its civil war ended, say the scores, Croatia took significant steps toward democracy. Estonia restricted political rights at first, but made a U-turn as civil liberties increased and then political rights expanded; even the regime's mildly discriminatory

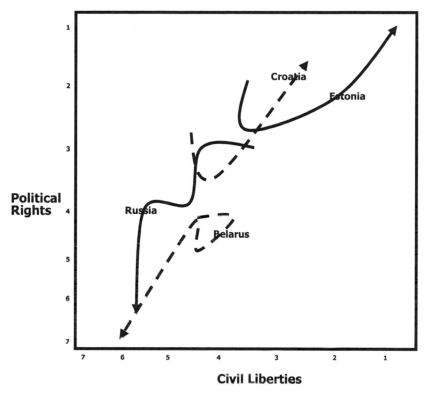

FIGURE 2-3. Freedom House Ratings of Four Post-Socialist Regimes, 1991–2006
Source: Compiled from Freedom House 2002, 2006

treatment of its substantial Russian minority did not keep Estonia from a rating of 1,1 – in the company of Europe's leading democracies.

Meanwhile, Russia and (especially) Belarus headed downward toward fewer political rights and diminished civil liberties. In Russia, the Yeltsin-Putin wars in the Northern Caucasus and the state's silencing of opposition voices pulled the beleaguered country back from the partial democratization Mikhail Gorbachev had initiated during the 1980s. Yeltsin and Putin concentrated their efforts on restoring the Russian state's internal capacity and external standing. They sacrificed civil liberties – or, more generally, democracy – as they did so. Putin used the state's control over valuable stores of oil and gas to pry his government free of popular consent. Inequalities of class and ethnicity became more salient in Russian public politics; Russian citizens disconnected their tattered trust networks even more definitively from public politics, as protection, breadth, equality, and mutually binding consultation diminished visibly (Fish 2005).

Belarus slid even farther. Belarus president Aleksandr Lukashenka won his office in a 1994 popular election as an anti-corruption watchdog. But as soon as he had consolidated his hold on the office, Lukashenka instituted censorship, smashed independent trade unions, fixed elections, and subjugated the legislature, thus compromising the country's previous small democratic gains. He benefited greatly from Russian aid, especially in the form of subsidized prices for Russian gas and oil. Like many an authoritarian ruler across the contemporary world, Lukashenka could avoid consulting his people by using mineral revenues to support state capacity.

Lukashenka did not, however, neglect internal repression. According to Kathleen Mihalisko,

Less than a year into his presidency, in April 1995, riot police acting on Lukashenka's orders beat up Popular Front deputies on the steps of the Supreme Council, in what was a first manifestation of regime violence. Ever since, the special interior ministry troops (OPMON) have become a most visible reminder of how Lukashenka prefers to deal with critics, being used against peaceful demonstrators with escalating brutality and frequency. In two years, the number of security forces is estimated to have risen to about 180,000, or double the size of the armed forces. (Mihalisko 1997: 237; see also Titarenko et al. 2001)

The use of specialized military forces to establish political control drew on an old Eastern European repertoire. By the presidential elections of 2006, Lukashenka was taking no chances of a "color revolution" in the style of Serbia, Georgia, and Ukraine. In fact, the head of Belarus's KGB justified repression by accusing the opposition "of planning to carry out a coup after the voting on Sunday, supported by the United States and Georgia" (Myers 2006: A3). Repression worked: only a few thousand protesters showed up on election night, as the government announced that Lukashenka had won 82.6 percent of the vote (Myers and Chivers 2006: A11). Although dwindling numbers of demonstrators continued to brave the cold for the next few days, on the sixth day riot police swept up the few hundred that remained (Myers and Chivers 2006). Post-socialist regimes that de-democratized after 1991 teetered between dictatorship and civil war.

Figure 2-3 reinforces a point that Figure 2-2 made visible. Regimes crowd along the diagonal, generally receiving broadly similar scores for political rights and civil liberties. When political rights and civil liberties change in any particular regime, furthermore, they tend to change together in the same direction – not in exact parallel, but in rough synchrony. In this book's terms, the installation of relatively broad, equal, and mutually binding popular consultation promotes the strengthening of protections against arbitrary action by governmental agents. Expanded protection, in its turn, promotes broader, more equal, more binding political participation. Not perfectly, as the erratic courses of Belarus, Russia, Estonia, and Croatia tell us, but enough so that democratization arrives as a simultaneous increase in political rights and civil liberties. That increase, as we have seen, often occurs with impressive rapidity in the aftermath of intense conflict.

What's to Explain?

We obviously have our explanatory work cut out for us. At least superficially, the histories of democratization and de-democratization we have surveyed lend themselves to completely contradictory explanations. We might, for example, think of democracy as an idea that someone (the Greeks?) invented, starting a centuries-long effort to implement the idea. We might take an opposite tack, arguing that only the conditions of industrial capitalism could support broad, equal, protective, and mutually binding political relations between states and citizens. We might also think that competing models of government, once familiar to national elites, attracted different sorts of ruling classes, and that some of these chose dictatorship and others democracy. Call these three approaches to explanation *idealist, structuralist*, and *instrumentalist*. You will have no trouble finding examples of each one in the vast recent literature on democracy.[1]

When taken separately, none of the three approaches come close to providing coherent explanations of the histories we have reviewed. In each case, we find ourselves asking "How?" and "Why?" *How* did ideas of democracy translate into concrete relations and practices? *How* did industrial capitalism generate pressures for democratization? *How* did self-interested rulers fashion democratic institutions? *Why* did it take so long? "How" and "why" questions spring up at every step of our historical way.

---

[1] For example, Acemoglu and Robinson 2006; Alexander 2002; Andrews and Chapman 1995; Arblaster 1987; Boix 2003; Collier and Levitsky 1997; Collier 1999; Cruz 2005; Dahl 1998; Diamond et al. 2004; Di Palma 1990; Engelstad and Østerud 2004; Geddes 1999; Gurr, Jaggers, and Moore 1990; Held 1996; Hoffmann 2003; Huntington 1991; Kurzman 1998; Lijphart 1999; Linz and Stepan 1996; Markoff 1996b; Morlino 2003; O'Donnell 1999; Ortega Ortiz 2001; Przeworski et al. 2000; Putnam, Leonardi, and Nanetti 1993; Rueschemeyer, Stephens, and Stephens 1992; Skocpol 2004; Sørensen 1998; Whitehead 2002; Yashar 1997.

Here is my claim: it will take a thoroughgoing process-oriented analysis of democratization and de-democratization to provide coherent answers to such questions. Available idealist, structuralist, and instrumentalist accounts of democracy do not offer adequate answers. We must dig much deeper into political processes. Later chapters will emphasize three kinds of political processes, those that alter relations between state-citizen interactions and 1) interpersonal trust networks, 2) categorical inequalities, and 3) autonomous power centers. They will also examine the effects of shocks such as domestic confrontation, revolution, conquest, and colonization in activating and accelerating those processes.

Looking closely at the effects of such shocks, furthermore, will clarify the extent to which popular struggle (rather than leaders' wise political deliberation) advances democratization. Before excavating our answers, however, we need a still clearer map of the terrain to be explored. The next chapter takes us much farther into the actual processes of democratization and de-democratization. This further exploration will equip us to examine how and why those fundamental processes occur.

3

Democratization and De-Democratization

Let's start with a really hard case: India. Since independence in 1947, India has occupied a position somewhere within the high-capacity, high-democracy quadrant of our capacity-democracy space. Both capacity and democracy have fluctuated somewhat over the sixty years, but in general India's national regime has resembled that of Canada, say, more than that of Jamaica or Kazakhstan. This country of 1.1 billion inhabitants nevertheless poses problems for any analysis of democratization and de-democratization. Those problems arise in a number of different ways:

- Despite extensive poverty and inequality among its people, the Indian economy is becoming one of the world's great makeweights.
- Its 25 states – many of them larger and more populous than most European states – vary enormously in wealth, social composition, and political character.
- Its public politics regularly features vivid displays of religiously tinged ritual.
- Hindu, Muslim, Sikh, and other religious militants all intermittently massacre one another and attack one another's sacred symbols.
- Around the country's edges (for example, in Kashmir and in the ethnically fragmented northeast) separatist groups regularly use armed force to attack government personnel and state security personnel regularly employ brutal repression.
- In the country's central regions Maoist guerrillas (commonly called Naxalites), who have some political presence in about a quarter of all Indian political districts, likewise use lethal means to massacre government forces and uncooperative villagers.

- Since independence in 1947 the regime has careened between emergencies and moments of accommodation.
- Finally, India remains by far the world's most populous democratic regime.

How can we possibly make sense of all this complexity?

News reports from India often portray the country as trembling at the edge of sectarian collapse. It was not always so. Independent India came into being in 1947 as partition from Pakistan left the country a predominantly Hindu population. (These days about 80 percent of Indians are at least nominally Hindu and another 12 percent are Muslim.) The new regime, headed by Jawaharlal Nehru, inherited a disciplined civil service and an effective army from its British colonial overlords. In both regards, the state could count on high capacity. Unlike its neighbor Pakistan, furthermore, Nehru's regime kept its military under effective civilian control. The regime's leaders came largely from the same group of elites that had used British-style contentious politics to win independence from Britain: people from well-heeled families in the upper castes, often educated in Britain.

Post-colonial India also inherited a federal system that accommodated the enormous diversity among the regions that Britain had assembled as subunits of government as it pursued its colonial conquests. Under normal conditions, the states retained substantial powers and responsibilities, although the central government and courts could restrict those powers in emergencies. Vast patron-client networks (notably within different segments of the Congress Party) connected most parts of India to the center

However, for all its centralized organization, even the vaunted civil service could not remain immune to political and financial influence. On the contrary, India's system of frequent transfers from one position to another brought political and financial pressure to bear on every transfer: Regional politicians balanced between rewarding their clients with better posts and taking payments for award of more attractive assignments, while civil servants themselves jockeyed for positions that advanced their careers, accommodated their kin, or provided larger opportunities for payoffs (de Zwart 1994).

Veteran observer Myron Weiner commented wryly:

Though a comparison between the old Soviet nomenklatura and India's political and administrative elites would not be apt given the openness of India's system of elite recruitment, it should be noted that those who exercise political power in India belong to a highly privileged class. Government officials are given virtually rent-free housing, low-interest loans, privileged access for their children to special governmental schools, priority seats on planes and trains, the private use of government vehicles, government-financed medical care, and good pensions. In the era of state regulation of the economy officials controlled the allocation of foreign exchange, the distribution of a wide variety of commodities including steel, coal, paper, and fertilizers, and determined what could and could not be imported. There was an elaborate system of patronage jointly controlled by elected politicians and officials that determined who got electric power, tube wells, schools, district colleges, railway stations, irrigation works, roads, bus lines, health center and jobs in government. Voters turned to politicians when they needed admission into a government hospital, or admission for their children into a local college. (Weiner 2001: 204)

Indian politicians were operating a classic patron-client system (for parallels, see, e.g., Auyero 2001, Bax 1976, Bearman 1993, Kettering 1993, Montgomery 1998, Schmidt et al. 1977, Willerton 1992).

Indeed, it may well have become the world's biggest patron-client system. Rajiv Gandhi himself complained in 1985 that "millions of ordinary Congress workers are handicapped, for on their backs ride the brokers of power and influence, who dispense patronage to convert a mass movement into a feudal oligarchy – corruption is not only tolerated – but [is] even regarded as a hallmark of leadership" (Kohli 1990: 5). The federal structure, furthermore, promoted the elaboration of parallel patronage networks at the level of each state (Manor 2004). Often a state's politics crystallized in opposition to those of the center. Nehru presided over a complex, delicately balanced political regime.

Despite almost immediate war with Pakistan over Kashmir and the assassination of liberation leader Mohandas Gandhi by a Hindu extremist (both in 1948), Nehru managed to contain sectarian conflict until his death in 1964. Relying on Nehru's prestige and political apparatus, as embodied in the Congress Party, his daughter Indira Gandhi became prime minister in 1966.

Indira Gandhi's nearly two decades in power coincided with, and to some extent caused, a deep shift in the character of India's public politics. Under Nehru, ethnic and religious zealots had little room to maneuver, whereas advocates for the poor and oppressed had great leverage. Raka Ray and Mary Fainsod Katzenstein speak of:

the dramatic swing from the early post-Independence symbiosis of state, party, and movement organized around democratic socialism on the left to its unraveling in the mid 1960s through the 1980s and the ascendance of its institutional mirror image on the right, the similarly synergistic nexus of state, party, and movement now organized, however, around religious nationalism and the market. (Ray and Katzenstein 2005: 3)

Once state founder Nehru disappeared from the scene, new forms of division and struggle emerged in India. The seamy web that held state, Congress, and far-reaching patron-client chains together began to tear (Kohli 1994).

Gandhi and her family certainly had less luck (or skill) than her father in managing religious and ethnic militants. Gandhi's own Sikh bodyguards assassinated her in 1984. In 1991, a suicide bomber acting on behalf of Sri Lanka's Tamil nationalists blew up her son and successor Rajiv Gandhi. Up to that point, Nehru's Congress had usually dominated the national parliament and served as the principal channel of government patronage. After Rajiv Gandhi's death, his Italian-born widow Sonia reluctantly became the head of the fragmented Congress Party. The party faltered. In the parliamentary elections of 1996, the Hindu nationalist Bharatiya Janata Party (BJP) emerged as the Indian parliament's largest single voting bloc.

By 1998, a new general election gave the BJP its first chance to win control over the government. During the run-up to the election, the normally sober *New York Times* reported that:

Whatever way the election goes, few Indians doubt that it will represent a historical turning point – made all the more poignant by Mrs. Gandhi's involvement and the coincidence of the election occurring in the 50th anniversary year of India's independence. If the Hindu nationalists win, their critics say, it will be a rejection of much India has stood for in its first half-century as a free nation. (Burns 1998: Y6)

As it turned out, the BJP surged ahead and formed a coalition government. It could not and did not, however, turn immediately to the programs of Hindu nationalism. It remained too busy simply keeping its hands on the levers of power. India certainly continued to struggle, but the country did not collapse. Somehow since independence, and perhaps long before, the Indian national state and its citizens have never fallen far from relatively broad, equal, protected, and mutually binding consultation. Even sensational displays of Hindu nationalism, civil war in Kashmir, and unending insurgency did not dislodge India from relatively high-capacity democracy. We might regard India either as a miracle or as a conundrum.

Puzzling India illustrates four problems for this chapter. First, given the sheer complexity of such an entity as India, how can we possibly place the regime as a whole on the continuum from undemocracy to democracy? Second, even if we can fix the regime's location since 1947 somewhere in high-capacity democratic territory, how can we identify India's phases of democratization and de-democratization? Third, having done so, can we

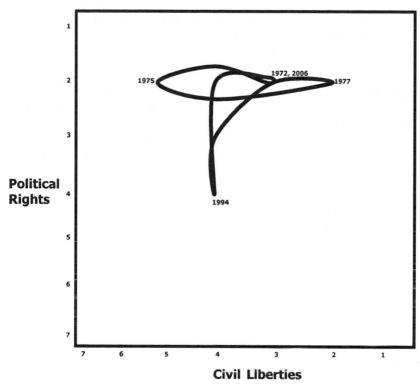

FIGURE 3-1. India's Freedom House Ratings, 1972–2006
Source: Compiled from Freedom House 2002, 2005, 2006

discover any empirical regularities within the two opposite processes, not only in India, but in the world as a whole? Fourth, having identified regularities in democratization and de-democratization, how do we explain them? This chapter neglects the fourth question – explanation – in favor of clarifying what we have to explain. It concentrates on measurement in a broad sense of the word: not so much precise numbers as careful placement of cases on analytically relevant continua. This placement makes it possible to examine change within cases and variation across cases.

Freedom House can again help us specify what we have to explain. Figure 3-1 traces India's shifts with regard to political rights and civil liberties since 1972, the beginning of Freedom House's annual evaluations. It dramatizes a series of major shifts:

> 1975: Accused of massive electoral fraud on behalf of Congress, Indira Gandhi declares a state of emergency; during the emergency, the government imprisons almost one thousand political opponents and

imposes a program of compulsory birth control; Freedom House maintains India's political rights rating at 2, but drops it from 3 to 5 (quite low) on civil liberties.

1977: With partial relaxation of emergency regulations, Gandhi calls a general election, but Congress loses badly and leaves power; Freedom House responds by moving India to a record high evaluation of 2 on political rights and 2 on civil liberties.

1980: After a split in Congress, Gandhi returns to power, heading her own segment of the party; Freedom House drops India's rating on civil liberties to 3.

1992: After Rajiv Gandhi's assassination by a Tamil militant (1991) and Hindu activists' sensational destruction of a mosque in Ayodhya, Uttar Pradesh, followed by Hindu-Muslim violence across India (1992), the government steps up repressive measures; Freedom House lowers Indian ratings to 3 on political rights and 4 on civil liberties; this move transfers India from the category Free to the middle category Partly Free.

1994: Further Hindu-Muslim clashes (notably in Bombay and Calcutta, 1993) kill 1,200 people; Freedom House lowers its estimate of Indian political rights to a record low of 4, for a total score of 4,4.

1997: The massive electoral defeat of Congress (1996) throws national politics into turmoil; Freedom House raises the Indian rating for political rights to 2 (its most common score over these years) but leaves civil liberties at 4.

1999: After the BJP forms its coalition government (1998), it undertakes widely condemned nuclear tests, but also gestures toward peace with Pakistan and holds back on anti-Muslim campaigns; commenting that "Observers rated parliamentary elections in 1996, 1998, and 1999 as the fairest in India's history," Freedom House returns India to its most common evaluation – 2,3 – which transfers the regime back into the Free category; India remains at that position into 2006.

Figure 3-1's flower shape reveals that Freedom House evaluations of political rights and civil liberties (which usually do correlate and change with each other) need not march in lockstep. According to the democracy-rating agency, Indian political rights plummeted during the Hindu-Muslim conflicts of the early 1990s but otherwise remained extensive. Civil liberties (the diagram's horizontal dimension) fluctuated much more, starting with Indira Gandhi's repressive emergency measures of 1975. According to Freedom House scores, even the tightening of central controls after the 1992 Ayodhya destruction and its bloody aftermath did not match the repression of 1975.

Can we translate the Indian chronology since 1972 into the terms of democratization and de-democratization? To do so, we must assume that Freedom House's measurement of political rights generally corresponds to our evaluation of breadth, equality, and mutually binding consultation and that its measurement of civil liberties generally corresponds to our consideration of protection. In these terms, we can reasonably think of 1975 (the Indira Gandhi emergency) and 1991 to 1994 (Rajiv Gandhi assassination, heightened Hindu-Muslim conflict, central government repression) as periods of rapid de-democratization. The years following each of these crises then count as slower periods of re-democratization.

At a scale unimaginable in any other existing democracy, the Indian regime trembles as it feels the tension among three mighty forces: 1) the formidable central power inherited from British colonial rule, reinforced by separation from Pakistan, consolidated by Nehru, and staffed by a powerful (if often venal) civil service; 2) the operation of immensely influential patronage networks, most obviously within the various branches of the Congress; and 3) the combination of intensely combative and fissiparous politics at the local and regional scales (Ganguly 1999).

Although the second element – intricate patronage networks extending from local to regional to national levels – lends India's bottom-up politics much of its complexity, from the top down national rulers generally work to coordinate their uses of patronage with their control of administrative power. As Paul Brass comments, this strategy produces a deep dilemma:

That dilemma is simply that it is impossible in such a diverse country within the framework of a federal parliamentary system to maintain a stable structure of national power for long. It is an extremely difficult, prolonged, and absorbing task to build national power in the country and it begins to disintegrate at the very point when it appears to have been consolidated. The task is so absorbing that, even with the best will in the world, it is impossible for the national leaders to focus their attentions on the goals of economic development and the fulfillment of the basic needs of the people. Indeed, those goals themselves must be subordinated to the imperative need of maintaining the power so laboriously constructed. (Brass 1994: 344; see also Brass 2003: 372)

Like rulers elsewhere, Indian rulers understandably equate the maintenance of order with protection of their own power. They choose how much weight to give the dilemma's two horns: maintaining power versus responding to popular will. The dilemma is genuine, as drastic weakening of central power – state capacity – also reduces the possibility of implementing popular will by means of state intervention.

During the postwar period, the Indian regime never exited from the high-capacity, high-democracy quadrant of our regime space; it simply changed locations within the quadrant. Earlier we saw regimes such as 18th-century France moving from a phase in which formidable obstacles to any sort of democratization existed to another phase in which volatile movement along the democracy-undemocracy axis became not only possible but likely. Very likely as a consequence of the long process in which Hindu and Muslim leaders challenged Britain's authoritarian rule, India seems to have passed that threshold well before independence in 1947. Combined with rulers' reliance on a huge patronage system, the new state's formidable capacity sustained the regime's incomplete but still impressive democracy.

We begin to identify connections between Indian post-colonial history and more general processes of democratization and de-democratization. As the cases we reviewed in Chapter 2 hinted, democratization and de-democratization do not work in strict symmetry. On the whole, de-democratization occurs in the course of rulers' and elites' responses to what they experience as regime crises, most obviously represented by threats to their own power. Democratization usually occurs in state response (however reluctant) to popular demands, after crises have eased. As a result, de-democratization generally occurs more rapidly, and with much greater central direction, than democratization.

As our search for explanations goes on, we will encounter exceptions to these generalizations, notably in cases in which military conquest or revolution led directly and rapidly to forced democratization. But on the whole we will find that democratic theorists have been correct: democratization and de-democratization pose the dilemma of central power versus popular will. Without significant state capacity, citizens' expressed collective demands cannot translate into transformations of social life. With significant state capacity, however, rulers inevitably feel the urge to use that capacity to reproduce their power positions, to pursue the programs they prefer, and to reward their supporters. Democracy involves negotiated consent in the exercise of concentrated state power. For that reason, it always involves popular mobilization. But what conditions will render that consent open, binding, and contingent on governmental performance?

Signs of Democratization and De-Democratization

The formidable case of India thus brings us back to this book's general mission. In broadest terms, we are trying to describe and explain variation and change in the extent to which the state behaves according to its citizens' expressed demands. To make the description manageable, it helps to break our inquiry into four components: how wide a range of citizens' expressed demands come into play, how equally different groups of citizens experience a translation of their demands into state behavior, to what extent the expression of demands itself receives the state's political protection, and how much the process of translation commits both sides, citizens and state. These four components lead directly to our working definition: A regime is democratic to the degree that political relations between the state and its citizens feature broad, equal, protected, mutually binding consultation. Democratization then means net movement toward broader, more equal, more protected, and more mutually binding consultation and de-democratization means net movement toward narrower, more unequal, less protected, and less mutually binding consultation.

But how can we know that such changes are actually happening? The problem breaks into two parts: principles of detection and available evidence that would allow us to apply those principles. Let us leave aside the second question – available evidence – for a moment in order to concentrate on principles. In a world of unlimited information, how would we go about detecting democratization and de-democratization according to these principles? Box 3-1 presents a summary of the guidelines discussed for detecting these processes.

My earlier analyses of France, post-socialist regimes, and India all applied these principles, however informally. The organizing ideas are simple: start with citizen-state interactions; concentrate on dynamics rather than static comparisons; average the changes in breadth, equality, protection, and mutually binding consultation, specify the range of cases within which you are working; standardize changes on that range; and let deviations from close correlation among changes signal important explanatory problems. In the case of India, for example, these principles call particular attention to the democratic crises of 1975 to 1977 and 1991 to 1994.

Let me not, however, raise your expectations too high. None of the analyses in the rest of the book reach the ambitious standard of measurement set by the examples in Box 3-1. Often I will propose an analytically

BOX 3-1. Principles for Description of Democracy, Democratization, and De-Democratization

1. Concentrate on observations of interactions between citizens and states; for example, observe what happens when groups of citizens make claims on state officials and when state officials seek to repress their enemies or rivals.

2. Invent or adopt measures that aggregate over many citizen-state interactions and/or sample a wide range of interactions; for example, analyze correspondence and meetings between officials and ordinary citizens.

3. Look for changes in breadth, equality, protection, and mutually binding consultation of state-citizen consultation; for example, analyze shifts in the frequency with which officials detain dissidents in the absence of due process.

4. Average those changes, on the assumption that alterations in breadth, equality, protection, and mutually binding consultation make equal contributions to democratization and de-democratization. For example, derive separate summary scores for changes in breadth, equality, protection, and mutually binding consultation before combining them into overall scores for democratization or de-democratization.

5. If the changes are distinctly heterogeneous (one element changes in the opposite direction, or one shifts far more or far less than the others), tag them for special attention. For example, if breadth, equality, and protection all increase while mutually binding consultation declines, investigate the possibility of a move toward benevolent despotism.

6. Set a clear range of comparison cases arrayed from least to most democratic, with the comparison cases ranging from all regimes that have ever existed to a quite narrow array, depending on your analytical purposes. For example, for an investigation of World War I's impact on democracy, compare all eventual belligerents year by year from 1915 to 1925.

7. Standardize changes in the case at hand on the range developed; for example, when looking at Germany from 1915 to 1925, score its degree of democracy relative to the highest (1) and lowest (0) democracy scores any of the war-affected regimes reached during the period.

8. Complement that comparison among regimes with detection of changes in the extent to which the state implemented the results of state-citizen consultation. For example, year by year from 1915 to 1925, compare German state performance with demands articulated by voting and social movement activity.

9. If this analysis reveals changes in implementation, investigate whether shifts in state capacity caused those changes. For example, determine whether postwar reparations, inflation, and reconstruction reduced the German state's ability to respond to citizen demands.

informed narrative in the style of my accounts for France and India, keeping the Box 3-1 principles in mind but without setting out numbers or even precise comparisons with other regimes. Repeatedly (as in the case of India) I will rely on annual Freedom House ratings of a regime's political rights and civil liberties, with political rights scores standing as rough proxies for breadth, equality, and mutually binding consultation while civil liberties stand in for protection. These measures fall far short of the precision it would take to verify – or falsify – this book's arguments. But they concretize my claims about particular regimes and thus open my analyses to confirmation, revision, or refutation by specialists.

Choice of comparison cases will obviously affect our understanding of the low to high democracy range. Suppose, for example, we wanted to emulate Adam Przeworski and his collaborators, who studied the performances of 141 independent regimes between 1950 and 1990. Przeworski and his colleagues estimated changes in the extent of democracy in a radically simple way. They adopted the most common strategy in recent quantitative analyses of democratization: with minor nuances, in any particular year they classified a regime as either authoritarian or democratic. A regime did not qualify as democratic unless it had an elected executive, an elected legislature, at least two competitive political parties, and some alternation in power (Przeworski et al. 2000: 18–36). They then asked 1) whether authoritarian and democratic regimes differed systematically in governmental performance, 2) under what conditions regimes crossed the threshold between authoritarian and democratic in either direction, and 3) what difference it made to performance whether a regime crossed the threshold.

Over the four decades studied, the great bulk of these regimes turned out to conduct formal elections, however fraudulent. Two conclusions follow. First, in the 1950 to 1990 study, the range runs essentially from sham elections to fully competitive electoral systems but involves no further distinctions beyond those limits. Second, in order to appropriate Przeworski and colleagues' results for the agenda in Box 3-1, we would have to assume that the character of elections correlates closely with other features of breadth, equality, protection, and mutually binding consultation.

Suppose, in contrast, that we were examining all western regimes on which we could collect evidence between 1750 and 1800. In France, the Dutch Republic, Great Britain, the nascent United States, and elsewhere, comparisons based on the characteristics of national elections would get us nowhere. By the end of the century, it is true, we would find restricted electorates choosing members of national legislatures in the United States and Great Britain. During some moments of the 1790s, we would observe something similar happening in France. But any scale treating characteristics of elections as the basic criteria for democratization and de-democratization would entirely distort the range, and therefore the comparisons, over the period from 1750 to 1800. We would have no choice but to fix on other sorts of rights, other forms of political participation, and other varieties of protection from arbitrary state action. We would find them (as my earlier account of France did) in more general political histories of citizen-state interaction.

During the next century, to be sure, electoral criteria would start to discipline any comparison of western regimes. Take three simple criteria: parliamentary representation based on consent of some significant portion of the population, manhood suffrage, and female suffrage. Assigning one point to each, we could construct a crude scale of democracy running from 0 (none of the three) to 3 (all of the three). Dynamically, we could think of the addition or subtraction of one element as a move toward or away from democracy. Drawing on the heroic compilations of Daniele Caramani (2000, 2003), Figure 3-2 presents data for construction of such a scale covering a number of European countries from 1800 to 1979.

For 18 political units (not all of which existed as autonomous states in 1815, and all of which shifted boundaries at least a bit after then), Caramani provides a wealth of information on suffrage. He distinguishes representation of whole classes through estates and similar institutions from general parliamentary representation, which means selection of deputies to a national assembly by an electorate, however large or small. Leaving aside discontinued earlier trials such as the French national assembly of 1789, Figure 3-2 distinguishes four configurations: 1) parliamentary representation exists without adult suffrage; 2) manhood suffrage exists, but continuous parliamentary representation has not yet begun; 3) both parliamentary representation and manhood suffrage exist from this point on; and 4) female suffrage joins manhood suffrage and parliamentary representation.

We can of course question Caramani's dates. Norway did not gain independence from Sweden – and thereby acquire a truly independent national parliament – until 1905. Although Finland did, indeed, install a democratic constitution in 1906, it remained part of the Russian Empire until 1917 and did not start operating as an independent democracy until after the civil war of 1917 to 1918 (Alapuro 1988). Louis Napoleon used

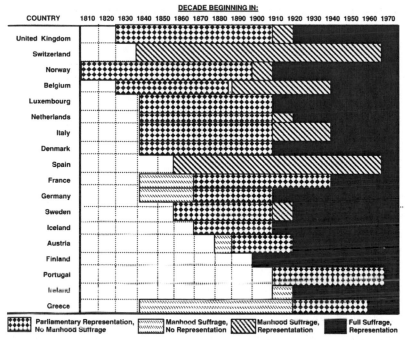

FIGURE 3-2. Representation and Suffrage in Selected European Regimes
Source: Compiled from Caramani 2000: 52–53

a wide array of devices to compromise the manhood suffrage that a revolutionary assembly had passed in 1848, so we might well place France's effective manhood suffrage in the early Third Republic. Italy as such did not become a unified country until 1870, so dating continuous parliamentary representation from Piedmont's reforms of 1848 might seem premature. We might also wonder whether 20th-century intervals of authoritarian regimes in Italy, Germany, Spain, France, and elsewhere interrupted parliamentary rule so thoroughly as to require new starting points after World War II. Nevertheless, Caramani's datings generally mark durable advances in representation as plausibly as any single alternatives we might propose.

The three minority cases in which manhood suffrage preceded a continuously functioning representative assembly – France, Germany, and (most dramatically) Greece – all resulted from moments during the revolutions of the 1840s when new regimes temporarily installed both representative legislatures and general male suffrage, but authoritarian regimes then took over, sapping legislative power without eliminating elections.

In France, Louis Napoleon cut back the National Assembly with his 1851 coup but did not quite dare to reinstate property qualifications for male suffrage.

In Germany, one might date parliamentary government from as early as 1808, as that is when Prussia established elections to a national assembly through a broad (but still property-restricted) male electorate. During the temporary unification of 1848 a German Union Bundestag adopted suffrage for independent adult males, although individual German states retained the right to define "independent" and "adult." Nevertheless, Caramani reasonably dates continuous parliamentary rule for Germany as a whole from German unification in 1871.

In Greece, the revolutionaries who wrested independence from the Ottoman Empire during the 1820s temporarily established a representative assembly chosen through manhood suffrage via an intermediate body of elite electors. But later authoritarian regimes soon removed all pretense of popular representation. Greek revolutionaries of 1843 brought back manhood suffrage and initiated a series of virtually powerless legislatures. Given a rocky history of coups and revolutions thereafter, exactly when we place the beginning of continuous parliamentary rule in Greece remains arbitrary, but Caramani's choice of 1926 plausibly marks the point at which the first legislature after the monarchy's abolition (1924) came to power through popular elections.

The timetables in Figure 3-2 make several important points.

- The great majority of Western European countries began parliamentary representation with restricted electorates.
- Manhood suffrage commonly arrived decades after the initial establishment of parliamentary representation.
- Although a few countries established full male and female suffrage simultaneously, on the whole women got the vote decades after men.
- The later the establishment of representative government, the shorter the duration of restricted suffrage.
- Transitions in different countries clustered together, notably in the 1840s (the revolutions of 1848 and their reformist counterparts) and the 1910s (World War I and its aftermath).

The expansion of representation during the revolutions of 1848 largely responded to popular demands for new rights. The concentration of innovations after World War I, however, reflected a somewhat different situation: citizens (including female citizens) who bore the terrible costs of war bargained with war-battered states for rights they had previously lacked, which their military and civilian service visibly justified.

As charted by landmarks of parliamentary representation and suffrage, European democratization occurred in fits and starts, concentrating especially in periods of international turmoil. Similar rhythms governed the establishment of workers' rights to organize and strike; both clustered around the revolutions of 1848 and World War I (Ebbinghaus 1995). Parallel changes also occurred in civil liberties – speech, press, assembly, and association (Anderson and Anderson 1967, chapter 6). In all these regards, regime crises and bottom-up mobilization converged to extract concessions from existing holders of power.

At least for Europe, available political histories provide some means of implementing the principles of Box 3-1: concentrating on observations of interactions between citizens and states; inventing or adopting measures that aggregate over many citizen-state interactions and/or sampling a wide range of interactions; looking for changes in breadth, equality, protection, and mutual binding of state-citizen consultation; averaging those changes on the assumption that alterations in breadth, equality, protection, and mutually binding consultation make equal contributions to democratization and de-democratization; and so on through the nine principles.

Nevertheless, our principles 6 and 7 – setting a clear range of comparison cases and standardizing on the range – do not tell us directly what measurements to adopt. They do not mark a clear path to the direct measurement of democratization and de-democratization. Item 2 on Box 3-1's agenda – invent or adopt measures that aggregate over many citizen-state interactions and/or sample a wide range of interactions – hides many a wayside bomb (Bollen and Paxton 2000, Inkeles 1991, Paxton 2000).

Obviously we cannot adopt checklists containing supposedly essential components of democratic systems such as competitive elections or a free press. Such checklists would take us back to yes-no comparisons seeking to distinguish what differentiates all democracies from all non-democracies. Instead, we need matters of degree that indicate a regime's movement toward greater or lesser democracy. At a minimum we would need shifts in the amount of press freedom and changes in the extent of participation in competitive elections, as measured by Tatu Vanhanen. But even those more dynamic measures would restrict our attention to regimes that have some sort of national press and hold competitive elections.

Ideally, we would like to have indicators that apply across the entire range from very undemocratic to very democratic regimes. Here are the sorts of indicators that would help:

Breadth: Increase (decrease) in the share of the population having legally enforceable rights to communicate complaints about governmental performance to high officials

Equality: Decline (rise) in the number of distinct legal categories defining rights and obligations of different population segments vis-à-vis the state

Protection: Decrease (increase) in the proportion of the population imprisoned without legal sentencing or legal recourse

Mutually binding consultation: Increase (decrease) in the share of all citizens' complaints regarding denial of legally mandated benefits that result in delivery of those benefits

No existing body of data contains these measures for any substantial number of regimes. Yet as they rate political rights and civil liberties on their scales of 1 to 7, Freedom House evaluators are actually processing information about just such changes (Gastil 1991). For the rest of this book, instead of trying to create a new set of numerical estimates, I will settle for adopting judgments from such sources as Freedom House and synthesizing political histories into my own judgments of shifts along the democracy-undemocracy scale.

Astonishing Switzerland

Let us see, for example, whether we can convert the unruly political history of Switzerland into something like a disciplined set of observations on democratization and de-democratization. We close in on Switzerland as a relatively unknown experimenter with both democratization and de-democratization. A close look at Swiss history between the late 18th century and the middle of the 19th century allows us to clarify the questions that have been emerging in this chapter so far: how we can trace movement along the democracy-undemocracy dimension, whether regimes that have entered the zone of possibility for democracy then become more liable to both democratization and de-democratization, and whether democratization and de-democratization typically occur at different tempos and with different forms of opposition between state and citizen power.

Swiss experience provides some surprises in all these regards, both because of the common assumption that the Swiss simply refashioned ancient Alpine local democracy into a national regime and because of Switzerland's reputation as a calm, smug, orderly country. In fact, the Swiss path to democracy led the country close to utter fragmentation and passed through nearly two decades of civil war.

The French Revolution shook Switzerland's economic and political ties to France while exposing Swiss people to new French models and doctrines. From 1789 onward, revolutionary movements formed in several parts of Switzerland. In 1793, Geneva (not a federation member, but closely tied to Switzerland) underwent a revolution on the French model. As the threat of French invasion mounted in early 1798, Basel, Vaud, Lucerne, Zurich, and other Swiss regions followed the revolutionary path. Basel, for example, turned from a constitution in which only citizens of the capital chose their canton's senators to another giving urban and rural populations equal representation.

In 1798, an expansive France conquered Switzerland in collaboration with Swiss revolutionaries. Under French supervision, the Swiss regime then adopted a much more centralized form of government with significantly expanded citizenship. The new regime incorporated the territories of cantons St. Gallen, Grisons, Thurgau, Ticino, Aargau, and Vaud on equal terms with the older cantons, but followed French revolutionary practice by reducing the cantons to administrative and electoral units. The central government remained fragile, however; four coups occurred between 1800 and 1802 alone. At the withdrawal of French troops in 1802, multiple rebellions broke out. Switzerland then rushed to the brink of civil war. Only Napoleon's intervention and the imposition of a new constitution in 1803 kept the country together.

The 1803 regime, known in Swiss history as the Mediation, restored considerable power to the cantons, but by no means reestablished the Old Regime. Switzerland's recast federation operated with a national assembly, official multilingualism, relative equality among cantons, and freedom for citizens to move from canton to canton. Despite some territorial adjustments, a weak central legislature, judiciary, and executive survived Napoleon's defeat. Survival only occurred, however, after another close brush with civil war, this time averted by Great Power intervention during 1813 to 1815.

In the war settlement of 1815, Austria, France, Great Britain, Portugal, Prussia, Russia, Spain, and Sweden accepted a treaty among 22 cantons (with the addition of Valais, Neuchâtel, and Geneva) called the Federal Pact as they guaranteed Switzerland's perpetual neutrality and the inviolability of its frontiers. As compared with the period of French hegemony, however, the Federal Pact greatly reduced the central state's capacity; Switzerland of the Federal Pact operated without a permanent bureaucracy, a standing army, common coinage, standard measures, or a national flag. It had to struggle with multiple internal customs barriers, a rotating capital, and incessant bickering among cantonal representatives who had no right to deviate from their home constituents' instructions. At the national scale, the Swiss lived with a system better disposed to vetoes than to concerted change.

At France's July 1830 revolution, anticlericalism became more salient in Swiss radicalism. Historians of Switzerland in the 1830s speak of a regeneration movement pursued by means of "publicity, clubs, and mass marches" (Nabholz et al. 1938 II, 406). A great spurt of new periodicals and pamphlets accompanied the political turmoil of 1830 to 1831 (Andrey 1986: 551–552). Within individual cantons, empowered liberals began enacting standard 19th-century reforms such as limitation of child labor and expansion of public schools. Nevertheless, the new cantonal constitutions installed during that mobilization stressed liberty and fraternity much more than they did equality.

Between 1830 and 1848, Switzerland underwent a contradictory set of political processes. Although the era's struggles unquestionably activated many convinced democrats, they pitted competing conceptions of democracy against each other. On one side, broadly speaking, we see the defenders of highland liberty: each village, city, and canton – or at least its property-holding adult males – should be free to control their collective destinies. On the other side we find the advocates of representative democracy at a national scale, who rejected the highland view in favor of greatly enlarged state capacity, equality across Switzerland as a whole, protection provided by federal authorities, and national consultation that would bind all parts of the country.

Behind the divisions between the two sides lay further divisions of religion, class, and integration into capitalist organization. The country's richer, more Protestant cantons struggled their way toward democracy. Those cantons installed representative institutions instead of the direct democracy of male citizens that had long prevailed in highland communities and cantons. Activists based in reformed cantons then used armed force to drive their unreformed neighbors toward representative democracy. They did so first in raids across cantonal boundaries, then in open, if short-lived, civil war.

The political problem became acute because national alignments of the mid-1840s pitted twelve richer and predominantly liberal-Protestant cantons against ten poorer, predominantly conservative-Catholic cantons in a diet in which each canton had a single vote. Ironically, the highland cantons that most prided themselves on direct democracy, Swiss style, dug in most fiercely against democratization that would involve population-based representation at a national scale. Thus liberals deployed the rhetoric of national patriotism and majority rule while conservatives countered with cantonal rights and defense of religious traditions. Three levels of citizenship – municipal, cantonal, and national – competed with one another.

Contention occurred incessantly, and often with vitriolic violence, from 1830 to 1848. Reform movements were already under way in Vaud and Ticino as 1830 began – indeed, Ticino preceded France by adopting a new constitution on July 4th, 1830 (Sauter 1972). Nevertheless, France's July Revolution of 1830 and its Belgian echo later in the year encouraged Swiss reformers and revolutionaries. As the French and Belgian revolutions rolled on, smaller-scale revolutions took place in the Swiss towns and cantons of Aargau, Lucerne, St. Gallen, Schaffhausen, Solothurn, Thurgau, Vaud, and Zurich. Thereafter, republicans and radicals repeatedly formed military bands and attempted to take over particular cantonal capitals by force of arms. Such bands failed in Lucerne (1841) but succeeded in bringing new administrations to power in Lausanne (1847), Geneva (1847), and Neuchâtel (1848).

The largest military engagement took place in 1847. Switzerland's federal Diet ordered dissolution of the mutual defense league (Sonderbund) formed by Catholic cantons two years earlier; when the Catholic cantons refused, the Diet sent an army to Fribourg and Zug (whose forces capitulated without serious fighting), then Lucerne (where a short battle occurred). The Sonderbund had about 79,000 men under arms, the federation some 99,000.

The Sonderbund War itself produced fewer casualties than the smaller-scale struggles that preceded it. Historian Joachim Remak titled his book on the subject *A Very Civil War* (1993). The war ended with 33 dead among Catholic forces and 60 dead among the attackers. Their defeat consolidated the dominance of liberals in Switzerland as a whole and led to the adoption of a cautiously liberal constitution, based on something like an American model, in 1848. The long negotiations of the peace settlement benefited greatly from two external factors: the distraction of Europe's major powers by their own 1848 revolutions and the unwillingness of Austria, Prussia, and France to let either of its rival powers gain political advantage in Switzerland.

The subsequent period resembled America's Reconstruction, the troubled time that followed the United States' own Civil War – grudging coexistence, persistent testing, but no more approaches to a definitive split. The "patriots" of 1848 led the country for years. General Guillaume Dufour, who led the federal troops that defeated the Sonderbund (and who had once taught Louis Napoleon at the Thun military school), for example, commanded the Swiss army for much of the first postwar decade. Between 1849 and 1870, all Swiss cantons terminated their profitable centuries-old export of mercenary units for military service outside of Switzerland. Thereafter, only papal guards and a few ceremonial military units represented Swiss soldiery outside of Switzerland itself. From that point onward, the image of tidy villages and orderly cities displaced the memory of incessant, bitter military strife.

Switzerland's complex history between 1790 and 1848 poses a serious challenge for the representation of democratization and de-democratization. Our capacity-democracy space helps to meet that challenge. Figure 3-3 traces Switzerland's astonishing trajectory from 1790 to 1848. Despite direct adult male democracy in a number of villages and highland cantons, the regime as a whole started its itinerary with low state capacity and little democracy. French intervention from 1798 onward boosted both capacity and democracy somewhat, but not permanently. At the 1815 peace settlement the Swiss regime both de-democratized and lost capacity. The energetic mobilizations of the 1830s restored some democracy to the regime as a whole without expanding the central state's capacity.

Soon Switzerland's divisions splintered first into civil wars at the cantonal and inter-cantonal levels before consolidating into the national civil war of the Sonderbund. By 1847 Switzerland had receded to its lowest levels of state capacity and democracy over the entire period. But with the military defeat of autonomist and conservative forces, the peace settlement of 1848 established a national regime of unprecedented democracy and state capacity. To be sure, late-19th-century Switzerland never came close to neighboring France, Prussia, or Austria with regard to central capacity. But it became a European model for decentralized democracy.

Before 1798, Switzerland had never come close to substantial capacity or democracy at a national scale. The French conquest of that year simultaneously imposed a much more centralized national government and connected Switzerland's advocates of national representative government with powerful French allies. At that point, Switzerland switched into a long phase of rapid, and often violent, alternation between democratization and de-democratization. Precisely because of the regime's

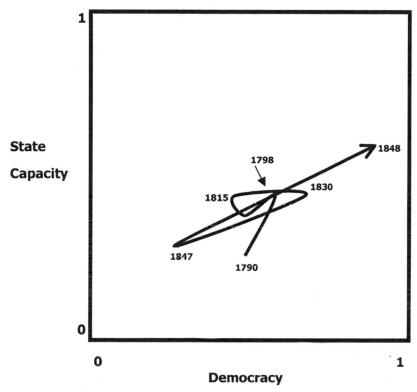

FIGURE 3-3. Fluctuations in Swiss National Regimes, 1790–1848

decentralized structure, variety, and sharp divisions, Swiss experience between 1798 and 1848 makes it difficult to divide national politics neatly into "state" and "citizens."

Swiss activists fought over that division for half a century. Yet a pair of generalizations that have been building up over other cases we have examined apply here as well: on the whole, Swiss de-democratization occurred more rapidly and violently than Swiss democratization, and in general, privileged elites backed de-democratization against the expressed will of most citizens. Formation of the Catholic-conservative Sonderbund (1845) and its engagement in outright civil war against liberal forces (1847) brought Switzerland's crisis of elite reaction. In Switzerland, as elsewhere, democratization and de-democratization turn out to have been asymmetrical processes.

Let me draw a methodological conclusion. As pleasant as it would be to manipulate quantitative measures of democratization, de-democratization, increase in state capacity, and decrease of state capacity, in the present state of knowledge, detailed analytical narratives of the kind we have just reviewed for Switzerland promise more for general explanations of democratization and de-democratization. They promise more because they allow us to match detailed changes in relations among political actors to alterations in their presumed causes. Although I will rely repeatedly on ratings such as those provided by Freedom House in chapters to come, the crucial matching of arguments and evidence will come in the form of analytical narratives.

What Next?

It is therefore time to move toward explanation of democratization and de-democratization. Almost inadvertently, we have accumulated a series of pressing explanatory questions. Answers to any of these questions, if correct, will provide major payoffs for today's studies of democracy. (If you yearn for fame and influence, and not necessarily fortune, as an analyst of democracy, answer one or more of these questions definitively.) Although I have phrased the questions in broadly historical terms, most students of the recent past are actually pursuing their own versions of the same questions. Box 3-2 summarizes the significant questions we have encountered so far.

The list does not, to be sure, exhaust every interesting question that contemporary students of democratization are taking up. These days, for example, many people are asking whether widespread religious fundamentalism among a regime's citizenry undermines or inhibits democratization, and whether there is some point of democratization at which ratchets fall into place that make de-democratization unlikely or impossible. But on the whole, the 13 questions sum up the problems for whose solution students of democratization and de-democratization would be inclined to award each other major prizes.

Saving questions 1 through 12 for later chapters, let me turn at once to number 13: necessary and sufficient conditions. Once you rule out conditions that belong to democratization and de-democratization by definition, I do not believe that any necessary, much less sufficient, conditions for either one exist. As we have already seen, comparison of cases in which democratization or de-democratization occurs with otherwise similar cases in which democratization or de-democratization does not occur can clarify what we have to explain. But it will not identify universal conditions. At least no one has identified such conditions so far.

BOX 3-2. Payoff Questions in the Study of Democratization and De-Democratization

1. In what ways did the truncated democratic institutions of city-states, warrior bands, peasant communities, merchant oligarchies, religious sects, and revolutionary movements provide models for more extensive forms of democracy? Given their availability, why did they never become direct templates for democracy at a national scale?

2. Why did Western Europe lead the way toward democratization, followed closely by the Americas?

3. How did (and do) such countries as France move from absolute immunity against national democratic institutions to frequent alternations between democratization and de-democratization?

4. Why, in general, did (and do) surges of de-democratization occur more rapidly than surges of democratization?

5. How do we explain the asymmetrical patterns of support for and involvement in democratization and de-democratization?

6. Why does democratization typically occur in waves, rather than in each regime separately at its own pace?

7. What explains the spread of democratization and de-democratization during the 19th and (especially) 20th centuries from its Western European starting points to the rest of the world?

8. Why (with the partial exceptions of Egypt and Japan) did democratization only start to occur in Asia and Africa well after World War II?

9. How can we account for the dramatically different experiences of postsocialist states with democratization and de-democratization?

10. Under what conditions, to what extent, and how does the growth of state capacity promote a regime's availability for democratization and de-democratization?

11. To what extent and how do an undemocratic regime's interactions with democratic regimes promote democratization in that regime?

12. How do the forms and sources of a state's sustaining resources (e.g., agriculture, minerals, or trade) affect its regime's susceptibility to democratization and de-democratization?

13. Do any necessary or sufficient conditions exist for democratization and de-democratization, or (on the contrary) do favorable conditions vary significantly by era, region, and type of regime?

I do think, however, that some necessary *processes* promote democratization, and that reversals of those processes promote de-democratization. For the moment, let us neglect de-democratization and concentrate on democratization to make this line of argument clear. For democratization to develop in any regime, changes must occur in three areas: trust networks, categorical inequality, and autonomous power centers.

Trust networks are ramified interpersonal connections, consisting mainly of strong ties, within which people set valued, consequential, long-term resources and enterprises at risk to the malfeasance, mistakes, or failures of others. Trading diasporas, kinship groups, religious sects, revolutionary conspiracies, and credit circles often comprise trust networks. Throughout most of history, participants in trust networks have carefully shielded themselves from involvement in political regimes, for justified fear that rulers would either seize their precious resources or subordinate them to the state's programs.

So long as they remain entirely segregated from regimes, however, trust networks constitute obstacles to democratization; their segregation blocks members' commitment to democratic collective enterprises. Democratization becomes possible when trust networks integrate significantly into regimes, and thus motivate their members to engage in mutually binding consultation – the contingent consent of citizens to programs proposed or enacted by the state (Tilly 2005b). Two large processes affecting trust networks therefore underlie democratization: 1) dissolution or integration of segregated trust networks and 2) creation of politically connected trust networks. In Switzerland, the violent struggles of 1830 to 1847 and the peace settlement of 1848 promoted both processes (Tilly 2004: 187–190).

Within the two processes appear a series of recurrent mechanisms, for example:

- Disintegration of existing segregated trust networks (e.g., decay of patrons' ability to provide their clients with goods and protection promotes withdrawal of clients from patron-client ties)
- Expansion of population categories lacking access to effective trust networks for their major long-term risky enterprises (e.g., growth of landless wage-workers in agrarian regions increases population without effective patronage and/or relations of mutual aid)
- Appearance of new long-term risky opportunities and threats that existing trust networks cannot handle (e.g., substantial increases in war, famine, disease, and/or banditry visibly overwhelm protective capacity of patrons, diasporas, and local solidarities)

In Switzerland, all three of these mechanisms reshaped trust networks between 1750 and 1848. Intensive growth of cottage textile production preceded 19th-century re-concentration in lowland cities, including Zürich. That two-stage industrial transformation swelled Switzerland's proletarian population as it shook the patronage-cum-control of landlords and parish priests (Braun 1960, 1965; Gruner 1968; Gschwind 1977; Joris 1994; Joris and Witzig 1992; Rosenband 1999). Successive French invasions, the 1815 great power settlement, and the struggles of 1830 through 1847 themselves had dual effects: They shook old relations between trust networks and public politics at the cantonal level, but – at least for Protestants and secular liberals – created new connections between interpersonal trust networks and the new half-regime that was emerging at a national scale within the Protestant-liberal coalition.

Each of the three mechanisms just listed promotes the dissolution of segregated trust networks and the creation of politically connected trust networks. The next chapter takes a detailed look at processes and mechanisms affecting trust networks' segregation from and integration into public politics.

What of categorical inequality? The term means organization of social life around boundaries separating whole sets of people who differ collectively in their life chances, as is commonly the case with categories of gender, race, caste, ethnicity, nationality, and religion and is sometimes the case with categories of social class. To the extent that such inequalities translate directly into categorical differences in political rights and obligations, democratization remains impossible. Any democratization process depends not necessarily on diminution of categorical inequality but on insulation of public politics from categorical inequality. Two main processes contribute to that insulation: equalization of the categories themselves in some regards and buffering of politics from the operation of those categories.

Here are the sorts of mechanisms that operate within the broader processes of equalization and buffering:

- Equalization of assets and/or well-being across categories within the population at large (e.g., booming demand for the products of peasant agriculture expands middle peasants)
- Reduction or governmental containment of privately controlled armed force (e.g., disbanding of magnates' personal armies weakens noble control over commoners, thereby diminishing nobles' capacity to translate noble-commoner differences directly into public politics)

- Adoption of devices that insulate public politics from categorical
  inequalities (e.g., secret ballots; payment of officeholders; and free,
  equal access of candidates to media forward the formation of cross-
  category coalitions)

These and similar mechanisms figured prominently in the Swiss history we have reviewed. In Switzerland, the regime that formed in 1848
established effective barriers between public politics and the categorical
inequalities over which Swiss activists killed each other during the previous 17 years.

Autonomous power centers operate outside the control of public politics and outside of regular citizen-state interactions. They can include
all those interpersonal connections that provide political actors – both
individuals and segments of the citizenry – with the means of altering
(or, for that matter, defending) existing distributions of resources, population, and activities within the regime. Sometimes they exist within
the state itself, most obviously when the military runs the state or operates independently of civilian authorities. The configuration of lineages,
religious congregations, economic organizations, organized communities,
and military forces in a given regime strongly affects the possibility that
the regime's public politics will move toward broad, equal, protected, and
mutually binding consultation. It does so both because that configuration
shapes what sorts of political actors are readily available and because it
affects which segments of the citizenry are directly available for participation in public politics. To the extent that power centers, especially those
controlling autonomous coercive means, remain detached from public
politics, democratization remains difficult or impossible.

Democracy-promoting processes involving autonomous power centers
include 1) broadening of political participation, 2) equalization of access
to political resources and opportunities outside the state, and 3) inhibition of autonomous and/or arbitrary coercive power both within and
outside the state. Although their weights and timing vary from one case
of democratization to another, to some degree all three must occur for
democratization to happen.

Mechanisms within these processes include:

- Coalition formation between segments of ruling classes and constituted
  political actors that are currently excluded from power (e.g., dissident
  bourgeois recruit backing from disfranchised workers, thus promoting
  political participation of those workers)

- Central co-optation or elimination of previously autonomous political intermediaries (e.g., regional strongmen join governing coalitions, thus becoming committed to state programs)
- Brokerage of coalitions across unequal categories and/or distinct trust networks (e.g., regional alliances form against state seizure of local assets, thus promoting employment of those alliances in other political struggles)

All of these mechanisms and more operated within the transition of Switzerland from enormous fragmentation to low-capacity partial democracy. Most important, the military victory and peace settlement of 1847 to 1848 definitively checked the longstanding capacity of communities and cantons to autonomously deploy their armed forces – which continued to exist.

Obviously larger changes in social life lie behind these crucial alterations of trust networks, categorical inequality, and non-state power. In later discussions we will pay attention to transformations of economic organization, mass communications, population mobility, and education. We will eventually see that four powerful political processes – domestic confrontation, military conquest, revolution, and colonization – have regularly accelerated transformations of trust networks, categorical inequality, and public politics, and as they have done so, these processes have sometimes produced rapid democratization or de-democratization.

All these changes will remain mysterious, and perhaps dubious as well, until we explore them in much more detail. In preparation for later chapters, however, let me simply lay out the argument in a straightforward series of points:

1. Trajectories of regimes within our capacity-democracy space significantly affect both the regimes' prospects for democracy and the character of their democracy if it arrives.
2. In the long run, increases in state capacity and democratization reinforce each other, as state expansion generates resistance, bargaining, and provisional settlements on one side, while on the other side democratization encourages demands for expansion of state intervention, which promotes increases in capacity.
3. At the extremes, if capacity develops farther and faster than democratization, the path to democracy (if it exists) passes through authoritarianism; if democratization develops farther and faster than capacity and the regime survives, the path then passes through a risky zone of capacity building.

4. Although the organizational forms – elections, terms of office, areal representation, deliberative assemblies, and so on – adopted by democratizing regimes often emulate or adapt institutions that have strong precedents in villages, cities, regional jurisdictions, or adjacent national regimes, they almost never evolve directly from those institutions.

5. Democratization depends on changes in three arenas – categorical inequality, trust networks, and public politics – as well as on interactions among those changes.

6. Regularities in democratization consist not of standard general sequences or sufficient conditions, but of recurrent causal mechanisms that in varying combinations and sequences produce changes in categorical inequality, networks of trust, and non-state power.

7. Under specifiable circumstances, revolution, conquest, colonization, and domestic confrontation accelerate and concentrate some of those crucial causal mechanisms.

8. Almost all of the crucial democracy-promoting causal mechanisms involve popular contention – politically constituted actors making public, collective claims on other actors, including agents of government – as correlates, causes, and effects.

9. Despite important alterations in the specific forms of democratic institutions such as legislatures and the relative impact of different causal factors such as international certification of democratic regimes, the fundamental processes promoting democratization have remained the same over democracy's several centuries of history.

These arguments center on a core idea. Democratization never occurs without at least partial realization of three large processes: integration of interpersonal trust networks into public politics; insulation of public politics from categorical inequalities; and elimination or neutralization of autonomous, coercion-controlling power centers in ways that augment the influence of ordinary people over public politics and increase the control of public politics over state performance. Substantial withdrawal of trust networks from public politics, increasing insertion of categorical inequalities into public politics, and rising autonomy of coercive power centers all promote de-democratization. Although delays occur in the effects of these processes as a function of institutions set in place in the past, the three large processes and their reversals always dominate moves toward and away from democracy.

Spelling out these arguments, the following chapters proceed in an obvious sequence. The next chapter (Chapter 4) deals with trust and distrust; Chapter 5 moves on to equality and inequality; and Chapter 6 takes up relations between public politics and autonomous power centers. We then turn to two syntheses. Chapter 7 analyzes alternative paths to democracy and undemocracy, whereas Chapter 8 offers general conclusions.

4

Trust and Distrust

With no deliberate plan, during the 19th century the American state built a huge, if clanking, machine for the integration of trust into public politics. Perhaps I should say the American *states*, since the mediation of national elections and other political activity by individual states provided opportunities for local and regional integration that a highly centralized system would have inhibited. As a result, three elements of American political life connected: 1) first-past-the-post elections in which victors gained the spoils while losers forsook the advantages of office; 2) patron-client chains tuned to the dispensation of jobs, political favors, and payoffs in return for political support; and 3) trust networks grounded in migration, ethnicity, religion, kinship, friendship, and work. American electoral campaigns in particular brought these elements together in vivid displays of partisanship.

The three elements represent much broader phenomena that figure in public politics everywhere: available forms of political participation; social relations among participants; and variable connections between trust networks and public politics. Their intersection matters because most historical combinations of political participation, social relations, and connections between trust networks and public politics have inhibited democratization rather than promoting it. Only certain combinations of the three make democratic politics possible. The next three chapters examine how those combinations come into being and how they produce their effects. This chapter concentrates on the place of trust and distrust in the formation of democratic regimes.

Let us pause for a moment to review the third element of 19th-century American political life: trust networks. For people who think of trust as a personal attitude – Joe is a trusting person, Jane tends to distrust everyone – the notion of a trust network sounds odd. We can, in fact, think of trust either as an attitude or as a relationship. For the purpose of studying democratization and de-democratization, it helps to concentrate on the relationship, leaving open what sorts of attitudes might motivate, complement, or result from a relationship of trust. Labels such as *kinsman, compadre, paisano, fellow believer*, and *co-member of a craft* provide a first indication of a trust relationship.

But we know a trust relationship more surely by the practices of its participants. People who trust each other lend one another money without security, provide favors without an immediate quid pro quo, allow one another to take care of their children, confide risky secrets to one another, ask one another to safeguard precious objects, and count on one another's assistance in emergencies.

Trust, then, consists of placing valued outcomes at risk to others' malfeasance, mistakes, or failures (Tilly 2005b). Trust relationships include those in which people regularly take such risks.[1] Although some trust relationships remain purely dyadic, they operate mainly within larger networks of similar relationships. Trust networks, to put it more formally, contain *ramified interpersonal connections, consisting mainly of strong ties, within which people set valued, consequential, long-term resources and enterprises at risk to the malfeasance, mistakes, or failures of others.*

How will we recognize a trust network when we encounter or enter one? First, we will notice a number of people who are connected, directly

[1] For surveys and particular studies of trust-sustaining practices, relations, and institutions, see Alapuro and Lonkila 2004; Anderson 1974; Anthony and Horne 2003; Auyero 2001; Bates et al. 1998; Bayat 1997; Bayon 1999; Besley 1995; Biggart 2001; Biggart and Castanias 2001; Buchan, Croson, and Dawes 2002; Burt and Knez 1995; Castrén and Lonkila 2004; Clark 2004; Cook 2001; Cordero-Guzmán, Smith, and Grosfoguel 2001; Curtin 1984; Darr 2003; Diani 1995; DiMaggio 2001; DiMaggio and Louch 1998; Elster 1999; Elster, Offe, and Preuss 1998; Feige 1997; Fernandez and McAdam 1988; Fontaine 1993; Gambetta 1993; Gould 1995, 1999, 2003; Granovetter 1995; Grimson 1999; Guinnane 2005; Guiso, Sapienza, and Zingales 2004; Haber, Razo, and Maurer 2003; Havik 1998; Heimer 1985; Hoffman, Postel-Vinay, and Rosenthal 2000; Landa 1994; Ledeneva 1998, 2004; Levi 1997; Levi and Stoker 2000; Light and Bonacich 1988; Lonkila 1999a, 1999b; MacLean 2004; Marques, Santos, and Araújo 2001; Meisch 2002; Morawska 1985, 1996, 2003; Muldrew 1993, 1998, 2001; Ogilvie 2005; Ohlemacher 1993; Opp and Gern 1993; Ostergren 1988; Ostrom 1990, 1998; Passy 1998, 2001; Pastor et al. 2002; Paxton 1999; Piipponen 2004; Portes 1995; Postel-Vinay 1998; Powell 1990; Powell and Smith-Doerr 1994; Rotberg 1999; Seligman 1997; Shapiro 1987; Singerman 1995; Solnick 1998; Stark 1995; Tilly 1990, 2000, 2005b; Tsai 2002; Uslaner 2002; Warren 1999; Weber and Carter 2003; White 2002; Wiktorowicz 2001; Wuthnow 2004; Yamagishi and Yamagishi 1994; Zelizer 2002, 2004, 2005a, 2005b.

or indirectly, by similar ties; they form a network. Second, we will see that the sheer existence of such a tie gives one member significant claims on the attention or aid of another; the network consists of strong ties. Third, we will discover that members of the network are collectively carrying on major long-term enterprises such as procreation, long-distance trade, transcontinental migration, workers' mutual aid, or practice of an underground religion. Finally, we will learn that the configuration of ties within the network sets the collective enterprise at risk to the malfeasance, mistakes, and failures of individual members. In 19th-century United States, many religious sects, artisanal groups, and migration streams maintained trust networks that eventually figured importantly in American public politics. In connection with the other two elements – competitive elections and patron-client networks – they put a distinctive stamp on 19th-century political struggles.

The three elements intertwined in Ohio's Thirteenth Electoral District during the congressional campaign of 1866 – just after the Civil War had ended. George Johns, a congressional employee, was helping organize the campaign of Republican candidate Columbus Delano. Among other local groups, he wanted to enlist the votes of Irish laborers, most of whom belonged to or supported the Fenian Brotherhood, the Irish nationalist revolutionary society founded in 1858. Since they had previously voted solidly Democratic, Fenians could help swing the Ohio election toward the Republicans. In particular, Johns wanted the help of Patrick Lamb, a saloonkeeper and sometime Democratic agent. Johns went to the saloon to seek out Lamb. As he later reported:

I asked the gentlemen who were with me if they would have something to drink. A glass of ale was taken, and I gave a five dollar bill in payment. Lamb was not present, and there being only a small boy he could not make the change. I told him it would do another time, but Lamb coming in shortly, the change was made. I had no conversation with him on this occasion, but I had heard him spoken of and referred to by others as a "Fenian." Later in the evening, after the close of the Butler meeting, he met me in Hughes' & Nichols's confectionery saloon, in this city; he took me outside and said that he had a considerable number of friends who were laborers, whom he wanted to get to vote for the republican party. I think he mentioned the number as between eighty and one hundred and twenty, and professed to have a considerable list of them – that it needed some work and attention and time to get them to the polls. He said that if he had fifty dollars to pay for his time and labor, and to pay his expenses, he would go and see them up and down the canal. (Bensel 2004: 70)

Lamb told a somewhat different story of his first meeting with Johns, but both agreed on the nature of their deal: money for votes. Lamb delivered a number of Fenian votes for Delano.

The openness and crassness of the Lamb-Johns transaction may shock 21st-century sensibilities. But it illustrates dramatically how the 19th-century American electoral process was integrating trust networks into public politics. In this case, ties formed by migration, ethnicity, religion, trade, and political conspiracy converged in connecting Ohio's Irish laborers. Their connections made them available to Lamb's brokerage. By no means did all voters receive payoffs or respond to brokers like Patrick Lamb. But in the American political arena, trust networks regularly formed the basis of people's involvement in politics.

The connection of politics with trust networks did not make 19th-century American politics benign. On the contrary, the salience of ethnicity, religion, race, migrant origin, and craft in political mobilization regularly generated violence as one organized group sought to cow or exclude another. Elections provided the high points – or, depending on your perspective, the low points. The presidential election of 1852, which pitted Democrat Franklin Pierce (the eventual winner) against Whig Winfield Scott, occurred as fights over slavery, the admission of new states, and immigration were bitterly dividing both parties, Indeed, the Whig party exploded during the next four years, and the Republicans arose as the anti-slavery party.

Ethnic alignments on all the issues became more salient. In the St. Louis elections of 1852, the First Ward's Democrat-supporting Germans simply prevented all Whigs from voting:

The election went forward with no more than the usual scuffling and shenanigans, possibly including [Whig agitator] Buntline's ripping down a Democratic poster and some stone-throwing. Then shots rang out – Whig supporters thought, from Neumeyer's tavern and house. Joseph Stevens was fatally hit and a few others hurt, either from this first shelling or as Buntline's group moved toward the tavern, which they sacked and burned. Authorities quickly turned out to quell the fighting, contain the fire, and much later in the evening, check the mob movement against the German newspaper. (Grimsted 1998: 230)

In St. Louis, Ohio's Thirteenth District, and elsewhere, elections offered repeated opportunities for mobilization on the basis of ethnicity, religion, migrant origin, race, and craft. In each case, local organizations based on or incorporating trust networks supplied the bases for mobilization.

Trust Networks Put Out Fires

Take the notorious case of 19th-century volunteer fire companies. Like the private militias that proliferated in the 19th-century United States, fire companies typically recruited from a single, local, urban, working-class, ethnic cluster. They regularly competed and fought with one another:

Fighting was a time-honored tradition among firemen. Most of the disputes flowed from functional differences. Hose companies fought for water plugs nearest a fire, and engine companies then did battle for prime hose locations. Being first to a fire engendered a great deal of pride, but the honor of extinguishing it was often achieved by fighting off later arrivals. Getting to a fire involved battling enthusiastic rivals who cut tow ropes and jammed carriage spokes with spanners to win the race. Fire companies were thus grass-roots institutions of the first order and competing units in every sense. (Laurie 1973: 77)

In Southwark, then a suburb of Philadelphia, during the 1840s, seven different fire companies operated from bases within a few streets of one another.

The American Republican Shiffler Hose Company drew its name from George Shiffler, an apprentice leather worker. Shiffler had been the first native-born American killed in Philadelphia's 1844 street fighting between Catholics and Protestants. As the rest of its name suggests, the hose company aligned with the recently formed nativist, anti-Catholic, and anti-slavery Republican Party. The Shiffler Company recruited its members from native-born Yankees. It fought most fiercely with the (Irish Catholic and Democratic) Moyamensing Hose Company and their gang allies, the Killers. The Killers often lit fires in Southwark and then waited to ambush the Shifflers as they arrived to extinguish the fires. But the Shifflers, in their turn, started carrying muskets and duck guns when they went to a new blaze. As a result, both Killers and Shifflers often left a fire with gunshot wounds (Laurie 1973: 79–82).

Eventually the tendency of volunteer fire companies to fight one another rather than fires and the frequency with which their more zealous members lit fires for the adventure of extinguishing them led American municipalities to professionalize their fire-fighting forces. But for decades volunteer fire companies, recruited from ethnically segregated trades, operated not only as guardians of public safety but also as workers' mutual benefit societies.

In Poughkeepsie, New York, Clyde and Sally Griffen's close accounting of fire company membership during the later 19th century reveals the great concentration of their members in locally concentrated trades, drawing especially on wage earners in their late twenties and early thirties who had little or no prospect of advancement from their positions as journeymen or laborers. (Alas, the Griffens did not analyze their fire companies' ethnic composition directly, but the companies' geographic distribution makes it seem likely that they divided mainly into Irish, German, and Yankee units.) "What their members lacked in future prospects," report the Griffens,

they made up in present excitement. Companies frequently made excursions to other cities, occasions full of conviviality sure to be recounted in detail in local newspapers. One company made an excursion to New Haven where "bonfires lit their parade routes on every corner...and they were feasted and welcomed by the Mayor." The next day the entire fire department of that city escorted them to the steamers for New York...A letter to the *Daily Press* complained in 1868 about the extensive coverage of "firemen's visits abroad, including tar-barrels, torchlights, collations, speeches, beautiful bouquets, pretty girls and all that sort of thing." (Griffen and Griffen 1978: 42)

Fire companies provided ordinary men with opportunities for public parade, celebration, and amusement. They also produced their own forms of mutual aid, including burial insurance. Commonly homogeneous in national origin as a function of their cities' residential segregation, they offered inviting pools for recruitment of votes and political activists. They played their parts in the integration of trust networks into American public politics organized around trade and ethnicity. Through ward committees, shop committees, and city-wide organizations, political parties and labor unions then aggregated political involvement into city, state, and national connections.

Lest this argument sound like warmed-over Tocqueville on the importance of voluntary associations to democracy in America, let me record my basic agreement with Jason Kaufman's analysis of fraternal orders and similar organizations since the later 19th century (Kaufman 2002). Kaufman's contrarian research documents the intensity of associational involvement in American cities during later decades of the 19th century. But it argues vigorously that:

1. Associational life declined after World War I.
2. The associations that declined served parochial interests rather than the general good.
3. For the most part, they thrived on combinations of exclusion, sociability, and security, for example, by providing mutual aid for recent immigrants from a single region.
4. They therefore contributed to the segmentation of American political and social life.
5. It was therefore on balance a good thing that associational life declined.

The first point challenges both Robert Putnam (who sees a decline in American voluntary participation, all right, but places it after 1950) and Theda Skocpol (who sees a vast organizational surge from the late 19th century involving the creation of national associations, their generation of local chapters, their absorption of and affiliation with previously existing local associations, and their increasing effectiveness as conduits for interest-based politics) (Putnam, Leonardi, and Nanetti 2000; Skocpol 2003; Skocpol and Fiorina 1999). The second, third, and fourth points confound latter-day admirers of Alexis de Tocqueville, who see civil society and voluntary association as crucial democratic assets and distinctive features of the American political heritage. The final point pronounces a surprising judgment on current calls for revival of voluntarism. It implies that a new proliferation of voluntary associations could easily advance parochial interests instead of serving democracy.

Fraternal orders, workers' mutual benefit societies, private militias, fire companies, and similar 19th-century organizations did serve parochial interests before they advanced democracy. In New York City during the 1850s, ethnic neighborhoods created their own militia units:

> By 1852, 4,000 out of 6,000 members were foreign-born, including: 2,600 Irish in the Emmet Guard, the Irish Rifles, the Irish-American Guards, and the Ninth and Sixty-ninth Regiments; 1,700 Germans in their own regiments; the Italian Garibaldi Guard, and the French Garde Lafayette attached to the Twelfth Regiment. On the other extreme, 2,000 "American" residents of the Lower East Side joined such stoutly nativist militia companies as the American Rifles and the American Guard. (Scherzer 1992: 199)

In frontier Milwaukee at the same time, public politics centered on organized rivalries among Yankees, Germans, and Irish, with the question of temperance sharply dividing sober Yankees from the rest (Conzen 1976, chapter 7).

Unlike the aggregating effects of catchall trade unions and political parties, political entities based narrowly on ethnic, religious, class, and craft differences inhibited the cross-group consensus and cross-cutting collective action promoted by thinner but broader forms of organization. But these narrowly based political entities produced two results those sorts of organizations rarely promoted: they integrated previously segregated trust networks at least partway into public politics, and they provided newcomers to associational life with experience in the give and take of organizational activity. To that extent they promoted American democratization.

Essential Concepts

In order to understand what was happening in the 19th-century United States, we now need to re-complicate the basic state-citizen relationship in three different ways: with regard to political resources that attach citizens to states, with regard to the place of intermediaries in the state-citizen relation, and with regard to political connections of trust networks.

First, *political resources* include benefits and penalties that influence people's participation in public politics. Political resources divide broadly into coercion, capital, and commitment. *Coercion* includes all concerted means of action that commonly cause loss or damage to the persons, possessions, or sustaining social relations of social actors. It features means such as weapons, armed forces, prisons, damaging information, and organized routines for imposing sanctions. Coercion's organization helps define the nature of regimes. With low accumulations of coercion, all regimes are insubstantial, while with high levels of coercive accumulation and concentration all regimes are formidable. As compared with its 20th-century counterparts, the 19th-century American state did not dispose of extensive coercive resources. Many of those resources, furthermore, fragmented into state and local versions such as militias and sheriffs.

Capital refers to tangible, transferable resources that in combination with effort can produce increases in use value, plus enforceable claims on such resources. Regimes that command substantial capital – for example, from rulers' direct control of natural resources, itself often undergirded by coercion – to some extent substitute purchase of other resources and compliance for direct coercion of their subject populations. As the center of an increasingly capitalist regime, the 19th-century U.S. state disposed of ample capital, but only in concert with its major capitalists.

Commitment means relations among persons, groups, structures, or positions that promote their taking account of one another. Shared language, for instance, powerfully links persons and groups without any necessary deployment of coercion or capital. Commitment's local organization varies as dramatically as do structures of coercion and capital. Commitments can take the form of shared religion or ethnicity, trading ties, work-generated solidarities, communities of taste, and much more. To the extent that commitments of these sorts connect rulers and ruled, they substitute partially for coercion and capital. But commitment can also turn against a government, as occurred in both the North and South during the prelude to the Civil War.

Second, *intermediaries*. Throughout most of history, few citizens have maintained direct contact with their states. They usually made contact with state authorities through privileged and partly autonomous intermediaries such as landlords, warlords, priests, and lineage heads. The new American state established some direct contact with its citizens through such national institutions as the postal service and its corps of tax collectors. But even in the 19th-century United States, most citizen-state interaction passed through two kinds of intermediaries: formal entities speaking for their putative interests and members of the elite who brokered government influence.

In the first category fell trade unions, political parties, special-interest associations, churches, and (more temporarily) groups of social movement activists. The second category included managers, officeholders, and a number of operatives – like George Johns – who dispensed favors in return for political support. With these two sorts of intermediaries, we begin to see that regimes do not reduce strictly to citizens and states but necessarily include a number of partly autonomous political actors. A regime consists of regularized interactions among states, citizens, and constituted political actors.

Third, *political connections of trust networks*. Throughout the same long stretch of human history during which state-citizen interaction remained mostly indirect, people were regularly carrying on valued, risky collective enterprises such as clandestine religious sects, long-distance trade, and maintenance of lineages by means of trust networks. Members of trust networks generally kept themselves insulated from state power as much as they could (Tilly 2005b). They knew that rulers who acquired control over trust networks commonly either subordinated those networks to their own state enterprises or crippled them by seizing their crucial resources: land, money, labor power, information, and more.

Yet now and then trust networks have become integrated into public politics. Box 4-1 identifies major exceptions to the historical insulation of trust networks from public politics. Those exceptions developed in one of three ways: indirectly through patrons, protectors, and other powerful intermediaries; more directly through actors publicly representing their collective interests; and even more directly via such state-controlled arrangements as theocracy, fascism, and social security.

Democracies necessarily accomplish partial integration of trust networks into public politics. If the basic trust networks that citizens deploy as they pursue their major collective enterprises remain segregated from public politics, then citizens have few incentives to participate in politics

BOX 4-1. Major Historical Exceptions to the Segregation of Trust
Networks from Public Politics

1. Trust networks in the form of religious sects, kinship groups, or mercantile networks have occasionally established their own autonomous
   systems of rule.

2. Regimes have sometimes conquered other regimes that were already run
   by trust networks.

3. Political actors organized as trust networks (e.g., religious cults) have
   sometimes seized power in already constituted regimes.

4. Once in power, rulers have often created their own trust networks in the
   forms of dynastic marriage alliances and internal patronage systems.

5. At least temporarily, totalitarian and theocratic regimes have managed
   extensive incorporation of existing trust networks into authoritarian systems of rule.

6. Democracies manage partial, contingent integration of trust networks
   into public politics.

and very strong incentives to shield their social relations from political
intervention. These conditions make effective, sustained translation of
citizens' expressed collective will into state action almost impossible, at
least outside of revolution. But total integration in the style of theocracies,
lineage-connected oligarchies, and fascism also squeezes out the possibility of democracy. It does so, as items 1 to 5 on Box 4-1's list suggest, by
inhibiting the negotiated translation of citizens' collective will into state
action.

How, then, would we know that trust networks were becoming integrated into public politics? Slanted toward indicators from our own time,
Box 4-2 identifies likely signs of that integration. They include the deliberate seeking of state protection or authorization for organizations embodying trust networks, the commitment of resources and members of trust
networks to state service, and – even riskier, in terms of historical experience – solicitation of direct state intervention in the operation of trust
networks. In general, these signs indicate that people are no longer working so hard to shield their trust networks from state surveillance and
intervention, that they are relying more heavily on state agencies for the
pursuit of their valued, long-term, high-risk collective enterprises, that in
practical ways they are displaying greater trust in government.

BOX 4-2. Signs of Trust Networks' Integration into Public Politics

In the contemporary world, we would be observing integration of trust networks into public politics if we saw many people in a given regime doing a number of the following things:

- Creating publicly recognized associations, mutual aid societies, parties, unions, congregations, and communities or seeking recognition for similar organizations that have existed underground
- Pursuing friendship, kinship, shared belief, security, and high-risk enterprises within such organizations
- Permitting family members to serve in national military and police forces
- Enrolling children in state-run educational institutions
- Promoting careers of family members in public service, including government office
- Seeking (or at least tolerating) government registration of vital events such as births, deaths, and marriages and then using the registration to validate legal transactions
- Providing private information to public organizations and authorities through censuses, surveys, and applications for services
- Entrusting private contracts to governmental enforcement
- Asking government agents to punish or prevent malfeasance by members of their own kin groups, religious sects, or economic networks
- Using government-issued legal tender for interpersonal transactions and savings
- Purchasing government securities with funds (e.g., dowry) committed to maintenance of interpersonal ties
- Relying on political actors and/or government agencies for vital services and long-term security

In European experience, we begin to catch glimpses of trust networks' integration in places like the Dutch Republic during the 17th century. Marjolein 't Hart points out that the new Dutch state, unlike its European rivals, already enjoyed excellent credit during the 17th century. The Netherlands' 17th-century revolt against Spain led to economic and organizational improvement of public finances in that supremely commercial regime. In the process, Dutch burghers began investing furiously in government securities, thus tying their families' fates to that of the regime:

In part, the Dutch success must be explained by the fact that the chief investors were magistrates and politicians themselves. They were close enough to their local receiver with whom they had contracted loans. At times, they were urged to invest by their political leaders so as to stimulate other buyers. The federal structure implied also a large degree of local political control. Other secure investments were found in land and houses, but already by 1700 the capital invested in government bonds exceeded all other. ('t Hart 1993: 178)

The segmented structure of the Dutch Republic, 't Hart reminds us, facilitated the work of brokers who simultaneously occupied municipal, provincial, and national positions of power. They helped make the Dutch Republic precocious in its integration of elite trust networks (Adams 2005, Davids and Lucassen 1995, Glete 2002, Prak 1991). It took another two centuries before ordinary Europeans and North Americans began investing major parts of their savings in government securities.

Sooner or later, however, it happened widely. Ordinary people face risks and carry on risky long-term enterprises even when their available trust networks fail to give them adequate protection. In those circumstances, governments or political actors that can either shore up existing networks or create new alternatives to them become more attractive – or at least less unattractive – allies. As the Dutch example suggests, some additional circumstances increase the attractiveness of politically connected trust networks to a broad public: creation of external guarantees for governmental commitments, as when a peace treaty or an occupying power backs up a defeated government's finances; increase in governmental resources for risk reduction and/or compensation of loss, as when commercial expansion generates new tax revenues; and visible governmental meeting of commitments to the advantage of substantial new segments of the population, as when non-citizens not only become eligible for welfare benefits but actually receive them.

The Democratic Dilemma

How do such connections affect democracy? Robert Putnam's work on Italy and the United States puts the connections between trust and democracy prominently on the agenda of democratic theory without actually stating a clear argument concerning the causal chain between trust and democracy. Putnam's *Making Democracy Work* provides evidence of a significant relationship between the extent of participation in non-governmental civic associations in an Italian region and the perceived effectiveness of governmental institutions in the same region: the greater the participation, the higher the effectiveness.

A theoretical slide then occurs at each end of Putnam's argument. On the side of governmental institutions, Putnam drifts into interpreting more effective institutions as more democratic. On the side of civic engagement, Putnam begins to treat organizational networks, social capital, norms of reciprocity, and fabrics of trust as closely connected or even equivalent elements. This double glissando leads to his book's final sentence: "Building social capital will not be easy, but it is the key to making democracy work" (Putnam, Leonardi, and Nanetti 1993: 185).

Similarly, in the United States Putnam moves hurriedly from civic involvement to democracy:

Modern society is replete with opportunities for free-riding and opportunism. Democracy does not require that citizens be selfless saints, but in many modest ways it does assume that most of us much of the time will resist the temptation to cheat. Social capital, the evidence increasingly suggests, strengthens our better, more expansive selves. The performance of our democratic institutions depends in measurable ways upon social capital. (Putnam, Leonardi, and Nanetti 2000: 349)

At best, then, we can draw from Putnam's analyses a much more modest conclusion: *within already relatively democratic regimes*, people who engage in civic organizations (or perhaps only in organizations oriented to the public good) are more likely to meet their collective obligations, to press for better government performance, and to trust their fellow citizens (Bermeo 2000). Such an argument may well be valid, but it tells us little about the causal connections between democracy and trust.

Recent democratic theorists have made four main claims about the bearing of trust on democracy as such:

1. As Margaret Levi's analysis of contingent consent (1997) indicates, collaboration with any government on the basis of commitment rather than coercion depends on expectations that others will bear fair shares of the governmental burden – pay their taxes, perform their military service, and so on.
2. Democracies are supposed to require higher levels of trust in government than other sorts of regimes because the voluntary delegation of powers to representatives and officials can only occur on the basis of extensive trust.

3. Alternation of factions in power depends on the trust of current non-incumbents that their turn will come, or at least that incumbents will honor their interests.

4. From the perspectives of most political actors, democracy is inherently a riskier, more contingent system than others; therefore only actors having significant trust in the outcomes of democratic politics will collaborate with the system at all.

All four claims make a certain level of trust a necessary condition for democracy. They imply that a significant decline in trust threatens democracy. All four imply that authoritarian and patronage-based regimes can survive with much lower levels of trust than democracies.

Mark Warren neatly knits together the four claims by pointing out the contradictions between public politics and trust. Politics, for Warren, combines conflicts over goods, pressures to associate for collective action, and attempts to produce collectively binding decisions (Warren 1999: 311). All these processes – goods conflicts, collective action, and bids for collectively binding decisions – occur more widely in the public politics of democracies. But precisely those processes threaten naturally accumulated trust: goods conflicts generate dissension, collective action brings us-them boundaries into play, and collectively binding decisions mean unequal realization of individual and group interests. Thus democracies require greater trust – at least with regard to outcomes of political struggle – than other sorts of regimes. We might call Warren's formulation *the democratic dilemma of trust*.

Warren identifies three competing theoretical solutions to the democratic dilemma: neoconservative, rational choice, and deliberative. The neoconservative view, typified by Francis Fukuyama, declares that the only way to mitigate the dilemma is to minimize the number of collective decisions made by political institutions and maximize those lodged where trust of one kind or another already exists: natural communities and markets. Rational choice approaches, exemplified by Russell Hardin, see trust as a belief that another (a person or an institution) has an interest in one's own welfare; hence institutions that guarantee beneficial performance help resolve the democratic dilemma.

The deliberative solution, which Warren himself prefers, bridges the gap by making democratic deliberation and trust mutually complementary: the very process of deliberation generates trust, but the existence of trust facilitates deliberation. The neoconservative theory identifies no necessary connection between democracy and trust, whereas the rational choice and deliberative theories make trust uniquely indispensable to democracy.

My argument likewise addresses the democratic dilemma, but radically recasts it and proposes a fourth solution. Treating trust as a relationship in which at least one party places valued enterprises at risk to the errors, failures, or malfeasance of another party, it recognizes that such relationships cluster in distinctive networks, especially as the duration and stakes of the valued enterprises increase. Although historically most trust networks have grown up outside of public politics, sometimes they originate within major political actors (e.g., trade unions) or in government itself (e.g., veterans' pension systems). Yet we should doubt that associations as such hold the key to democratic participation. Instead, we should recognize that the forms of relations between trust networks and public politics matter deeply. They govern the possibility of contingent consent, hence the effective translation of citizens' expressed collective will into state action.

Surprisingly, a kind of *distrust* therefore becomes a necessary condition of democracy. Contingent consent entails unwillingness to offer rulers, however well elected, blank checks. It implies the threat that if they do not perform in accordance with citizens' expressed collective will, citizens will not only turn them out but also withdraw compliance from such risky government-run activities as military service, jury duty, and tax collection. In Albert Hirschman's terms, democratic citizens may display loyalty during recognized state crises, but ordinarily they employ voice backed by the threat of exit (Hirschman 1970).

The democratic dilemma, in this view, concerns how to connect those valued enterprises and the networks that sustain them to public politics without damaging either trust networks or public politics. The connection will only work well with contingent consent on the part of trust network members. A state's shift away from coercion toward combinations of capital and commitment promotes contingent consent. The trajectory of democratization therefore differs greatly depending on whether the previous relationships between trust networks and rulers are those of authoritarianism, theocracy, patronage, or outright evasion.

For example, democratization depends on movement away from coercion and on relaxation of governmental controls over visible trust networks as an exit from authoritarianism. From a starting point of patronage, in contrast, democratization depends on weakening of patrons' mediation and on more direct integration of trust networks into public politics. Matthew Cleary and Susan Stokes offer a "stylized scenario" illustrating both the operation and the limits of patron-client systems:

A poor and class-divided society democratizes. Poverty and inequality tempt political parties to deploy a strategy of clientelism: the trading of votes and political support in return for small, private payoffs to voters. Clientelism functions only when both voters and political brokers are tightly enmeshed in personal networks, networks that allow the brokers to punish individual voters who defect from their implicit contract – to hold them "perversely accountable" for their votes. Clientelism is then, by necessity, a highly personalized form of politics. It also requires that voters take actions that cannot be fully monitored by the patron party, such as voting for their candidates in exchange for handouts. To improve compliance, parties cultivate relations of friendship and trust with their clienteles. (Cleary and Stokes 2006: 10)

Cleary and Stokes rightly point out that such a system sacrifices accountability in favor of loyalty. If my analysis of the American 19th-century experience is correct, however, it plays a crucial part in connecting previously insulated trust networks with public politics.

Of breadth, equality, mutually binding consultation, and protection, integration of trust networks into public politics most directly affects mutually binding consultation. To the extent that people integrate their trust networks into public politics, they come to rely on governmental performance for maintenance of those networks. They also gain power, individual and collective, through the connections to government that those networks mediate. They acquire an unbreakable interest in governmental performance. The political stakes matter. Paying taxes, buying governmental securities, yielding private information to officials, depending on government for benefits, and releasing network members for military service cement that interest and promote active bargaining over the terms of its fulfillment.

Interested citizens participate more actively, on the average, in elections, referenda, lobbying, interest group membership, social movement mobilization, and direct contact with politicians – that is, in consultation. Conversely, segments of the population that withdraw their trust networks from public politics for whatever reasons weaken their own interest in governmental performance, hence their zeal to participate in democratic public politics. Furthermore, to the extent that rich, powerful people can buy public officials or capture those pieces of government bearing most directly on their interests, they weaken public politics doubly: by withdrawing their own trust networks and by undermining the effectiveness of less fortunate citizens' consultation.

Three main processes integrate trust networks into public politics: dissolution of segregated trust networks, integration of previously segregated trust networks, and creation of new politically connected trust networks. These processes qualify as necessary causes of democratization. They are necessary because without them, citizens lack incentives to face the adversities of democratic politics and can easily exit from public politics when things go against them. Integrated trust networks encourage citizens to choose voice and loyalty over exit.

Reversals of those processes produce withdrawals of trust networks from public politics. Remember the analyses of differences between democratization and de-democratization we encountered earlier: the usually greater speed of de-democratization than of democratization and the disproportionate influence of power holders on de-democratization. Both result to an important degree from the greater ease with which powerful people can withdraw their own trust networks from direct involvement in public politics. They can do so by such means as creating private control over pieces of the state, purchasing such services as education and protection rather than using those supplied to the public, and buying cooperation of state officials instead of seeking to influence them through established political institutions.

Integration of trust networks into public politics is not, however, a *sufficient* condition for democratization; authoritarian regimes and theocracies, after all, likewise integrate trust networks. For a full explanation of democratization, we also have to consider two other clusters of processes: 1) insulation of categorical inequalities (for example, by class, gender, and race) from public politics and 2) transformation of non-state power through a) broadening of political participation, b) equalization of political participation, c) enhancement of collective control over government, and d) inhibition of arbitrary coercive power by political actors, including agents of government. Together, the integration of trust networks, insulation of categorical inequalities, and transformations of non-state power produce the broad, equal, binding, and protective relations between citizens and states that constitute democracy.

Back to the United States

As we look closely at 19th-century American politics, to be sure, we discover plenty of racism, nativism, bigotry, violence, crass competition, and corruption. As Cleary and Stokes suggest, America's client-based politics depended heavily on personal acquaintance, sacrificed accountability for loyalty, and imposed serious scale limits on politically based collective action. It also rested on exclusion, often forcible, of non-clients.

Concluding his superb survey of contested elections during the later 19th century, Richard Bensel recognizes the stringent limits of American political participation. The characteristic voter of the time, he points out,

was the northern, rural, native-born, white, Protestant male. Facing almost no barriers at the polls, such males voted at rates higher than any other group in American history. Others faced formal barriers or social discrimination of one kind or another. Southern and border state whites, for example, were often disabled on grounds of suspect loyalty. Blacks, both North and South, were thought to be mentally and culturally deficient. Western Mormons were viewed as immoral heretics (although they turned the tables in Utah). Urban immigrants were incompletely assimilated, thus possessing flawed understandings of American institutions and ideals. It did not help that many of them were Catholic. When these groups claimed suffrage rights – and they all did – the polls became charged with passion and, all too often, violence, fraud, and intimidation. (Bensel 2004: 287)

Bensel concludes that the use of physical violence to exclude competitors and pariahs from the polls compromised democratic freedoms (Bensel 2004: 290). Yet the conflict-filled process he describes was paradoxically increasing the stakes of elections, stimulating organizational efforts on behalf of excluded categories, and creating ties between those categories' trust networks and public politics.

Despite massive exclusion of slaves and women from the electorate, over the 19th century, levels of political participation rose significantly in the United States. Property and taxpaying qualifications for the vote declined rapidly as U.S. states multiplied during the first half of the century (Keyssar 2000: 50–51), but involvement of those who were eligible to vote also increased election by election. Figure 4-1 provides a crude indication. It plots the proportion of the total population voting in presidential elections against that total population (from U.S. Department of Commerce 1975: I, 8 and II, 1073–1074). Before the election of 1824 state procedures for casting electoral votes varied too much for an accurate reckoning of the popular vote. But from that point on, we have reasonable counts. In 1824, Andrew Jackson beat John Quincy Adams in the popular vote, with Henry Clay and W. H. Crawford far behind. But in the absence of a majority of electoral votes, the House of Representatives chose Adams over Jackson.

In 1824, about 356,000 men voted, around 3.5 percent of the total population (male and female, adults and children) of 10.4 million. By the

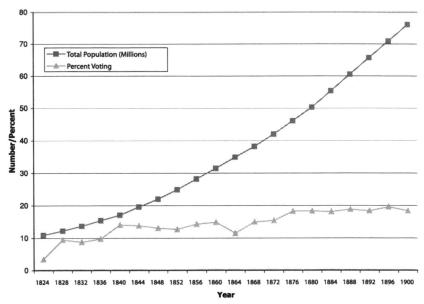

FIGURE 4-1. Total Population and Popular Vote in U.S. Presidential Elections, 1824–1900

election of 1828 (again Jackson vs. Adams, with Jackson winning this time), the number of voters more than tripled to almost 1.2 million, or 9.4 percent of the total population. From that point onward, as the total population grew rapidly, the proportion voting for president rose overall, reaching close to 20 percent in the 1870s. (Of course, the emancipation of slaves greatly increased the number of adult males eligible to vote, but in fact violence-backed discrimination kept most black men from the polls for decades longer.) The major exceptions to expansion occurred during the Civil War in 1864, when Confederate states Alabama, Arkansas, Florida, Georgia, Louisiana, Mississippi, North Carolina, South Carolina, Tennessee, Texas, and Virginia obviously did not vote in the Union, and then in 1868, when Mississippi, Texas, and Virginia had not yet formally reentered the Union.

What do these numbers mean? Even at century's end, a fairly small number of adult males were electing American presidents. As Ohio's 1866 election illustrates, furthermore, many of those adult males were exchanging votes for favors rather than deeply deliberating the qualities of presidential candidates. Political brokers were becoming very skilled at collecting votes for their own parties, and not necessarily to the benefit of their constituents. Nevertheless, two changes of great importance for American democracy were occurring. First, overall participation in public politics, however ill-informed, was increasing. Second, precisely because they drew directly on local workplace, ethnic, religious, and kinship ties, political organizations and brokers were integrating trust networks into American public politics.

New York City's Italians, for example, began their organizational lives in the city by creating entirely Italian mutual aid societies and Catholic parishes. But soon they connected with public politics by organizing political clubs. "[B]y the turn of the century," reports Samuel Baily,

well-organized and effective political machines – whose leaders were willing to accommodate to some extent the diverse social and economic groups of the city – had come to play an increasingly important role in politics. The formation of Italian political clubs affiliated with these machines was an important initial step in the long-term process of Italian incorporation into the political system in New York. In a manner similar to the role played by ethnic parishes in the church, Italian political clubs proved over time to be the most effective mechanism with which to recruit Italians into the political system. (Baily 1999: 210)

The clanking American political machine was busy incorporating immigrant trust networks into national politics by means of entirely local links.

The process sometimes reversed. During the 1850s, divisions between the often simultaneously anti-slavery, anti-Catholic, and anti-immigrant advocates of free labor and their Democratic opponents blocked the process of incorporation. For example, a group of nativists called Know-Nothings had a million members by 1854 (Keyssar 2000: 84). The Civil War itself ruptured the integration of southern trust networks into the national state, and Reconstruction only painfully knit them back together. After the Civil War, threatened elites in both the South and North regularly tried to reverse the increasing involvement of blacks, organized workers, and immigrants in American public politics. In the South, they largely succeeded in disfranchising blacks starting in the 1890s. Residency requirements, poll taxes, exclusion for minor crimes, and Jim Crow intimidation all subverted black males' constitutional rights to vote. In the process, many poor southern whites also lost their rights (Keyssar 2000: 111–113).

Reversals have also occurred in our own time. In *Diminished Democracy*, Theda Skocpol argues persuasively that over the last few decades, American civic life has become impoverished as company managers have replaced grassroots participation with specialized fund-raising and influence-wielding organizations quite prepared to accept your money but not your direct involvement. "As long as centralized and professionally managed institutions and advocacy groups retain special access to government and the media and as long as advocacy groups and pollsters have more to offer office-seeking politicians than other kinds of actors, American civic democracy will not become much more inclusive – and local voluntary efforts will remain detached from national centers of power" (Skocpol 2003: 281). Although she uses different wording, Skocpol is describing the insulation of trust networks from national public politics. As she says, that insulation diminishes democracy.

Trust and Distrust in Argentina

Despite large differences in the two political systems, some parallel processes occurred in Argentina. With the country's political history of caudillos, colonels, and repressive regimes, we might have expected Argentina to resemble Greece, Chile, or Portugal more than the United States. In fact, the country's very uneven relationship between center and periphery left space for islands of democratic activity. At least in Buenos Aires, elements of democratic politics became visible quite early. The Argentine constitution of 1853 implied universal male adult suffrage, and legislation of the following quarter century generally specified that native-born males twenty-one or older (plus younger National Guard members and married men nineteen or older) had the right to vote.

More so than in the United States, military service played a significant part in integrating rural and immigrant populations into national public politics. Fernando López-Alves dates that process from the presidency of Juan Manuel de Rosas, governor and sometime dictator of Buenos Aires province from 1829 to 1852. It continued through the following decades:

In contrast to what happened in Uruguay and Colombia, by the early 20th century Argentine elites clearly saw the army as an instrument for integration of the lower classes. In 1895, when a quarter of the population was of foreign origin, contemporaries declared that obligatory conscription would promote construction of the nation and "nationalize" the first generation of Argentines who were "sons of the immigrants who have flooded the country with their foreign culture." (López-Alves 2003: 205; see also Forte 2003: 146–162)

Argentina did not enact universal military service, but it did draw large numbers of poor men into national politics indirectly through military service.

Ordinary people also joined public politics more directly. By the 1860s, Buenos Aires elections often resembled their rough-and-tumble U.S. counterparts. Held in parish churches, they became the sites of fierce rivalries between members of hostile political and parish clubs that supported competing candidates. As reported by witness Félix Armesto, municipal elections at the parish church of La Merced in December 1863 went like this:

One of the parties "owned" the polls and, with that force, it did not exclude any means – however fraudulent they might be – to win the election. . . .

The indignation of the vanquished was such that they tried to attack, a usual practice in those days; but the winners . . . had introduced their own party elements, and some in the church galleries and others on the roof retaliated by throwing rocks at the assailants.

The pistols and other portable firearms were monopolized by the rich, and so was the revolver, then very imperfect. The battle was therefore fought by means of the simple and primitive rock, as most of the fighting was done at a distance, and knives were reserved for face to face encounters.

The besiegers, more numerous than those within, used paving stones and brought piles of rocks from the Bajo [the riverside], while the latter tore apart the bricks from the walls and used anything that came to their hands; no tiles were left in the dome. . . .

[The neighboring buildings] were the refuge of the enemy forces and from there, as well as from the tower of the church, each party made accurate impact on the heads and eyes of the respective warriors. . . . Around the block, not one windowpane or glass remained in place, and not one of the combatants remained unharmed. (Sabato 2001: 38)

In contrast to the United States, however, only a small and declining proportion of the total population actually voted. With a rapidly growing metropolitan population, turnout dropped from highs of around 7 percent of the total during the 1820s and 1830s to 2 or 3 percent during the 1870s (Sabato 2001: 64).

Surely a significant share of that decline resulted from the swelling of immigration and hence the swelling of the proportion of the population lacking citizenship. During the late 19th century, for example, only 4 percent of Spanish immigrants – the major in-migrant stream, along with the Italians – acquired citizenship (Moya 1998: 305). Of the entire foreign-born population, only 0.2 percent had acquired citizenship by 1895, and by 1914 the figure had only risen to 2.3 percent (Baily 1999: 198). In contrast with New York, Baily reports, Italian immigrants in Buenos Aires did get involved in public politics, but almost entirely through their participation in organized labor. Argentina did not build nearly so effective a machine for integrating immigrant trust networks into public politics as the United States did during the same period.

Nevertheless, Argentine associational politics expanded. In 1889, Buenos Aires students formed an organization called the Youth Civic Union (*Unión Cívica de la Juventud*) to oppose government policies. The organization soon attracted non-student followers and evolved into a general Civic Union. In 1890 the Union staged a Buenos Aires demonstration with 30,000 participants. Later that year a popular militia aligned with the Union attacked government forces in a failed rebellion, only to discover that the major politicians who had encouraged the attack had made a deal behind its back to change the government. The 1890s brought organization-based popular politics onto the national scene, but against a distinctive Argentine background of military and strongman maneuvering. At the same time, mass immigration from Europe – in 1914, 80 percent of Buenos Aires' population consisted of immigrants and their children – transformed social life and popular politics.

Between 1890 and 1914, associational life flowered in Argentina. A broad, semi-conspiratorial movement of people who called themselves Radicals connected numerous local middle-class political clubs with a hierarchy of party committees. They adopted standard social movement means, including mass meetings and demonstrations. Several anarchist federations organized workers in the Buenos Aires region. In addition to their own demonstrations on such occasions as May Day and New Year's Day, anarchists originated half a dozen general strikes in and around Buenos Aires between 1899 and 1910. When they threatened to sabotage festivities for the centennial of Argentine independence in 1910, however, the government began arresting anarchists as vigilantes and smashed their meeting places.

Meanwhile, Argentine socialists initiated standard social movement campaigns for working-class credit, housing, education, divorce, women's suffrage, and an eight-hour day. Their Socialist Party, founded in 1894, brought together workers, professionals, and some small manufacturers. By the time the party elected its first member of Argentina's Chamber of Deputies in 1904, elements of democratic politics had taken root in the country. These elements long preceded the formal democratic transition that Ruth Berins Collier marks at 1912, when the Sáenz Peña Law enacted suffrage and the secret ballot for men 18 and over (Collier 1999: 30).

By no means did the 1912 reforms end Argentina's alternation of democratization and de-democratization. The country suffered repeated military takeovers:

1930–1932:   General José Uriburu

1943–1945:   General Pedro Ramirez, with Colonel Juan Perón a rising star

1955–1958:   Successive military juntas, displacing Perón, who had been elected president in 1946

1962–1963:   Military coup, bringing in military-backed government of Senate president José Maria Guido

1966–1973:   Multiple coups and military or military-backed regimes

1976–1983:   New coups and military regimes, in the first of which General Jorge Videla replaced Perón's widow Isabelita, who had become president at Perón's death in 1974

Humiliated by British forces after they invaded the disputed Malvinas (Falkland) Islands in 1982, the Argentine military then retreated definitively — at least for the time being – from the country's public politics.

Meanwhile, Juan Perón's long presence had transformed Argentine politics. During the 1930s, army officer Perón had sympathized with Europe's fascist regimes. In 1946, he launched his own revolutionary movement – *peronismo* – calling for import-substitution industrialization and national discipline. With the support of the military (temporary) and organized labor (more or less permanent), he won election as president in 1946. Perón's followers built up immense, effective patronage networks. After being removed by the military and exiled to Spain in 1955, Perón returned to Argentina and won the presidency again in 1973. He died, at the age of 78, the following year. But the Peronist Party outlived him, continued as a major force in national politics, and still runs an impressive network of patronage today.

Argentine-American scholar Javier Auyero has become a close observer of Peronist patronage and its political consequences (Auyero 1997, 2001, 2002, 2003). In the Buenos Aires metropolitan area shantytown he calls Villa Paraiso, Auyero documents the work of Peronist *punteros* and *punteras*, the frontline workers who deliver goods and services to poor people in exchange for political support. After Perón's ouster in 1955, governments both military and civilian defined Villa Paraiso as a social blight, deserving destruction. Local Peronists led the locality's successful resistance to clearance and then enlisted inhabitants in more general resistance to Argentina's authoritarian regimes. The ruthless military regime that took over the country in 1976 laid siege to Villa Paraiso in 1978, arresting dozens of people. Local lore counts a dozen inhabitants as "disappeared" *(desaparecidos)* during those terrible years (Auyero 2001: 61).

Nonetheless, Peronist networks survived in Villa Paraiso. During the mass unemployment of the 1990s, Peronist agents far overshadowed the Catholic Church as a source of aid for local residents. They organized *Unidades Básicas* (UBS: grassroots committees) that do the party's day-to-day local work:

In Villa Paraiso, there are five UBS, each controlled by a broker: Medina's UB Chacho Peñaloza, Pisutti's UB The Leader, Andrea's UB Fernando Fontana, Cholo's UB 27 de Abril, and Matilde's UB Three Generations. The UBS are dispersed through Paraiso (although Matilde's is located outside the administrative limits of the shantytown, its political/social work targets the shantytown population). Their work extends beyond politics and election times. Many serve as centers from which food and medicine are distributed, and brokers can be approached for small favors all year round. During recent years, these UBS have become the most important sites of survival problem solving. (Auyero 2001: 83)

Peronist clients not only vote for the party's candidates but also attend rallies, paint graffiti, hang banners, and provide other local services when the party needs them. Female brokers ostentatiously imitate lady bountiful Evita Perón in their enactment of Peronist generosity (Auyero 1997). In the midst of a democratic regime, an extensive patron-client system continues to flourish.

Looking much more broadly at politics in Mar del Plata, Buenos Aires, Córdoba, and Misiones, Matthew Cleary and Susan Stokes have demonstrated a negative relationship between Peronist influence and what they regard as evidence of informed democratic participation: getting political information from newspapers, splitting tickets, speaking openly about their votes, showing respect for the rule of law, and so on. In both Mexico and Argentina, they report, people in less democratized regions (Cleary and Stokes 2006: 178):

- Identified the character of politicians, and not institutional constraints, as the chief determinant of government responsiveness
- Were more prone to clientelism and saw their neighbors as more prone to it
- Were less inclined to voice unconditional support for the rule of law

To use terms that none of them employ, Auyero, Cleary, and Stokes are remarking on the greater mediation of trust networks' integration into public politics through patrons in those places where PRI (in Mexico) and the Peronist Party (in Argentina) recruit their support through the daily operation of patron-client ties.

In the United States, Mexico, and Argentina, however, the evidence indicates that patron-client politics played an indispensable intermediate role. However much we may deplore political participation on the basis of personal ties and group prejudice, the absorption of newcomers into politics through patronage facilitated the integration of previously segregated trust networks into public politics, just as it promoted the involvement of the same newcomers in new trust networks created by the state itself and by major political actors such as trade unions.

Contingent integration of trust networks into public politics does not exhaust the processes on which democracy depends. Alterations of inequality and of non-state power must also occur for extensive democratization to take place. Other alterations of inequality and public politics can forward de-democratization. Let us turn to the second major necessary process: insulation of citizen-state interactions from categorical inequality. Chapter 5 focuses on equality and inequality.

5

Equality and Inequality

Political ethnographer Adam Ashforth has reached a startling conclusion concerning democratization in South Africa: witchcraft is threatening the country's hard-won democracy. From 1990 to the recent past, Ashforth has spent much of his time sharing the public and private lives of Soweto (South West Township), a huge black suburb of Johannesburg. His Soweto sojourn has therefore taken him through what most observers hail as South Africa's transition from authoritarianism to democracy.

Before he started working in Soweto, Ashforth wrote an impressive historical analysis of the legal process by which apartheid took shape (Ashforth 1990). But preparation for a book on witchcraft, violence, and democracy plunged him shoulder-deep into ethnography. Through first-hand observation, personal intervention, and incessant interrogation of his acquaintances, Ashforth built up a powerful picture of coping, strife, and hope amid vicious violence. Ashforth's ethnographic involvement forced him to abandon many a preconceived category and explanation of struggle during and after apartheid.

Ashforth argues persuasively that witchcraft is hobbling South African democratization. Sowetans and South Africans at large commonly believe that evil persons can call up occult forces to harm others they envy or dislike; that calling up such occult forces constitutes witchcraft; that some individuals inherit or learn the skills of witchcraft, thus becoming witches; and that only counter-use of occult forces can overcome witchcraft's damaging effects. Witchcraft can kill, cause personal suffering, and destroy careers. Fear of witchcraft, counteraction of witchcraft, and initiation of witchcraft pervade daily life. In a national population of 44 million, perhaps half a million South African "prophets" specialize in combating witchcraft (Ashforth 2005: 8). In their combat, they appeal to supernatural forces, especially those mediated by ancestors.

Witchcraft long preceded South Africa's democratization. As a fact of African life for at least a century, it mingled with religious practice and belief, including those of the many Christian sects that organized spiritual life in black townships. During the vast anti-regime mobilizations of the 1980s in those townships, accusations of witchcraft often accompanied accusations of being the state's paid informers. Crowds of youths often attacked suspected informers and witches – without making too fine a distinction between them – by filling tires with kerosene, placing the tires around suspects' necks, and lighting them on fire. During the post-Apartheid era, the burning-tire attacks focused primarily on witches (Ashforth 2005, chapter 5; Bozzoli 2004, epilogue). But in Soweto democratization has not caused witchcraft to fade away. On the contrary, according to Ashforth it has become more pervasive and dangerous since the 1990s.

How could that be? Ashforth offers two related explanations. First, before the 1990s, essentially all Sowetans lived with the certainties of hardship and oppression, under the fist of South Africa's authoritarian state. Since then life has become more uncertain precisely because new opportunities for escape and advancement have opened up. Second, in Soweto and elsewhere a minority of black people have gained educations, jobs, and incomes of which they could not previously have dreamed. A black bourgeoisie consisting largely of former African National Congress (ANC) activists is emerging (Johnson 2004: 224–225). But the vast majority of black Africans have stayed behind. Between 1991 and 1996, in South Africa as a whole, the richest 20 percent of black households increased their real incomes by 15 percent, while the poorest two fifths lost 21 percent (Terreblanche 2002: 388). As a consequence, inequality has risen within the black population. Hence the resentment and jealousy that feed witchcraft have started to poison relations among neighbors, friends, and relatives.

The prevalence of witchcraft poses multiple threats to South African democratization. It greatly complicates public response to the medical scourge that is devastating the country's poor: AIDS. In 2003, an estimated 21.5 percent of the South African population aged 15 to 49 were HIV positive; one thousand people per day were dying of AIDS (Johnson 2004: 227, UNDP 2005: 248). Of pregnant women attending KwaZulu province's prenatal clinics in 2004, a full 40.7 percent tested HIV positive (Avert 2006: 1). To the extent that AIDS victims and their families see the disease as a result of witchcraft – the extent is large – an already reluctant state's capacity to deal with the menace declines and health inequality increases. More generally, the disconnect between what ordinary people experience as the major threat to their security and success, on one side, and the state's problem-solving programs, on the other, discredits the state as a guarantor of protection and mutually binding consultation.

South Africa's rulers face a painful dilemma. If they acknowledge witchcraft as the major problem their citizens confront in their daily lives, what can they do about it? Wouldn't any serious effort to root out witches and witchcraft compromise human rights, privacy, and the rule of law? If they deny witchcraft's reality and seek to eliminate its influence through propaganda and education, however, they align themselves against long-established beliefs and practices. South African democrats who call for enlightenment, concludes Ashforth, risk separation from the bulk of the people:

They risk alienating themselves from the everyday concerns of their citizens, citizens who find themselves living in a world with witches. Leaders who are alienated in this way may find themselves struggling to create an image of the democratic state as a regime embodying the true interests of the people they are governing. If they neglect to deal with the witches, those who seek to rule may end up being perceived as agents of evil forces themselves. Thus, the challenge for those who would govern a democratic state in a world of witches, is to promote doctrines of human rights while not being perceived as protectors of witches, who perpetrate occult violence within communities. (Ashforth 2005: 15)

To be sure, every democracy faces moral and political dilemmas produced by the discrepancy between premises of public politics and widespread understandings among the citizenry: if a majority of a regime's population opposes same-sex cohabitation or high executive salaries, does the state have an obligation to outlaw them? If most citizens consider religious law more valid than secular law, should the state institute religious law? The South African dilemma overshadows these common democratic problems because no simple compromise among conflicting rights will reduce its net harm. As a result, South African politicians remain silent on the problem of witchcraft.

South Africa's recent conflicts took place against the backdrop of one of the 20th century's most momentous national political struggles. Before the revolution of the 1980s, South Africa had no serious experience with democracy. On the contrary, well before the formation of South Africa as a relatively unified state during the early 20th century, successive

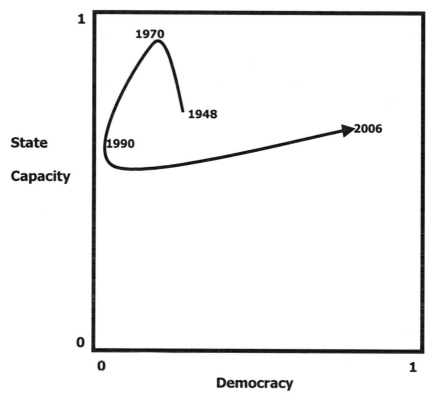

FIGURF 5-1. South African Regimes, 1948–2006

regimes built on racial oppression. Furthermore, the Afrikaner-dominated coalition that came to power in the 1948 national elections tightened racial controls, elaborated the official grid of racial-ethnic distinctions, and stepped up an already formidable state's capacity. South Africa de-democratized visibly from an already undemocratic position.

Figure 5-1 sketches the regime's trajectory in the democracy-capacity space from 1948 onward. The figure shows de-democratization and increase in capacity from 1948 until around the 1970s, further de-democratization combined with declining capacity during the swelling popular resistance of the next two decades, followed by spectacular democratization plus some mild recovery of state capacity after 1990. The rapidity and extent of these fluctuations recall France after 1789 and Switzerland in the 1840s. They describe revolutionary change.

The problem we face here is how South Africa's capacity-democracy trajectory interacted with categorical inequality. Both recently and over the long run, South Africans have suffered greatly as a result of the regime's extraordinary intersections of inequality and public politics. In recent years, however, South Africa has also produced the world's most spectacular combination of democratization with stark inequality. How should we sort out these complex interactions?

Before looking more closely into those intersections, let us think much more generally about relations among equality, inequality, democratization, and de-democratization. This chapter offers a broad account of these relations and then seeks to make that account credible by means of concrete historical examples, including South Africa during the 20th and 21st centuries. The account looks at 1) how categorical inequality arises in general, 2) parts played by states and regimes in the creation and transformation of categorical inequality, and 3) implications of 1 and 2 for democratization and de-democratization.

What problems does inequality pose for democratization? As a glance at Brazil, the United States, and India will verify, more or less functioning democracies can both emerge and survive in the presence of massive material inequalities. Social inequality impedes democratization and undermines democracy under two conditions: first, the crystallization of continuous differences (such as those that distinguish you from your neighbor) into everyday categorical differences by race, gender, class, ethnicity, religion, and similar broad groupings; second, the direct translation of those categorical differences into public politics. Before the 1990s, the South African regime not only fostered crystallization of everyday differences by what it treated as "race" into massive material inequalities, but it also built those distinctions directly into political rights and obligations.

To the extent that citizen-state interactions organize around categorical differences also prevailing in routine social life, those differences undermine broad, equal, protected, mutually binding consultation. They block or subvert democratic politics because they inevitably install large resource disparities in the political arena. They inhibit coalition formation across categorical boundaries. Meanwhile, they give members of advantaged categories both the incentive and the means to evade outcomes of democratic deliberation when those outcomes counter their interests. Before the democratic revolution of the later 1980s, as we will see, South Africa's whites repeatedly used their leverage to subvert even the simulacra of democratic institutions they installed to divide and conquer the country's non-white population.

Creation of Categorical Inequality

Democracy works better, and democratization is more likely to occur, when political processes reduce translation of everyday categorical inequalities into public politics. Our explanatory problem, then, concerns how insulation of public politics from categorical inequality occurs. To explain that insulation process, however, it helps to step back and take a look at the processes that create categorical material inequality in the first place.

Inequality is a relation between persons or sets of persons in which interaction generates greater advantages for one than for another. At a small scale, we might trace out the unequal relations that characterize a shop, a household, or a neighborhood. At a large scale, multiple relations of this kind compound into vast, connected webs of inequality. At either scale, the interpersonal networks involved approximate single hierarchies only under extraordinary circumstances – for example, when some powerful institution such as an army, a corporation, or a church clumps people into distinct levels. More often people become clumped into categories without forming neatly ranked hierarchies. Members of those categories differ, on the average, in their advantages, but categorical boundaries are important because people use them to organize social life and to reproduce inequality between members of different categories.

Durable categorical inequality refers to organized differences in advantages by gender, race, nationality, ethnicity, religion, community, and similar classification systems (Tilly 1998). It occurs when transactions across a categorical boundary (e.g., male-female) 1) regularly yield net advantages to people on one side of the boundary and 2) reproduce the boundary. Although forms and degrees of categorical inequality vary dramatically across times and places, all large human populations have always maintained substantial systems of categorical inequality.

Here is a barebones account of how such systems emerge and operate:

- Material inequality results from unequal control over value-producing resources (e.g., some wildcatters strike oil, while others drill dry wells).
- Paired and unequal categories such as male-female or white-black consist of asymmetrical relations across a socially recognized (and usually incomplete) boundary between interpersonal networks; such categorical pairs recur in a wide variety of situations, with the usual effect being unequal exclusion of each network from resources controlled by the other (e.g., in U.S. urban ghettos, immigrant merchants often make

their living by selling mainly to black people, but never integrate into the black community).

- An inequality-generating mechanism we may call *exploitation* occurs when persons who control a resource 1) enlist the effort of others in production of value by means of that resource but 2) exclude the others from the full value added by their effort (e.g., before 1848, citizens of several Swiss cantons drew substantial revenues in rents and taxes from non-citizen residents of adjacent tributary territories who produced agricultural and craft goods under control of the cantons' landlords and merchants).

- Another inequality-generating mechanism we may call *opportunity hoarding* consists of confining disposition of a value-producing resource to members of an in-group (e.g., Southeast Asian spice merchants from a particular ethnic-religious category dominate the distribution and sale of their product).

- Both exploitation and opportunity hoarding generally incorporate paired and unequal categories. The boundaries between greater and lesser beneficiaries of the value added by effort committed to controlled resources (e.g., the distinction between professionals and non-professionals – registered nurses and aides, scientists and laboratory assistants, optometrists and optical clerks, architects and architectural drawers – often marks just such boundaries).

- Over a wide range of circumstances, mobility across boundaries does not in itself change the production of inequality, but it alters who benefits from inequality (e.g., so long as college degrees remain essential for engineering jobs, acquisition of those degrees by immigrants reinforces the exclusion of non–degree holders, even among immigrants).

- Inequalities produced in these ways become more durable and effective to the extent that recipients of the surplus generated by exploitation and/or opportunity hoarding commit a portion of that surplus to reproducing 1) boundaries separating themselves from excluded categories of the population and 2) unequal relations across those boundaries (e.g., landlords devote some of their available wage-labor to building fences and chasing off squatters).

Those are the theory's bare bones (for more detail, see Tilly 2005a). Taken in these terms, the theory does not provide direct explanations for individual-by-individual variation in success and failure or for change and variation in the overall distribution of a country's wealth and income. But it does explain the creation of categorical inequality.

BOX 5-1. Historically Prominent Inequality-Generating Resources

- Coercive means, including weapons, jails, and organized specialists in violence
- Labor, especially skilled and/or effectively coordinated labor
- Animals, especially domesticated food- and/or work-producing animals
- Land, including natural resources located in and on it
- Commitment-maintaining institutions such as religious sects, kinship systems, patron-client networks, and trade diasporas
- Machines, especially machines that convert raw materials, produce goods or services, and transport persons, goods, services, or information
- Financial capital – transferable and fungible means of acquiring property rights
- Information, especially information that facilitates profitable, safe, or coordinated action
- Media that disseminate such information
- Scientific-technical knowledge, especially knowledge that facilitates intervention – for good or evil – in human welfare

---

Exploitation and opportunity hoarding always set crucial barriers in place. A first take on inequality in any setting begins with specification of the value-generating resources on which exploitation and opportunity hoarding are operating. Box 5-1 lists the main classes of resources whose control has supported inequality in one setting or another across the long sweep of human history. It does not exhaust the possibilities. Control of precious metals or minerals has, for example, sometimes figured centrally in exploitation and opportunity hoarding; here I have folded those situations into the topic of control over land containing the minerals. But the list does identify the main classes of resources that have supported large-scale systems of inequality over the last 5,000 years.

All of these resources lend themselves to production of benefits for some recipients by means of coordinated effort. When they are in short supply and relatively easy to circumscribe, they all lend themselves to exploitation and opportunity hoarding, hence to the generation of inequality. Coercive means, for example, have underlain many systems of inequality for thousands of years and still play at least some part in the maintenance of inequality throughout the world despite the rising importance of items later on the list. Land ownership still constitutes the fundamental basis of inequality in the world's poorer agricultural regions.

In the World Bank's broad survey of poor people's experiences, Bangladesh provides a striking case in point. In the Bangladeshi village of Kalkerchar, according to local testimony, rich people "have their own land and other properties, livestock for cultivation, and money for investments, and can afford sufficient meals, wear good clothes, send their children to school, have jobs and mobility, and are free from disability" (Narayan and Petesch 2002: 120). Middle categories own or sharecrop one or two acres of land, while the "social poor" combine sharecropping with wage labor for the rich. The "helpless poor," in contrast,

are largely landless, without homesteads or farmland. Wage labor and sharecropping are their main means of earning a living. Study participants say the helpless poor are identifiable by their old clothes and pained faces. They can afford neither health care nor education for their children, they do not have the means to entertain guests, and many cannot afford a dowry to marry daughters. (Narayan and Petesch 2002: 121)

Over the last five millennia, most human beings have lived in the lower levels of just such land-based inequality systems. Machines, financial capital, information, and media are historical latecomers. Only recently has control over scientific-technical knowledge become a major basis of inequality across the world.

If the notion that scientific-technical knowledge may one day rival wealth as a basis of categorical inequality strikes you as far-fetched, however, consider how the Persian Gulf emirate Qatar is investing income from its huge but exhaustible supply of natural gas. The emir, Sheikh Hammad bin Khalifa Al-Thani, is investing billions in scientific education and research, with the intent of making Qatar the Middle East's research magnet. The emir's wife, Sheikha Mozah bint Nasser Al-Misnad, runs the Qatar Foundation for Education, Science, and Community Development, worth billions in its own right. She has committed the proceeds from an entire oil well, perhaps $80 million per year, to a scientific research fund. In a principality of 800,000 people, the 500 students at the fledgling university, Education City, stand every chance of becoming a national elite (*Science* 2006). If the emir's program succeeds, control over land (and in this case the fossil fuels beneath it) may well give way to control over scientific-technical knowledge as the chief basis of Qatar's inequality.

Prevalence of one combination of inequality-sustaining resources over another strongly affects patterns of individual and collective mobility.

Where coercive means prevail, individuals and groups that acquire arms and warriors gain crucial mobility advantages. In agrarian systems, acquisition or loss of land (which often occurs, to be sure, through someone's use of coercive force) makes the great difference. Only in recent eras of wage labor and extensive commerce has it been widely possible for workers to save money from wages and then invest it in such small enterprises as craft production and retail trade.

By themselves, prevailing resources strongly differentiate systems of inequality. Across the contemporary world, for example, the great prominence of land plus coercive means in the inequality of such countries as Uganda and Cambodia contrasts greatly with the sorts of inequality based on financial capital and scientific-technical knowledge in France or Japan. Brazil is moving from a system of inequality based chiefly on enormous differences in control over land to another one – no less unequal – based much more heavily on control over financial capital and scientific knowledge. China is experiencing widespread rural conflicts as it shifts from a land-coercion inequality system to one in which control over machines, financial capital, and scientific-technical knowledge looms large.

Prevalent inequality-generating resources and their current control strongly affect the viability of authoritarian rule. Regimes that rely on control of land, labor, and coercive means – the most common varieties over the last 5,000 years – lend themselves handily to tyranny. But within such regimes rulers inevitably face limits to their personal consolidation of power. Limits stem from the invariable reliance of such regimes on powerful, partly autonomous intermediaries such as warlords, landlords, and lineage heads. Much more rarely, regimes relying especially on commitment-maintaining institutions such as shared religions impose authoritarian control over their citizens in the names of gods, priests, and prophets. Resources later in the list – machines, financial capital, information, media, and scientific-technical knowledge – only figure in state authoritarianism when rulers monopolize the production and/or distribution of those resources. Most of the time, rulers incorporate the producers and distributors of those resources into their regimes and thus accept limits on their own authoritarianism.

We begin to understand why capitalist economies host democratic regimes more frequently than other sorts of economies. The connection does not lie in the ideological compatibility of democracy and free enterprise, but in the material basis of rule. Look back at the resources listed in Box 5-1. Items early on the list – coercive means, labor, animals, land, and commitment-maintaining institutions – have not only underlain categorical inequality across the bulk of human history but also served most commonly as the direct bases of rule (Tilly 2005b).

Large-scale regimes, for example, have commonly depended on the contingent allegiance of large landlords who deployed their own armed force, enjoyed extensive autonomy within their own domains, drew their main revenues from the land and labor they controlled within those domains, and supported the military enterprises of their overlords, but only within stringent limits. To the degree that a regime incorporates coercion-wielding warlords or labor-exploiting landlords directly into its system of rule, it simultaneously builds in the everyday inequalities around which people organize social life. Such a regime exercises power through the very people who have both the means and the interest to block the populations they control from resisting tyranny. It builds in obstacles to broad, equal, protective, mutually binding consultation.

Look at the items later on the list: machines, financial capital, information, media, and scientific-technical knowledge. All undergird enormous material inequalities in the contemporary world. They do not figure in capitalist economies alone; such non-capitalist giants as China and Iran likewise rely heavily on machines, financial capital, information, media, and scientific-technical knowledge. In both capitalist and non-capitalist economies, reliance on those resources generates broad categorical inequalities between those who control them and those who either lack access to them or fall under their influence. But on neither side of the divide do regimes build categorical distinctions produced by control over the resources directly into their systems of rule.

Why, then, does capitalism give democratization a better chance? Because regimes in relatively prosperous non-capitalist economies maintain the political integration of categorical distinctions that are organized around resources earlier on the list, notably coercive means, land, and commitment-maintaining institutions. Under state socialism, all three implemented the state's rule, despite nominal commitment to a fourth resource, labor. In states prospering through their monopolies of salable resources such as oil, rulers typically defend their monopolies by using significant shares of their revenues to reproduce boundaries between members of their own commitment-maintaining institutions and all others. In Iran, Saudi Arabia, Sudan, Bolivia, and Venezuela, we see oil-rich rulers broadcasting very different ideologies but using abundant oil revenues to build up rulers' support networks and to exclude their opposition. In all these cases and more, rulers block the way to thoroughgoing capitalism.

Full-fledged industrial and financial capitalism, in contrast, permits rulers to rule without nearly so heavy a reliance on the unequal categories of everyday life. Whether they rely on a small circle of capitalists or a large circle of taxpayers, they must simply acquire enough capital to pay for their states' major activities. One might imagine a capitalist regime that assigned distinctly superior political rights to possessors of capital, media magnates, or specialists in scientific-technical knowledge. Orwellian dreams about the future often involve one or more of the three. But the paths by which capitalism actually developed made it much easier and attractive for rulers to maintain a rough balance between the mass of consumers and the mass of citizens. Under capitalism, citizens, workers, and consumers coincide (Cohen 2003, Montgomery 1993).

Regimes and Inequality

Nevertheless, all regimes, democratic or otherwise, inevitably intervene in the production of inequality. They do so in three distinct ways: by protecting the advantages of their major supporters; by establishing their own systems of extraction and allocation of resources; and by redistributing resources among different segments of their subject populations. Compared to undemocratic governments, broadly speaking, democratic governments offer protection for advantages received by larger shares of their subject populations, create systems of extraction and allocation that respond more fully to popular control, produce more collective benefits, organize broader welfare programs, and redistribute resources in favor of vulnerable populations within their constituencies more extensively (Bunce 2001, Goodin et al. 1999, Przeworski et al. 2000).

These very activities, however, involve democratic states in perpetuating some kinds of categorical inequality. Most obviously, democratic states devote extensive effort to maintaining boundaries – and differences in benefits – among their own citizens and between their citizens and citizens of other countries. But to the extent that they secure property and existing forms of social organization, they also sustain the inequality already built into property and existing forms of social organization. State maintenance of inheritance rights, for example, passes racial and ethnic differences in wealth from one generation to the next (Spilerman 2000). Within democratic regimes, a great deal of political struggle centers on the extent to which the state should sustain or alter existing categorical inequalities.

If democratic regimes live with extensive material inequality and democratic states invest in maintaining existing forms of material inequality, then the absence of inequality cannot be a necessary condition of democracy or democratization. Instead, the democratic accomplishment consists of *insulating* public politics from whatever material inequalities exist. Democracy can form and survive so long as public politics itself does not divide sharply at the boundaries of unequal categories. Conversely, political rights, obligations, and involvements that divide precisely at categorical boundaries threaten democracy and inhibit democratization. Democracy thrives on a lack of correspondence between the inequalities of everyday life and those of state-citizen relations.

Note the corollary: Both the organization of major political actors around the boundaries of significant categorical inequalities and the enactment of rules for political participation that correspond to such boundaries – especially if excluded parties are those whom existing categorical inequalities already disadvantage in general – undermine democracy. In western political regimes, categorical differences by nobility, religious status, gender, race, and property ownership have supplied the primary bases of unequal rights and obligations, but elsewhere ethnicity and kinship have figured as well. To the extent that such distinctions dominate public politics, democracy falters.

Changes in the overall degree and character of categorical inequality also affect democracy's prospects. Any substantial increase in categorical inequality that occurs without some compensating adjustment in public politics poses a serious threat to existing democratic regimes. Increasing categorical inequality threatens democracy because it gives members of advantaged categories means and incentives to:

- Opt out of democratic bargains
- Create beneficial relations with state agents
- Shield themselves from onerous political obligations
- Intervene directly in state disposition of resources
- Use their state access to extract more advantages from unequal relations with non-state actors
- Use their influence over the state for further exploitation or exclusion of subordinate categories, and thus
- Move their regimes even further away from broad, equal, protected, mutually binding consultation.

Democracy and democratization depend on some combination of 1) material equalization across categories and 2) buffering of public politics from categorical inequality.

Negative versions of these mechanisms (e.g., proliferation of privately controlled armed force and formation of class-segregated political

BOX 5-2. Mechanisms Insulating Public Politics from Categorical Inequality

1. Dissolution of state controls (e.g., legal restrictions on property-holding) that support current unequal relations among social categories (e.g., wholesale confiscation and sale of church property weakens established ecclesiastical power)

2. Equalization of assets and/or well-being across categories within the population at large (e.g., booming demand for the products of peasant agriculture increases number of middle peasants)

3. Reduction or state containment of privately controlled armed force (e.g., disbanding of magnates' personal armies weakens noble control over commoners, thereby diminishing nobles' capacity to translate noble-commoner differences directly into public politics)

4. Adoption of procedural devices that insulate public politics from categorical inequalities (e.g., secret ballots; payment of officeholders; and free, equal access of candidates to media forward the formation of cross-category coalitions)

5. Formation of politically active coalitions and associations for cross-cutting categorical inequality (e.g., creation of region-wide mobilizations against state property seizures crosses categorical lines)

6. Wholesale increases of political participation, rights, or obligations that cut across social categories (e.g., state annexation of socially heterogeneous territories promotes categorically mixed politics)

coalitions or associations) facilitate translations of categorical inequality into public politics and thus reverse democratization.

Major processes combining these mechanisms include 1) equalization of categories (as seen chiefly in mechanisms 1, 2, and 3) and 2) buffering of public politics from categorical inequality (as seen chiefly in mechanisms 3 to 6).

Box 5-2 lists specific mechanisms that promote equalization and/or buffering. They describe rare historical occurrences. Over most of history, for example, rulers and their main supporters resisted any dissolution of state controls that supported the unequal relations among social categories at the time; on the contrary, when they had the capacity they acted to reinforce those controls. Again, one of the last things rulers and their major supporters have ever given up is their private control over armed force; private armies and secret police still flourish in many low-capacity undemocratic regimes of Asia, Africa, and Latin America.

Yet sometimes several of these mechanisms have activated at once, promoting equalization and/or buffering. The formation of settler colonies such as Argentina and Australia, for example, equalized material conditions as compared with the colonizing countries. Although they regularly subordinated, massacred, or excluded indigenous people, the settlers' shared endeavors promoted accommodations buffering public politics from inequalities among settlers. Any historical explanation of democratization must specify the sequences and combinations of these mechanisms as they insulated public politics from categorical inequality.

Inequality and Democracy in South Africa

Most states accommodate, or even benefit from, the forms of inequality that prevail among their citizens. Few, however, have ever undertaken to engineer categorical inequality as a means of rule. In the recent past, South Africa's rulers undertook the world's most extensive effort to integrate racial categories directly into their system of political control. For a few decades, that effort succeeded; it sustained exploitation and opportunity hoarding by a white ruling class without bringing economy or polity to a halt. It used coercion to back the power of capital. Then, with strategic external allies, the victims of oppression increased their resistance to the point of stalemating economic life and bringing down the regime. During the 1980s, a revolution occurred in South Africa.

South Africa's experience with categorical inequality makes vividly visible a set of processes implied by the theory just laid out, but rarely occurring elsewhere with such deliberation and observable public effect. The regime's imposition of racial categories on public politics destroyed insulation of politics from existing categorical inequalities, thereby de-democratizing an already undemocratic regime. But the revolutionary struggles of the 1970s and (especially) the 1980s built up some insulation between racially defined categorical inequality and public politics, and thus promoted conditions for eventual democratization. It did so in two ways: by producing sustained popular resistance against the direct inscription of racial categories into politics, and by forging powerful (if temporary) coalitions across racial and ethnic categories. Reforms of the 1990s and thereafter then promoted partial democratization by causing a modest decline of material inequality across racial categories, by generating greater inequality within the African category, and by introducing new buffers between existing inequalities and South African public politics.

In his sweeping history of South African inequality, economist Sampie Terreblanche summarizes the main features in these terms:

One of the clearest patterns is that, during the long period of colonialism and imperialism, the colonial masters were mostly the victors in group conflicts, and the indigenous population groups mostly the losers. A second pattern – closely linked to the first – is that in the post-colonial period local whites (the descendants of the settlers from erstwhile colonial Europe) were again (at least until 1974) mostly the conquerors, and therefore in a position to enrich themselves, mostly at the cost of indigenous people.

The colonial powers and white colonists did so in mainly three ways: firstly, by creating political and economic power structures that put them in a privileged and entrenched position *vis-à-vis* the indigenous population groups; secondly, by depriving indigenous people of land, surface water, and cattle; and, thirdly, by reducing slaves and indigenous people to different forms of unfree and exploitable labor. These three threads have run ominously through South Africa's modern history, from the mid-17th until the late 20th century. (Terreblanche 2002: 6)

Over three centuries, then, whichever Europeans ran South Africa used their political power not only to subordinate the indigenous population but also to stamp their own definitions of unequal categories on social life in general. In broadest terms, most systems sharply distinguished Afrikaners, British, Asians (especially of Indian origin), Africans, and Coloured – those non-white people who fit into none of the other categories. Only under the system called apartheid, or apartness (1948–1990), did the state itself take pains to organize public life around further distinctions within the African population. It did so with a vengeance: it inscribed categorical inequality directly into public politics.

Box 5-3 presents Terreblanche's convenient periodization of changes in South Africa's political economy from 1652 to 2002. Each of his "systemic periods" generated a somewhat different pattern of inequality among racial and ethnic populations. Installation of apartheid from 1948 onward modified, and then reinforced, categorical differences previous administrations had created. It did so with greatly increased intensity: uprooting Africans and Coloured people from long-established urban residences; herding Africans into small, fragmented, overpopulated homelands; even segregating European children into different schools according to the language spoken at home, English or Afrikaans.

White demand for black labor in cities, mines, and farms, however, subverted all plans for total containment of South Africa's populations.

BOX 5-3. Six "Systemic Periods" of South African Inequality, According to Sampie Terreblanche

1. The mercantilistic and feudal system institutionalized by Dutch colonialism during the second half of the 17th and most of the 18th centuries (1652–1795). During this period the *Trekboere* created a semi-independent feudal subsystem, with its own power and labor relations. But this feudal subsystem was not fully independent and must therefore be regarded as part of the Dutch colonial system.

2. The systems of racial capitalism institutionalized by British colonialism and British imperialism during the "long 19th century" (1795–1910). The legal, political, and economic patterns introduced by the British destroyed the mercantilistic, feudal, and traditional patterns of the Dutch East India Company, the Afrikaners, the Khoisan, and the Africans, in that order.

3. During the 19th century the Voortrekkers succeeded in creating relatively independent republics north of the Orange River, in which they adapted labor patterns that were by then regarded as illegal in the Cape. The power constellations of the two republics were precarious, but they were still independent enough of the colonial authority in the Cape to practice a separate feudal system.

4. After the discovery of diamonds (in 1867) and gold (in 1886), British colonialism was transformed into an aggressive and more comprehensive version of imperialism and racial capitalism. To successfully exploit South Africa's mineral resources, the British had to create a new power constellation and political and economic system. To institutionalize a system conducive to the profitable exploitation of gold, the British fought several wars at the end of the 19th century, including the Anglo-Boer War (1899–1902). The new power constellation was not only maintained but also more thoroughly institutionalized during the first half of the 20th century, when political, economic, and ideological power was mainly in the hands of the local English establishment, which had close ties with Britain. It is necessary to distinguish between the systemic period of colonial and agricultural racial capitalism during British colonialism (1795–1890) and the systemic period of colonial and mineral racial capitalism during British imperialism and the political and economic hegemony of the local British establishment (1890–1948).

5. When the Afrikaner-oriented National Party (NP) won the general election of 1948, it used its political power to intensify unfree labor patterns. Although the NP did not drastically transform the economic system of racial capitalism institutionalized by the English establishment, it used its political and ideological power to institutionalize a new version of it.

During the last 20 years of Afrikaner political hegemony (1974–1994), a crisis developed surrounding the legitimacy and sustainability of white political supremacy and the profitability of racial capitalism. In the early 1990s Afrikaner political hegemony collapsed rather dramatically as a prelude to the rise of African political hegemony.

6. Since 1990 we have experienced a transition from the politico-economic system of white political domination and racial capitalism to a new system of democratic capitalism. Over the next 12 years (1990–2002) a democratic political system – controlled by an African elite – was successfully institutionalized. Unfortunately, a parallel socioeconomic transformation has not yet taken place.

Adapted from Terreblanche 2002: 14–16

Growth of manufacturing and services promoted rapid expansion of the black urban population, until by 1945 manufacturing had surpassed mining's contribution to South African GDP (Lodge 1996: 188). By 1960, a full 63 percent of the African population lived at least temporarily outside African reserves (Fredrickson 1981: 244). Around that time, furthermore, what had been an urban labor shortage shifted to a labor surplus, so that African unemployment concentrated increasingly in cities and townships rather than rural reserves. South Africa's rulers had to manage the contradiction between treating Africans as conquest-formed Natives and recognizing them as capitalist-created Workers. The contradiction led to costly efforts to segregate blacks from whites residentially and socially while drawing more and more Africans into the urban and industrial labor forces (Murray 1987, chapter 2; Terreblanche 2002, chapter 9).

Establishment of tribally defined segregation, furthermore, responded not only to official conceptions of history but also to political convenience. In Thembuland, paramount chief Sabata Dalindyebo led opposition to the state's apartheid land redistribution plans but found himself displaced by a state-backed candidate:

The new system provided an expedient opportunity for the NAD [Native Affairs Department] to dilute the influence of chiefs it regarded as uncooperative. The popularly acknowledged Paramount Chief Sabata Dalindyebo, for example, saw his chiefdom arbitrarily split into two regions, Thembuland (later renamed Dalindyebo) and Emigrant Thembuland. In the latter region, Kaizer Matanzima, a once obscure chief who early showed a genuine interest in the philosophy and practice and soon the material rewards of apartheid, was elevated to paramount chief. (Evans 1990: 44)

When the regime created the new homeland of Transkei in 1963, it made Matanzima homeland chief. Transkei then became a formally independent republic, under Matanzima's headship, in 1979 (Davenport and Saunders 2000: 402, 432).

Urbanization, industrialization, and political expediency did not keep South African authorities from building racially defined categories deeply into the country's legal and economic structures. Even partial legalization of African unions in 1979 inscribed the government's own racial divisions into the law. Recipients of this organizational largesse faced an acute dilemma: accept state-endorsed categorization and retain meager claims to land and employment or reject it and abandon all state-enforced rights whatsoever.

Take the case of M. G. Buthelezi, who became leader of the Zulu homeland encircling Durban called KwaZulu. Buthelezi started out as an ANC (African National Congress) activist, expelled from Fort Hare University for participating in an ANC demonstration. He split with the party over his own ambition to run the homeland and created the Inkatha Freedom Party. His Inkatha Freedom Party activists dominated the export of migrant labor from the region and collected protection from merchants inside it. The party also received clandestine subsidies from the apartheid state. During the 1980s and well into the 1990s, Inkatha and ANC activists fought running battles for control of KwaZulu localities. Buthelezi's movement exemplifies that even some Africans had a stake in the categories earlier imposed by white South Africans to sustain their domination (Davenport and Saunders 2000: 434–435, 500–501). We should therefore avoid any supposition that the political actors of 20th-century South Africa had somehow formed prior to and independently of the successive regimes within which they lived and struggled (Jung 2000). The state engaged energetically in the very production of the unequal categories it imposed on public life.

The state's determination did not, of course, guarantee that its actions produced the effects its rulers desired. One might have thought, for example, that the strict hierarchy of apartheid would produce economic homogeneity within each racial category. On the contrary, by excluding possible competition, the state-backed system of exploitation and opportunity hoarding generated wide disparities between successful and unsuccessful whites. Within the African population, a large gap separated impoverished rural areas beset by massive, rising unemployment and urban or mining regions, where Africans had work, albeit badly paying work.

Consequence: great inequality within the white population and substantial inequality within the African population.

When affirmative action moved a small number of Africans into previously all-white positions after 1990, their presence did not transform previously existing hierarchies and promotion channels. Instead, those few Africans benefited from the same inequality-generating mechanisms that had prevailed among their white predecessors. At the same time, however, the great mass of Africans remained in poverty, and rising unemployment hit Africans disproportionately. Racial categorization declined, but material inequality persisted or even increased. Jeremy Seekings and Nicoli Nattrass sum up this phenomenon in these terms:

The apartheid distributional regime provided full employment for white people (by means of a combination of racially discriminatory labour-market, industrial, and educational policies) while channeling cheap African labour to unskilled jobs in the mines and on farms. But the very success of this regime in advantaging white people allowed the basis of exclusion to shift from race to class: white South Africans acquired the advantages of class that allowed them to sustain privilege in the market and ceased to be dependent on continued racial discrimination. The consequence of this was that some classes of black South Africans could become insiders while others remained largely excluded from the benefits of prosperity. (Seekings and Nattrass 2005: 6)

These consequences, however, did not become visible until massive resistance, confrontation, and revolutionary transformation had destroyed the state-imposed racial system of apartheid.

Resistance, Confrontation, and Revolution

Separatist policies had unanticipated political consequences as well. First, they drove Africans, Asians, Coloureds, and dissident whites into a common front as apartheid governments increasingly deprived the Asian and Coloured populations of distinctive rights they had previously enjoyed. Second, the apartheid regime's attempt to impose new chiefs and territorial units that would perform the work of indirect rule actually stimulated popular resistance to chiefly authority and beyond it to governmental control (Olivier 1991). From around 1970 the state's control of black settlements weakened, its ability to impose labor discipline declined, and violent encounters pitting citizens against repressive forces consequently multiplied.

Separatist policies finally made government-defined African identities available as bases of political mobilization. In 1983, a shaken apartheid regime attempted to expand its support by establishing a very unequal tricameral legislature that incorporated representatives of the Asian and Coloured populations into separate chambers. That measure, however, spurred mobilization among black Africans and among other non-black challengers of the regime. At street level, informal groups of young activists called "comrades" alternately collaborated and fought with members of community organizations called "civics." The formation of a national United Democratic Front from 575 disparate organizations drew on connections established by the now-illegal BC (Black Consciousness movement) and ANC, but went well beyond them. At its peak, the UDF claimed 2 million members (Johnson 2004: 187).

In 1985 a similar (and, in fact, overlapping) coalition of trade unions formed COSATU, the Congress of South African Trade Unions. Those well-brokered organizations coordinated widespread resistance to the regime. Threatened, the government declared successively more repressive states of emergency in July 1985 and June 1986. The latter declaration:

gave every police officer broad powers of arrest, detention, and interrogation, without a warrant; they empowered the police commissioner to ban any meeting; and they prohibited all coverage of unrest by television and radio reporters and severely curtailed newspaper coverage. The government had resorted to legalized tyranny. (Thompson 2000: 235)

The government detained thousands of suspects without trial. Despite the state of emergency, despite banning of many community organizations, and despite preventive detention of activists by the thousands, black mobilization actually accelerated during the later 1980s. Resistance combined with international sanctions to shake white control of public politics.

Under domestic and international pressure, even the once-solid Afrikaner bloc began to crack. Stigmatized, boycotted, deprived of new investment, and cut off from credit by many Europeans and Americans, including the European Community and the U.S. Congress, big capitalists lost much of their enthusiasm for apartheid (Price 1991, chapter 7). In 1982 National Party Members of Parliament (MPs) opposed to any compromise had already bolted the NP to form a smaller, determined Conservative Party (CP). For five more years, NP governments (now harassed by right-wing pressure and the threat of autonomous Afrikaner military action) tried to subdue their opponents on both flanks by legal means and clandestine assaults. During 1988, the government intensified its attacks on the ANC and the government's liberal opposition, as the ANC's own sabotage campaign accelerated.

After the NP beat the CP badly in the white municipal elections of October 1988, however, president and NP head P. W. Botha announced dramatic concessions. They included reprieves of six ANC activists under death sentences and transfer of ANC leader Nelson Mandela from the hospital where he was being treated for tuberculosis to house arrest rather than back to the island prison where he had suffered for 25 years.

The following year brought decisive steps toward settlement of South Africa's domestic standoff. In 1989, NP leader and premier F. W. de Klerk undertook negotiations with the previously banned ANC, including Mandela himself, freeing most of the ANC's imprisoned leaders. De Klerk's toleration of a 35,000-person multiracial protest march–cum-celebration in Cape Town (September 1989) not only signaled a major shift of strategy but also encouraged multiple marches on behalf of reconciliation through the rest of South Africa. A welcome-home celebration for freed ANC prisoners at Soweto's Soccer City "became in effect the first ANC rally in 30 years" (AR 1989: 295).

By 1990, de Klerk was governing in close consultation with the ANC. Released from house arrest, Mandela became a major participant in national politics. In 1991, COSATU activist Cyril Ramaphosa won election as the ANC's general secretary. Meanwhile, KwaZulu homeland chief Buthelezi's Inkatha Freedom Party, which had previously received clandestine support from the government and the National Party, found itself increasingly isolated. Inkatha stepped up attacks on its ANC rivals, but by the 1994 elections was only receiving about 6 percent of the national black vote, as compared with the 75 percent that went to the ANC. (Of the total vote, all racial categories together, the ANC got 63 percent, the NP 20 percent, and Inkatha 11 percent.) In a triumph that would have astonished almost any South African of any political category ten years earlier, ex-prisoner Nelson Mandela became president of South Africa.

"As the South African state in 1990 began to shift away from formal racial exclusion and segregation, toward 'non-racial' democracy," notes Anthony Marx,

racial identity and mobilization has lost some of its salience. In its place, political entrepreneurs have increasingly relied on "tribal" or "ethnic" identities as the basis of mobilization, as indicated by Zulu nationalism and "coloured" fears of African domination under the ANC. (Marx 1995: 169)

Disaggregation occurred at two levels: the non-white front cracked; by 1996, for example, Coloured voters in the Cape were opting massively for the National Party, former architect of apartheid. But the categories

African, Coloured, and Asian also lost unifying force in favor of smaller-scale distinctions.

Nevertheless, the ANC also had to negotiate between 1990 and its electoral triumph of 1994. The Soviet Union's partial disintegration in 1989 had two crucial effects in South Africa. First, it reduced the credibility of the conservatives' claim to serve as a bulwark against an international communist conspiracy. Second, it reduced external diplomatic and financial support for the ANC. Together, the two effects encouraged the United States to press both sides for a compromise solution other than a revolution. To assert its presence, the ANC declared 1991 its "year of mass action," calling its supporters to peaceful, disciplined strikes; boycotts; marches; and rallies (Jung and Shapiro 1995: 286).

Step by step, the ANC presence undermined the NP plan of establishing some sort of power sharing. Yet the ANC also worked to avoid complete polarization. It accepted "proportional representation for elections, job security for white civil servants, and an amnesty for security forces that admitted to crimes under the old regime" (Bratton and van de Walle 1997: 178). Thus a semi-revolutionary situation yielded to a remarkable negotiated compromise.

As the ANC came to power, significant splits occurred within the former resistance movement. Not only did many ANC leaders move directly into governmental positions and businesses previously closed to Africans, but divisions occurred at the local scale as well. Civic organizations had played crucial parts in initiating boycotts and other mass actions during the 1980s, but they lost much of their political weight, in part because their leaders left for opportunities in the new regime, but also in part because the ANC imposed strict tests of loyalty on those it continued to sponsor (Zuern 2001, 2002). Some street-level comrades who had used their muscle to defend their townships against white forces turned to gang rivalries and petty crime. "Since 1994," reports Richard Wilson,

in the absence of political and economic opportunities, ANC para-militaries have become criminals as a means of economic survival. Sharpeville gangs still calling themselves Special Defense Units run protection rackets, promising security from other criminals and SDUs in return for regular payments from terrorized residents. The ANC repeatedly attempted to arrange a cease-fire between feuding factions, but could neither maintain nor enforce it. (Wilson 2001: 179)

In parallel to the departure of a small but prosperous new bourgeoisie, black communities have seen a dramatic split between those swept into the ANC state and those left behind.

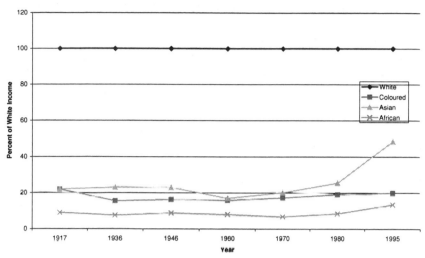

FIGURE 5-2. Relative per Capita Income by Racial Category, South Africa, 1917–1995

Source: Terreblanche 2002: table 10.8

Figure 5-2 shows one result of an extraordinarily unequal political system. From 1917 to 1995, it compares the per capita incomes of Coloured, Asian, and African citizens with those of whites. Although the South African regime kept Africans at the bottom throughout the eight decades, until the recent past it also held the Asian and Coloured populations at very low levels. The installation of apartheid from 1948 onward did not much affect the relative position of the Coloured population, but it clearly hurt both Asians and Africans; by 1970, the per capita income of Africans had fallen to 6.8 percent of white income; the average white earned almost fifteen times more than the average African.

Then the system began to shatter. After 1980, Asians nearly doubled their relative position (rising to 48.4 percent of white income), and Africans finally began to gain as well. In contrast, the Coloured population (largely neglected by ANC patronage and frequently joining the political opposition to ANC hegemony) made no relative gains at all. Since 1995, African mobility into higher income categories continued, so that "by 2000, there were about as many African people as white people in the top income quintile" (Seekings and Nattrass 2005: 45). Since Africans made up about 75 percent of the population and whites about 14 percent, of course, those numbers fell far short of parity. Nevertheless, class inequality began to displace racial inequality in economic life. The shattering of apartheid and the black acquisition of political power started to make a significant difference to South Africa's material inequality.

The dismantling of apartheid did not entirely eliminate racial categories from South African public life. Whereas the coalition against apartheid had aligned African and Coloured citizens shoulder to shoulder, the ANC state's affirmative action program on behalf of "formerly oppressed" people generally referred to Africans alone (Jung 2000: 202). Shakeup of the civil service removed a number of Asian and Coloured officials from lower-level bureaucratic positions (Johnson 2004: 214). Abe Williams, the Western Cape's Coloured provincial minister for welfare, complained:

> But you see what is happening to Coloured people is that they are feeling the hurt of affirmative action against them. When they fought apartheid they were considered part of the struggle against apartheid. But now that apartheid is out of the way, they are not getting the benefit of the new system because they are again being seen as "you're not Black." And that is very heartbreaking. (Jung 2000: 203)

In the Western Cape and elsewhere, indeed, considerable numbers of Coloured voters turned to the ANC's opposition, the formerly racist National Party. Given overwhelming ANC power over the state, we can hardly speak of 21st-century South Africa as a thoroughgoing democracy. It is not obvious, furthermore, that the new regime will avoid substituting sharp class divisions for the racial divisions that long defined South Africa's public politics. But as compared with the 1970s, the regime has moved dramatically toward broader, more equal, better protected, mutually binding consultation between state and citizens. Through its partial buffering of public politics from categorical inequality, the regime has democratized.

Mechanisms at Work

One case does not constitute a general argument. South Africa, furthermore, is an extreme case: one in which the state deliberately, openly, and for a while successfully inscribed categorical inequalities that already prevailed across everyday social life into national public politics. The pervasiveness of witchcraft and of HIV infection, furthermore, could compromise South Africa's gains from democratization, and even cause the beleaguered regime to de-democratize. Yet South Africa has two advantages for the advancement of this book's analysis. First, it shows that there exists at least one important national experience that does conform to this book's unfamiliar line of explanation. Second, it indicates what we might expect to find in less extreme cases if the argument is valid.

If you look back at Box 5-2, for example, you will find that all the mechanisms for insulating public politics from categorical inequality listed there came into play at one stage or another of South Africa's great transformations after 1970:

- Dissolution of state controls that support current unequal relations among social categories
- Equalization of assets and/or well-being across categories within the population at large
- Reduction or state containment of privately controlled armed force
- Adoption of procedural devices that insulate public politics from categorical inequalities
- Formation of politically active coalitions and associations cross-cutting categorical inequality
- Wholesale increases of political participation, rights, or obligations that cut across social categories

These mechanisms' mere presence does not prove that they actually promoted democratization in South Africa. Yet the overall narrative of South African political change lends plausibility to my main causal account: State efforts to use categorical inequality as an instrument of rule unexpectedly generated powerful cross-category coalitions, which eventually created buffers between public politics and inequality. That South African democratization remains incomplete goes without saying.

In less extreme cases, we will have to dig even deeper to trace precise cause-effect connections. Among other things, it will often be difficult to separate processes connecting trust networks to public politics from those that produce buffers between public politics and inequality. Nevertheless, the preceding six-item checklist of crucial mechanisms applies just as clearly to the 19th-century United States or 20th-century India as to South Africa since 1970. Moreover, each item points to a corollary mechanism that should, in principle, promote de-democratization. Disintegration of cross-class coalitions in favor of political actors firmly entrenched within unequal categories, for example, threatens reversal of democracy. Spain during the period between 1930 and 1936 looks like a case in point. In Spain, the bourgeois republic's exclusion of organized peasants and workers broke up the coalition that made the democratic revolution of 1930 to 1931 and re-inscribed class differences directly into public politics at the same time that military men led by Francisco Franco were threatening the republic from the right (Ballbé 1985, González Calleja 1999, Soto Carmona 1988).

The memory of Spain in a period of looming civil war raises new questions about connections between autonomous power centers and public politics, as distinguished from the influence of trust networks and categorical inequality. Chapter 6 takes us into that complex realm.

6

Power and Public Politics

Russia once lived in a vital, vigorous moment of democratic hope. Aspirations rose impressively in 1988. At that point, to be sure, the Russian Republic still dominated the Soviet Union rather than existing as an independent state. Russian Mikhail Gorbachev, general secretary of the USSR's Communist Party and (since that year) chairman of the Supreme Soviet's presidium, was then leading the drive toward *glasnost'* (political openness) and *perestroika* (economic and political rebuilding). During the historic 19th party conference that opened at the end of June 1988, Gorbachev delivered an intensely hopeful three-and-one-half-hour address.

The sober *Annual Register* summarized Gorbachev's speech as rejecting Stalinism and calling for a new society that would preserve the benefits of socialism:

Although it was impossible to describe such a society in a detailed way, a socialism of this kind would be a system of 'true things.' The purpose of all social development, from the economy to spiritual life, would be the satisfaction of popular needs. There would be a dynamic and advanced economy based upon a variety of forms of property and worker participation, combining a broad measure of central planning with a great degree of autonomy for individual enterprises. The basic needs of all would be provided, including health, education and housing, but individual talent would also be rewarded, where appropriate, in both moral and material terms. A society of this kind would have a high degree of culture and morality, and would be managed by a system of 'profound and consistent democracy.' (AR USSR 1988: 106)

Gorbachev claimed to be setting the Soviet Union, including his own Russia, on the path to democratization. The *Annual Register*'s reporter noted, however, that economic performance was declining in the USSR and that widespread demands for autonomy or even independence were arising among the Union's non-Russian nationalities. Despite Gorbachev's promotion of openness and rebuilding, no smooth transition to democracy had begun at a national scale.

Nine years later, in 1997, the Soviet Union had splintered and Russia had gone through fierce struggles for political control. Playing Russian nationalism against Gorbachev's effort to preserve what remained of the Union, Russian party leader Boris Yeltsin had seized power in 1991. In 1993, Yeltsin had consolidated his grip by putting down a right-wing parliamentary coup. Yeltsin won the presidential election in 1996, but by 1997 his health was faltering, a fact that caused feverish maneuvering for influence within the presidential circle. The *Register* then broadcast little good news about the domestic political situation:

Continuing into 1997, the struggle was conducted between the country's major financial-industrial groups, embracing the largest banks, key sectors of the economy and the newspapers and television stations in which they had acquired a controlling interest. The wider political situation was one of relative stability, apart from a far-reaching government reshuffle in the spring; but this was set against a background of continuing economic decline and widening social differences, accompanied by an increase in organized crime and corruption. (AR Russia 1997: 135–136)

Russia's fledgling democracy had fallen on hard times.

An enfeebled Yeltsin resigned the presidency at the end of 1999, opening the path to his prime minister, Vladimir Putin. A career intelligence officer who had headed the Federal Security Bureau (the KGB's postcommunist successor), Putin made no effort to promote democracy. During his victorious electoral campaign of 2000, he even refused to debate his rival candidates. But his public statements stressed the necessity of restoring a strong state and a properly functioning market. He also promised strong action against the "Islamic fundamentalists" he portrayed as threatening Chechnya and other sections of the Caucasus. Soon after taking office, he reduced the powers of regional governors, started restraining the mass media, and undertook a broad effort to tame the country's "oligarchs" – the capitalists in business and media who had made billions and acquired enormous autonomy during the 1990s. Putin emphasized state capacity at the expense of democracy (Fish 2005).

Reinforcement of central control continued. As the *Annual Register* of 2004 put it:

Russia ended the year on a trajectory towards a more authoritarian state, and it seemed unlikely – despite the hopes of the liberal groups that had largely been sidelined in Russian politics – that the country would repeat the experience of its neighbor Ukraine and see the political establishment give way before a popular revolution. Developments in Russia in 2004 were dominated by two factors: the government's response to the terrorist reprisals carried out by Chechen separatists beyond the borders of the republic, most horrifically in September against children in the school of Beslan in North Ossetia; and the government's campaign against the "oligarchs" to regain control over energy interests, epitomized by the Yukos saga. The campaigns against Chechnya and against the oligarchs generally won popular approval. (AR Russia 2004: 105)

Consider the Putin government's arrest, prosecution, and imprisonment of Mikhail Khodokorsky, head of Yukos, the country's largest privatized energy company. It exemplified Putin's relentless campaign to recapture control of oil and gas supplies as a means of consolidating his personal political power and eliminating wildcat capitalism "oligarchs" from his possible political opposition. Soon the state-controlled energy corporation became the world's largest producer of natural gas. With nearly a quarter of the world's known natural gas reserves, Putin's Russia used its energy to buttress its international influence. As of 2006, Slovakia was importing 100 percent of its gas from Russia, Bulgaria 94 percent, Lithuania 84 percent, Hungary 80 percent, Austria 74 percent, Germany 40 percent, Italy 30 percent, and France 25 percent (Schmitt 2006: 61). Clearly, the state's monopolization of energy supplies was lending it tremendous clout both domestically and internationally.

Russian citizens felt the domestic clout. In 2004, Putin's government extended its surveillance of media as it began prosecuting both academics and businessmen who showed signs of mounting political opposition or embarrassing state authorities. In April 2004, for example, the Moscow City Court sentenced 41-year-old Moscow researcher Igor Sutyagin to 15 years in prison for high treason and espionage. During the later 1990s, Sutyagin had helped run a Canadian-sponsored research project on civilian-military relations in 12 post-Soviet and post–Warsaw Pact countries, including Russia. Sutyagin had no access to military or intelligence secrets. Working from Moscow's Institute of USA and Canada Studies (once a major center of planning for *glasnost'* and *perestroika*), Sutyagin organized interviews with leaders across 12 countries using a standardized survey instrument. The court convicted him – unjustly, by all external accounts – of passing state secrets to British and U.S. intelligence.

In 2005, the Putin government passed a series of state-strengthening laws. The new laws abolished direct election of governors, ended single

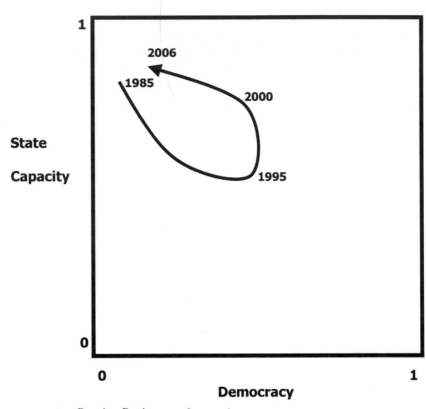

FIGURE 6-1. Russian Regimes, 1985–2006

constituency voting in parliamentary elections, tightened requirements for registration of political parties, and raised the threshold for party representation in parliament. The government also began considering laws to restrict radically the autonomy of non-governmental organizations. Human rights organizations working in the Caucasus found themselves under extreme pressure, with the Russian-Chechen Friendship Society the object of criminal cases for inciting racial hatred and violating tax laws (Human Rights Watch 2006). In terms of breadth, equality, protection, and mutually binding consultation, Putin's regime was visibly de-democratizing Russia. Without following the twists and turns from Gorbachev to Yeltsin to Putin, Figure 6-1 schematizes Russia's astonishing trajectory from 1985 to 2006.

According to the sketch, Russia moved toward democratic territory after 1985 while losing substantial state capacity, then began reversing its direction in both regards. As Chapter 2 reported, in 1991 through

1992, Freedom House placed Russia at 3 both on political rights and civil liberties – certainly not democratic by Freedom House standards or ours, but far above the regime's 6,5 for political rights and civil liberties in 2005. A fixed 2004 presidential election in which Putin received 71.4 of the vote (his nearest competitor received 13.7 percent) removed even openly contested elections from Russia's claims for recognition as a democracy. Responding to Russia's snuffing out of opposition voices, for 2005 Freedom House shifted the regime's overall classification from Partly Free to Not Free.

Freedom House's ratings illustrate Russia's de-democratization but miss the arc of state capacity: from high in the period before the Gorbachev reforms to declining during the Yeltsin years, then back sensationally to high levels under Putin. The two trends obviously connected; Putin's regime was aggressively expanding state capacity as it squeezed out democracy. Yet in one regard Putin may surprisingly have been promoting longer-term changes that will eventually facilitate Russian democratization. Although he was permitting the Russian military dangerously broad autonomy in the Caucasus, he was also subordinating capitalists who had acquired extraordinary independence from state control. If, in the future, the Russian state again becomes subject to protected, mutually binding consultation in dialogue with a broad, relatively equal citizenry, we may look back to Putin as the autocrat who took the first undemocratic steps toward that outcome.

Transforming Power Configurations

In order to appreciate that ironic possibility, we must look at power configurations within and around whatever regime we are studying. Throughout this book, we are analyzing changes in public politics: state-citizen interactions that visibly engage state power and performance. After insulating public politics from categorical inequality and contingently integrating trust networks into public politics, the third essential alteration behind democratization consists of reducing autonomous power clusters within the regime's operating territory, especially clusters that dispose of their own concentrated coercive means. The clusters may operate outside the state (e.g., warlords) or within it (e.g., military rulers). Their reduction subordinates states to public politics and facilitates popular influence over public politics.

This chapter takes up a fairly complex set of causal connections. Its logic runs from 1) specific causal mechanisms to 2) recurrent causal

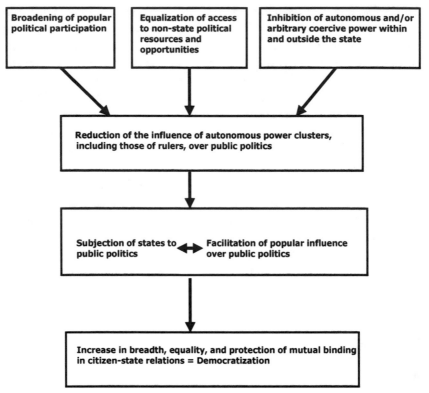

FIGURE 6-2. Causal Connections between Changing Power Configurations and Democratization

processes to 3) effects of those processes on autonomous power clusters to 4) effects of changes in autonomous power clusters on states and public politics to 5) further effects of those changes in states and public politics on democratization and de-democratization. Figure 6-2 omits detailed mechanisms for the moment but schematizes the connections from 2 to 3 to 4 to 5. Its central logic runs like this: a recurrent set of alterations in power configurations both within states and outside of them produces changes in relations among states, citizens, and public politics, which in turn promote democratization. Reversals anywhere in the causal sequence promote de-democratization.

We are studying transformations in which autonomous clusters of power such as warlords, patron-client systems, religious communities, armies, and large kinship groups dissolve and/or become subject to public politics with extensive popular participation. These transformations, as

Figure 6-2 emphasizes, include both direct curbing of such power centers' autonomy and citizens' acquisition of collective capacity that indirectly checks or bypasses autonomous power centers. On the first count, Putin was reining in the autonomous power of capitalists, private protection services, gangsters, and ethnic separatists who had all gained ground during the turbulent 1990s. On the second, however, he was actually reversing citizens' acquisition of collective capacity. As he himself advertised, he was pursuing an aggressively statist program.

Three connected processes reduce autonomous power clusters:

1. Broadening of political participation (which, after all, has often occurred by force in authoritarian regimes and therefore does not belong to democratization by definition)
2. Equalization of access to non-state political resources and opportunities (which has frequently resulted from expansion of mass media and acceleration of geographical mobility rather than changes in political institutions as such and therefore qualifies as a cause rather than a component of democratization)
3. Inhibition of autonomous and/or arbitrary coercive power both within and outside the state (e.g., through military defeat, bureaucratic containment of previously autonomous armed forces, or truces between the state and sometime rebels)

If these three big processes promote democratization, their importance contradicts a widespread view of democratization: that it depends fundamentally on the assent, however grudging, of people currently in power. Bargaining models of democratization (e.g., Acemoglu and Robinson 2006, Alexander 2002) ordinarily incorporate such a view. Although democracy does by definition entail a degree of elite assent in the long run, elite assent is not a precondition for democratization. In fact, the three processes regularly occur in the utter absence of any demands for democracy. They even occur at the initiative of power holders, in efforts to maintain their power.

But the three processes do involve new citizen-state bargains; Figure 6-2's midsection summarizes the outcomes of new bargains as 1) subjection of states to public politics and 2) facilitation of popular influence over public politics. Putin's anti-democratic smashing of oligarchs to reestablish state control over energy supplies helped eliminate rival centers of coercive power within the Russian regime. As of 2006, however, Putin's regime was not striking bargains that subjected the Russian state to public politics or facilitated popular influence over public politics. On the contrary, the state's actions between 2000 and 2006 de-democratized Russia. Elsewhere, however, the three processes of broadening, equalization, and inhibition do regularly cause democratization to occur.

Why and how do these processes promote democratization? Why and how do their reversals promote de-democratization? Remember that our fundamental standard for democracy is the extent to which the state behaves in conformity to the expressed demands of its citizens, and that democratization therefore consists of an increase in conformity between state behavior and citizens' expressed demands. Earlier chapters have made the case that the contingent integration of trust networks into public politics and the insulation of public politics from categorical inequality increase the conformity of states' behavior to citizens' expressed demands. Over and above the effects of changes in trust networks and categorical inequality, positive versions of the three processes just identified have a two-part effect: they subject the state to control by public politics, and they facilitate popular influence over public politics. Their reversals – narrowing of political participation, and so on – reduce external control over the state and popular influence over public politics; so doing, they cause de-democratization.

By breaking the three big processes into specific mechanisms, Box 6-1 identifies concrete and relevant changes that have recurrently subjected states to control by public politics and facilitated popular influence over public politics. They range from obvious to obscure. It should be obvious, for example, that coalitions between segments of ruling classes and excluded political actors (mechanism number 1) both subject states to public politics and facilitate popular influence over public politics. As seen in Chapter 2, France's turbulent long-term moves toward democracy repeatedly involved such coalitions: urbanites' backing of the dissident aristocrats who led the Fronde (1648–1653); tense alliances among segments of the nobility and *haute bourgeoisie*; dissenting sovereign courts, law clerks, and again city-dwellers (1787–1789); and repeated insider-outsider alignments during the 19th century.

In retrospect, we easily think of those coalitions as proto-democratic (Westrich 1972). But note two crucial features of their politics: first, participants were often defending threatened rights or interests rather than calling for broad, equal, protected mutual consultation; second, when their actions did move the regime toward democracy (as they did not in 1648 to 1653 but did in 1787 to 1789), they did so indirectly, by subjecting the state to public politics and facilitating popular influence over public politics (Markoff 1996a, Nicolas 2002, Tilly 1986).

BOX 6-1. Mechanisms Subjecting States to Public Politics and/or Facilitating Popular Influence over Public Politics

1. Coalition formation between segments of ruling classes and constituted political actors that are currently excluded from power (e.g., dissident bourgeois recruit backing from disfranchised workers, thus promoting political participation of those workers)

2. Central co-optation or elimination of previously autonomous political intermediaries (e.g., regional strongmen join governing coalitions, thus becoming committed to governmental programs)

3. Dissolution or transformation of non-state patron-client networks (e.g., great landlords become commercial farmers, expelling tenants and bond workers from the land)

4. Brokerage of coalitions across unequal categories, distinct trust networks, and/or previously autonomous power centers (e.g., regional alliances form against governmental seizure of local assets, thus promoting employment of those alliances in other political struggles)

5. Expansion of state activities for which sustaining resources are only available through negotiation with citizens (e.g., a war-making state creates a mass national army through military conscription)

6. Mobilization-repression-bargaining cycles during which currently excluded actors act collectively in ways that threaten survival of the regime and/or its ruling classes, governmental repression fails, struggle ensues, and settlements concede political standing and/or rights to mobilized actors (e.g., negotiated settlement of resistance to governmental seizure of land establishes agreements concerning property rights)

7. Imposition of uniform governmental structures and practices through the state's jurisdiction (e.g., creation of uniform nationwide taxes increases likelihood of equity, visibility, and conformity)

8. Bureaucratic containment of previously autonomous military forces (e.g., incorporation of mercenaries into national armies reduces their independent leverage as political actors)

Negative versions of these mechanisms (e.g., multiplication of autonomous political intermediaries and creation of special regimes for favored segments of the population) promote declines in breadth, equality, and protection of mutually binding consultation and hence cause de-democratization.

Major processes combining these mechanisms include 1) broadening of political participation (as seen chiefly in mechanisms 1 to 4), 2) equalization of access to non-state political resources and opportunities (chiefly mechanisms 3, 5, and 7), and 3) inhibition of autonomous and/or arbitrary coercive power both within and outside the state (chiefly mechanisms 1, 6, 7, and 8).

For a more complex, less obvious democracy-promoting mechanism, consider item 6: mobilization-repression-bargaining cycles during which currently excluded actors act collectively in ways that threaten survival of the regime and/or its ruling classes, governmental repression fails, struggle ensues, and settlements concede political standing and/or rights to mobilized actors. Such cycles typically occur as a state expands through conquest, as previously subjugated regions or power holders bid for autonomy, and as a state demands increased resources from subject populations through taxation, conscription, or confiscation of property. Most often such confrontations end at neither extreme – neither successful evasion of state power nor total state victory. Instead, bargaining usually produces some compliance with state demands in return for some reduction in those demands combined with some specification of the parties' future rights.

The mechanism is important because it affects the state's long-term viability. States fail without continuing supplies of sustaining resources: money, goods, and labor power. They acquire those supplies in three main ways: 1) through direct operation of enterprises that produce the resources, 2) through exchange of goods or services over whose production and/or distribution they exert control, and 3) through extraction of necessary resources from their subject populations. The first two bypass any significant consent to the state's actions on the part of citizens. The third depends on at least a modicum of consent. It results from mechanism 5 in Box 6-1: expansion of state activities for which sustaining resources are only available through negotiation with citizens. In these circumstances, rulers have no choice but to extract resources from an often reluctant citizenry and therefore to bargain with citizens (Levi 1997). Extraction therefore opens the way to new citizen-state bargains that subject states to public politics and facilitate popular influence over public politics. To that extent it promotes democratization over the long run.

How? As Chapter 5 indicated, it depends to some extent on the major resources on which the regime's economy builds. A regime relying primarily on control of land, labor, animals, and coercive means typically draws its sustaining resources through regional holders of power who retain great autonomy within their own domains but yield a portion of their surplus to the state or assist the state in collecting that portion of the surplus. A highly capitalized and commercialized economy, in contrast, makes it easier for the state to draw resources from capital, wealth, wages, and commercial transactions.

Kingdoms, for example, have commonly operated land-coercion systems in which royal domains yielded significant shares of the money, goods, and labor power required by state activities. By doing so they were adopting the first strategy: direct operation of the enterprises that produce the resources. More recently, states have regularly monopolized the production of precious goods such as oil and exchanged those goods for other state requisites. This is the second strategy: exchange of goods or services over whose production and/or distribution they exert control. But ever since the beginning of state rule, most states have also requisitioned or otherwise acquired goods and services directly from their own subject populations. Those states adopted the third strategy: extraction of necessary resources from citizens. Russia moved away from the first strategy as the largely self-sufficient economy of the Soviet Union and its satellite states disintegrated. It pushed the third strategy – direct extraction – harder, but with mediocre success. Under Putin, it has put greater emphasis on the second strategy, especially by exchanging energy supplies for other national necessities.

Taxation, Negotiated Consent, and Avoidance of Consent

Taxation follows the third strategy. State taxation poses interesting questions for political analysts because in general taxpayers receive little or no individual quid pro quo when they pay. They may receive nothing at all, or they may receive small shares of collective goods. Why should they ever contribute (Herzog 1989, Levi 1988)? Yet states have regularly built themselves up through taxation, forced or otherwise (Ardant 1971, 1972; Brewer 1989; Daunton 2001; Kozub 2003; Tilly 1992, chapter 3; Webber and Wildavsky 1986). As they have extracted taxes, they have often initiated mobilization-repression-bargaining cycles ranging from small-scale resistance to mass rebellion.

Those cycles impose hidden political costs on states: although they commonly increase the flow of resources to the state, they also make the state dependent on that flow and set terms for the next round of extraction. In both these ways, they subject states to public politics and facilitate popular influence over public politics. Without, for the most part, promoting democratic consultation in the short run, they set conditions for democratization in the long run. As we saw previously, over the long run of French history, the shift of a state toward dependence on citizens' compliance with continued extraction increases the susceptibility of the regime to alternation between democratization and de-democratization. Mobilization-repression-bargaining cycles push regimes across the susceptibility threshold.

Such cycles continue in contemporary China. Thomas Bernstein and Xiaobo Lü have surveyed Chinese rural tax resistance and its resolution during the 1990s. Despite governmental secrecy on such matters, Bernstein and Lü accumulated substantial evidence of rising resistance to arbitrarily imposed taxes and fees. Moreover, the peasants sometimes succeeded, received concessions from local authorities, drew the attention of high state officials to local abuses, and renegotiated the terms of future extraction.

A famous series of struggles in Renshou, Sichuan, during 1992 and 1993 incorporated a mobilization-repression-bargaining cycle of this sort. There, local cadres continued to impose heavy taxes and forced labor for road-building on peasant households despite a state campaign for "burden reduction." When they could not get workers or cash, they seized household goods, including TVs, grain, and hogs. But under the leadership of peasant Zhang De'an, local people began fighting back. The county prosecutor tried to have Zhang arrested for tax evasion, but:

Zhang publicly tore up the arrest warrant as seven to eight hundred peasants carrying farm tools and shoulder poles gathered in Xie'an township. They drove the arresting officers out and burned a police vehicle. Violence erupted the Xie'an township in January and February. Stores closed and the government was paralyzed. "Hundreds of peasants were said to have been involved in a 'guerrilla war' of throwing stones." Farmers marched to the county seat and jostled into the government compound, loudly demanding justice.

This popular mobilization aroused the Sichuan Party and government leaders to send a work team to Renshou in February. Given the national offensive on excessive burdens, the provincial and Renshou county officials "affirmed that Zhang De'an was reasonable in giving publicity to the policy about lessening peasants' burdens and calling on people to refuse to pay the excess cash levy." (Bernstein and Lü 2002: 132–133)

Cadres fought back, and struggles continued in Renshou. By 1994, nevertheless, provincial and national authorities were clearly making concessions. They released peasants who had beaten cadres and police, replaced numerous officials, and contributed provincial funds for the building of local highways (Bernstein and Lü 2002: 136).

Let me be clear: the Renshou events did not establish that China was democratizing rapidly during the 1990s, much less that the Chinese state was collapsing. Since they provided a widely publicized model for state-citizen negotiation, nevertheless, these events did activate a mechanism that subjected the state to public politics and, to a small degree, facilitated popular influence over public politics. In this case, the crucial mechanism was the mobilization-repression-bargaining cycle. The accumulation of such confrontations and resolutions creates openings for democratization that did not exist before. As more Renshou-style cycles appear in China, the regime moves closer to broad, equal, protected, mutually binding citizen-state consultation – to democracy.

With the collapse of state socialism outside of China and North Korea, states that acquired their sustaining resources by producing those resources themselves practically disappeared. But the second state-sustaining strategy – exchange of goods and services over whose production the state exerts control – has survived and even thrived. Earlier we saw Vladimir Putin moving toward such a strategy by recapturing the state control over oil and gas production that had largely escaped into private hands during the 1990s. Over the same period, many oil-rich states avoided bargaining for citizen consent by seizing control of oil production (often in collaboration with obliging foreign capitalists), selling on international markets, buying coercive means on other international markets, and paying off their main local supporters with the surplus.

During the 21st century, Libya, Chad, Sudan, Venezuela, Bolivia, Uzbekistan, Kazakhstan, and a half-dozen Middle Eastern states pursued different versions of the basic consent-avoidance strategy. This book opened with a picture of undemocratic Kazakhstan, where in December 2005 President Nursultan Nazarbayev gained a democratically incredible 91 percent of the presidential vote. The Kazakh state's control of production and distribution of the country's immense energy supplies permitted Nazarbayev to avoid bargaining for citizen consent to his rule.

Kazakhstan represents an extremely successful version of a more general strategy on the part of energy-rich states. Consider Algeria, where in 2004 President Abdelaziz Bouteflika won re-election with a suspicious 84.99 percent of the vote. In 1999, army-backed Bouteflika had run unopposed after all opposition candidates withdrew from an election they called a "charade." In effect if not in form, Algeria's army has controlled the state through a long series of compliant presidents since independence from France in 1962. Algerians often refer to the military power structure as *la boîte noire* – the black box. During the 1990s, military control strengthened as the army first aborted a 1992 election in which an Islamist front seemed likely to win a parliamentary majority and then pursued a bloody but ultimately victorious campaign to wipe out Islamist guerrillas. Both the army and government-backed militias responded to the Islamists' attacks with massacres and disappearances.

After 1999 a massive rise in oil revenues was giving Bouteflika room to maneuver. Algeria's state-owned energy company Sonatrach has become the world's twelfth largest oil producer and a major supplier of natural gas to Europe as well. By 2006, rising international oil prices had built the Algerian treasury up to $55 billion in official reserves, enough to cover two years of the country's imports (Séréni 2006: 8). Using that revenue and allying with a small circle of civilian tycoons, Bouteflika had leverage to reduce the general staff's prominence in the regime. But he did so by building up the power of another military branch, the Département de renseignement et de sécurité – the Algerian KGB (Addi 2006: 7).

The *Annual Register* for 2004 portrayed Bouteflika's move as a power grab:

During the summer, emboldened by his overwhelming election victory, he moved to consolidate his position by making changes among the senior ranks of the armed forces, promoting a number of his own protégés to key posts, and appointing new governors of most of Algeria's provinces. The military changes began with the departure in July of General Lamari, chief of staff for more than a decade and one of the leading military décideurs, "on grounds of ill health". He was replaced by General Salah Ahmed Gaid, commander of land forces, who was reported to be less hardline and politicized than Lamari. Four out of the six regional commanders were also replaced. Later there was speculation in the local press that Bouteflika intended to transfer control over the intelligence and security services from the military command to the presidency, and appoint a Cabinet minister to the Defence portfolio. (AR Algeria 2004: 222)

Like Putin in Russia, then, Bouteflika was taking advantage of his vast energy revenues to move toward containment of the military's autonomous power, without in the least directly subjecting the state to public politics or increasing popular influence over public politics. If a civilian-ruled Algeria democratizes, nevertheless, we may eventually see Bouteflika as the ruler who for entirely undemocratic reasons took a crucial step toward democracy.

Spanish Democratization

After all these cases of de-democratization and blocked democratization, we need to think about cases in which the mechanisms and processes under review actually promoted substantial democratization. We are now re-entering familiar terrain. In many contemporary regimes we observe not only the mechanisms reviewed earlier – insider-outsider coalitions, mobilization repression-bargaining cycles, and expansion of state activities for which sustaining resources are only available through negotiation with citizens – but also other mechanisms listed in Box 6-1 such as:

- Dissolution or transformation of non-state patron-client networks
- Imposition of uniform governmental structures and practices through the state's jurisdiction
- Bureaucratic containment of previously autonomous military forces

Spain's experience since World War I provides an ideal opportunity for thinking through how such mechanisms work. The troubled country went through multiple crises and reversals, but finally became democratic during the later 20th century (Ortega Ortiz 2000). Indeed, Spain's rapid adoption of democratic institutions after dictator Francisco Franco's death in 1975 made the regime a prominent test case and poster child for theories of democratization.

Analysts of Spanish democratization typically adopted four moves that we have encountered before. First, in their search for causes, they concentrated closely on regime changes immediately preceding and during the crucial period of transition – defined most often as the period from Franco's death to the early 1980s. Second, they tried to identify not democracy-promoting processes but necessary conditions for democracy. Third, they distinguished between background factors and immediate causes of democratization. Fourth, they centered the inquiry on what they commonly called consolidation: not the initial adoption of democratic forms but the creation of conditions making massive de-democratization both difficult and unlikely.

Pursuing that four-part agenda, Nikiforos Diamandouros identifies these conditions as favoring Spanish democratization (Diamandouros 1997: 5–19; see also Linz and Stepan 1996, chapter 6; Maravall and Santamaria 1986):

Background Factors
- Other European states' increasing disapproval of undemocratic regimes
- Socioeconomic development
- Prior democratic learning
- Social pluralism, fostered by economic growth in the 1950s and afterward
- Franco's civilianization of his regime

Immediate Causes

- Readiness of power holders to relinquish some of their power if they retained substantial advantages
- Restriction of major negotiations to the national elite, which means exclusion of popular mass actors from consideration except as threats to any compact that might emerge
- Decoupling of political from economic demands (e.g., wage demands on the part of organized labor)
- Leadership by Prime Minster Adolfo Suarez, King Juan Carlos, and Prime Minster Felipe González
- Clever solutions to the problem of balancing central power and regional rights

This miscellaneous list of factors does not reflect a systematic theory of democratization. But it does incorporate a commonsense explanation of this sort: in favorable international and domestic circumstances, wise national leaders who were prepared to compromise saw that they could negotiate a transition to a fairly stable political system without devastating conflict and without losing much of their power; preferring that outcome to chaos, they negotiated the transition.

As descriptions, most features of the checklist make considerable sense. Surely a postwar European and Atlantic environment that granted rewards to democratizing regimes while penalizing holdouts weakened the Franco regime's authoritarian position. Certainly economic growth deeply altered citizen-state relations. Economic growth of the 1950s and 1960s undoubtedly urbanized the Spanish population, raised the standard of living, lifted educational levels, increased mass media exposure, and thus facilitated popular political participation.

Unlike Algeria or Kazakhstan, furthermore, Spain did have experience with democratic regimes in the past, however transient and troubled. From this book's point of view, however, such a summary remains frustratingly vague about mechanisms and processes. Except for pointing out its effect on historical memory, the summary also fails to specify how this historical experience affected both public politics' relation to the state and citizens' control over public politics – the two interacting loci of changes promoting democratization itself. Our task, then, is not so much to reject the Diamandouros analysis as to refine and systematize it.

Let us step back a bit before concentrating on Spain's major spurts of democratization. Using what he regards as phases that occurred in regime after regime elsewhere in Europe, Stanley Payne schematizes Spain's history from the end of the Napoleonic occupation to 1976 as follows (Payne 2000: 6):

Early Convulsive Liberalism: 1810–1874
Stable Elitist Liberalism: 1875–1909
Democratization: 1909–1936
Authoritarianism: 1923–1930 and 1936–1976

For Payne, the Tragic Week of 1909 (when protests against the inequalities of conscription for military service in Morocco mutated into revolutionary action, anticlerical attacks, and a general strike in Catalonia) marks the point of transition to democratization. Whether we place the pivot at 1909 or (as I will in a moment) at 1917, the main point remains: early in the 20th century, Spain moved from a long stage of oligarchic rule with frequent military intervention to a new phase of susceptibility to both democratization and de-democratization.

What historical changes must we explain? From around World War I to the late 20th century, Spain made a spectacular series of shifts between democratization and de-democratization. Spain de-democratized significantly with Primo de Rivera's 1923 military coup, and catastrophically with Francisco Franco's military victory in the civil war of 1936 to 1939. In contrast, Spain democratized weakly as Primo de Rivera's regime relaxed its central control during the mid-1920s, spectacularly with the revolution of 1930 to 1931, and again dramatically after Francisco Franco's death in 1975. At least so far, the democratization of 1975 through 1981 has not reversed. To what extent do our three basic processes – broadening of popular political participation, equalization of access to non-state political resources and opportunities, and inhibition of autonomous and/or arbitrary coercive power within and outside the state – and their consequences explain Spain's long-term experience with democratization and de-democratization?

In the form of a chronology from 1914 to 1981, Box 6-2 illustrates what we must explain.

The chronology describes repeated encounters with both democratization and de-democratization. Only during the 1970s do we see more than a decade pass without significant reversals of direction. The chronology also makes clear that, as had been true long before 1914, military intervention in Spanish national politics occurred frequently and almost always damaged democracy. More so than elsewhere in Europe, furthermore,

---

BOX 6-2. Democratization and De-Democratization in Spain, 1914–1981

1914–1918 Spain neutral during World War I, with consequent industrial expansion, especially in Catalonia

1917   Under constitutional monarchy, military regime suspends constitutional guarantees, Catalans agitate for home rule, workers stage general strike

1923   Mutiny of Barcelona garrison, military coup of Primo de Rivera, weakened monarchy

1925   Partial civilianization of Primo de Rivera dictatorship, but continuation of military rule under weak monarchy with Primo de Rivera's prime minister

1930   Resignation and death of Primo de Rivera, interim government of Damaso Berenguer

1931   Municipal elections produce landslide for republicans, king flees country without abdicating, provisional government declares republic, establishes universal male suffrage for ages 23 and over, bans army officers and clergy from presidency

1932   Military rebellion quelled, Catalan charter of autonomy

1933   Radical uprisings in Barcelona and elsewhere, elections produce center-right rule, female suffrage established, fascist Falange forms

1934   Catalan declaration of independence, radical risings, miners' insurrection in Asturias, all repressed

1936   Popular Front victory in national elections, strike waves and occupations in agricultural and industrial sectors, Spanish government grants home rule to Basque region, military rising in Morocco spreads to Spain, civil war begins, rebels name Franco chief of state, Germany and Italy aid rebels while USSR supplies leftists

1939   Franco's forces win civil war and establish authoritarian state, German and Italian forces withdraw

1939–1945 Spain neutral during World War II; through successive struggles and administrative reforms, Franco subordinates military to civilian control

1948   Ten-year-old prince Juan Carlos, heir to throne, arrives in Spain for education under the regime

1950   After long diplomatic isolation, both the United States and the UN open diplomatic relations with Spain

1953	United States establishes military bases in return for economic and military aid; after long tension over state control of the Spanish church, Franco signs Concordat with the Vatican extending church autonomy
1960–1974	Unprecedented industrialization and economic growth
1968	Franco names Juan Carlos his eventual successor as head of state
1973	ETA (Basque nationalist) assassination of Franco's prime minister, Carrero Blanco
1975	Franco dies and Juan Carlos becomes king, extensive worker mobilization begins
1976–1978	Under Prime Minister Adolfo Suarez, Spain initiates democratic reforms, elects new parliament, and adopts democratic constitution, with voting age lowered first to 21, then to 18
1979	Basque and Catalan autonomy statutes
1981	Attempted military coup defeated, new regional autonomies, beginning of continuous (if often turbulent) democratic rule

demands for regional autonomy or independence complicated Spain's national democratic programs throughout the 20th century.

The chronology itself omits another factor that greatly influenced the texture and course of Spanish democratization and de-democratization. From the late 19th century onward, both agricultural and industrial workers organized and politicized in Spain to a remarkable degree. Integration of organized workers (both industrial and agricultural) into Spain's national public politics generally marked the country's periods of democratization, just as their collective exclusion signaled periods of de-democratization.

As we have seen in earlier cases, Spanish democratization generally occurred through substantial expansion of popular political participation, and de-democratization through defection of elites from burdensome democratic consultation. Spain's timetable of democratization and de-democratization therefore clarifies what any analysis must explain: how the Spanish military finally lost its notorious autonomy and fell under civilian control, how excluded workers finally became durably integrated into the national regime, but also how elites withdrew from democracy during the Primo de Rivera regime and the Civil War.

Analytically, these problems generalize into a quartet of questions about Spain's phases of democratization:

1. Did our three crucial processes – broadening of popular political participation, equalization of access to non-state political resources and opportunities, and inhibition of autonomous and/or arbitrary coercive power within and outside the state – actually cause subjection of the state to public politics and facilitation of popular influence over public politics?
2. Did the mechanisms listed in Box 6-1 – coalition formation, central co-optation, and so on – contribute to the three crucial processes, as the box argues?
3. Did subjection of the state to public politics and facilitation of popular influence over public politics play indispensable parts in democratization?
4. Did reversals of the three crucial processes cause de-democratization?

Without pinning down all the details, the historical narrative that follows replies "Yes" to each of the four questions.

Despite the massive return of military power under Franco, Spain went through important phases of the three crucial processes during the period between World War I and the revolution of 1931 – the period Spanish historians commonly call the crisis and decline of the Restoration. After the abortive First Republic of 1873 to 1874, a constitutional monarchy (the Restoration), generally backed by the military, governed Spain without direct military intervention from 1874 to 1917. The regime installed manhood suffrage in 1890 but the "existing patronage and party-boss system, commonly known as *caciquismo*, largely contained or deflected popular voting for about thirty years" (Payne 2000: 5). Loss of the Spanish-American War (1898) weakened the military's political position, but by no means eliminated it as a national political actor.

Prior to World War I, nevertheless, workers and nationalists began to organize in a dazzling array of ideological formations, from anarchism to Catalan separatism. In parallel with developments elsewhere in Europe, 1917 brought violent confrontations between the right and left, with the military temporarily seizing power and forcing suspension of constitutional guarantees. At that point, we can reasonably say that Spain had entered a phase that earlier chapters have shown us in French and other regimes: a phase in which rulers depended for their survival on citizens' compliance and in which alternation between democratization and de-democratization became possible as never before. We cannot, of course, date Spain's democratic "consolidation" at 1917 or 1931. But we can identify the span of years between those dates as crucial for the transformations of public politics that undergird democratization.

Introducing his subtle, deeply documented study of Spanish political conflict from 1917 to 1931, Eduardo González Calleja makes a telling observation:

> Study of public order, subversion, and violence during the three brief phases that signal the Restoration's definitive collapse is marked by the presence of various factors that seem to confirm the full establishment in our country of a modern repertoire of collective action: linking of protest to political activity in general, its almost exclusive channeling by formally organized groups (especially parties, unions, and large corporatist actors) pursuing objectives well matched to defined political programs, and adoption of forms of struggle that were more flexible, autonomous with respect to power holders, modular (that is, consisting of basic routines that could be used and combined by a wide variety of actors in pursuit of very different goals), with national and even international scope and impact. (González Calleja 1999: 17)

The repertoire change coincided with a great expansion of political organization among workers and other citizens. Even while elites were defecting from the modest democratic gains of 1917 to 1923 under Primo de Rivera's protection, popular participation in public politics was increasing energetically.

Once Primo de Rivera's dictatorship ended in 1925, for example, the number of organized workers shot up rapidly, then accelerated with the peaceful revolution of 1931 (Soto Carmona 1988. 303-305). In that abrupt transfer of power, republicans won overwhelming majorities of Spain's urban voters in the municipal elections of April 1931. The king (no longer assured of support by an increasingly unenthusiastic general staff) fled the country. Republicans declared the monarchy defunct.

The break with the previous regime came quickly. No formal act of the exiting regime endowed the new one with legitimacy. The new Republic's national assembly included only four members of the Primo de Rivera legislature, 1.2 percent of the total seats (Genieys 1997: 123). In terms of control over the state, a revolution had occurred (González Calleja 1999: 627). The new rulers took control of a state with weak infrastructure but powerful means of top-down intervention:

> Republican rulers inherited a state that disposed of formidable despotic power, greatly superior to that of any other organization within the territory, but lacking sufficient infrastructural power to apply its rulers' policies when it came to the production and distribution of goods and services. (Cruz 2006: 333)

Revolutionary bases remained quite narrow, and the new regime lacked the means of either incorporating its opposition or containing its own allies. Popular attacks on churches, disestablishment of the Catholic Church, and extensive land reform soon alienated both rural landlords and the Catholic hierarchy (Malefakis 1970, chapter 6). These groups, as well as the military, soon began to defect.

Indeed, Gerard Alexander argues that the Spanish right never really committed to the Republic. By *right*, Alexander means mainly secular liberals in existing political parties plus Catholic politicians, especially those affiliated with the Confederación Española de Derechas Autónomas (Alexander 2002: 106). The right did not commit to democracy and the Republic therefore failed to consolidate, Alexander claims,

> because rightists detected high risks in democracy. These high risks were the result of the perceived susceptibility of millions of landless laborers and industrial and mining workers to revolutionary political appeals threatening the right's safety, property, income, control of the workplace, and church. Many on the right traced these risks to Spain's underlying social structure. (Alexander 2002: 103)

In short, not only the military but also the old civilian ruling classes understood that the revolution seriously challenged their power.

The new rulers acted on precisely that assumption. Despite shrinking the army's active officer corps rapidly, the new regime continued to apply the old regime's instruments of exclusion and control (Payne 1967: 268–276). The provisional government installed on 14 April 1931 pursued an exclusive line, denying the right of public assembly to monarchists, anarchists, and communists alike (Ballbé 1985: 318). The bourgeois republic that then came to power regularly used military force to repress leftist and striking workers, thus excluding them from the new regime (Ballbé 1985, chapter 11). As rulers cried anarchy, excluded actors cried persecution (Cruz 2006: 334–335). The small Spanish Communist Party withdrew within its shell; it took the position that the revolution of 1931 could at best serve as a wedge for a true proletarian revolution and that collaboration with bourgeois rulers would delay the coming revolution (Cruz 1987: 127–128).

Yet, on the whole, workers – especially those represented by the Socialist Party – stuck with the republic. Significantly, the first group of workers to defect from the republican coalition and align themselves with the military in 1935 and 1936 was the small but active Catholic workers' union (Soto Carmona 1988: 313). Peasants and agricultural wage laborers benefited from the extensive land reforms of 1931 and generally continued to support the regime. Indeed, they soon went beyond it by occupying uncultivated fields and striking against low-wage landlords.

By 1936, rural strikes and land occupations were threatening the precarious republican regime as the regime also faced military opposition from Francisco Franco and his collaborators (Malefakis 1970, chapter 14). Military support from Germany and Italy greatly facilitated Franco's invasion of the Spanish mainland from Morocco. At the same time, already fragile elite support for the republican regime was fragmenting. In Aragon, for example, mobilization of landless laborers turned landowners fiercely against the new rulers (Casanova et al. 1992: 86–87). Aragon landlords got their revenge: counter-revolutionaries eventually killed 8,628 suspected supporters of the republican cause (Casanova et al. 1992: 213). As Franco came to power, his regime's violent repression snuffed out Aragon's previously energetic democratic mobilization. Across the country as a whole, however, deaths from combat, executions, and murders hit Franco's supporters harder than they did republicans: about 132,000 deaths for nationalists and 96,000 for republicans (Payne 2000: 219). The civil war left vivid scars on both sides.

Franco and After

Once in power, Franco built a regime in alliance with the military, the clergy, the authoritarian Falange, and the syndicalist movement the Falange controlled. From the viewpoint of long-term democratization, Franco's most significant move was to subordinate the military so thoroughly to his control that it lost its fabled, dangerous autonomy. Spain's Cold War alliance with the United States (which had previously shunned the Franco regime) furthered that subordination by increasing U.S.-backed military expenditure, sending thousands of officers to the United States for training and generally making military careers more attractive to those officers who were willing to conform.

During the 1950s, Franco also managed to strengthen his ties with the church through a papal concordat and to sidetrack the Falange's post-Franco political ambitions by governing increasingly through technocrats and bureaucrats rather than zealots. An era of compromise and of clerical reform muted the furious anticlericalism that had been one of the most striking features of republican activism during the Republic and the Civil War (Cruz 1997). All this became easier because during the same period Spain was entering the most rapid period of economic growth in its entire history and was attracting foreign capital as never before. Managing the new industrial economy left less room in the regime for military officers and political traditionalists.

At the same time, the transformation of Spanish social life undermined the bases of Franco's rule. Stanley Payne sums up:

Though Franco was never seriously challenged as long as he lived, the surviving government administrators would find that by the time of his death, the kind of society and culture on which the regime had primarily been based had largely ceased to exist, and that would make it impossible for the regime to reproduce itself. Ultimately, the economic and cultural achievements that took place under the regime, whether or not they were intended to develop as they did, deprived the regime of its reason for being. (Payne 2000: 493)

Domestic opposition grew during the 1960s, and the physically depleted Franco's reactions were nothing like the repressive steps that had made him fearsome in the 1930s. Industrial workers, students, regional nationalists, and – more surprisingly – lower-level clergy began voicing dissent. Formal designation of Prince Juan Carlos as Franco's successor in July 1969 signaled that regime transition had already begun. Overthrow of the authoritarian Portuguese regime in 1974, furthermore, threatened Spain's conservatives and encouraged its progressives.

In most regards, Franco's death on 20 November 1975 was therefore an anticlimax. Nevertheless, only after Juan Carlos' succession did the regime implement the formal institutions of parliamentary democracy as westerners generally understand them: freedom of press and association, broad electoral competition, independent judiciary, and more. In that sense, students of the Spanish transition are correct to consider the years from 1975 to 1981 a wonder of political engineering.

Figure 6-3 sketches what the political engineers wrought. After minor increments of democratization and enhancement of state capacity between World War I and 1930, Spain's Second Republic brought dramatic democratization combined with substantial loss of state capacity and Franco's regime built state capacity to unprecedented levels at the total expense of democracy, but from the 1960s onward democratization proceeded at an increasing pace with only minor losses of central capacity.

Spain therefore underwent two major cycles of democratization, an interrupted and ultimately reversed cycle from World War I to the mid-1930s and another more continuous cycle from Franco's postwar years to the 1970s. Each cycle corresponded roughly to the causal sequence sketched in Figure 6-2:

- Broadening of popular political participation, equalization of access to non-state political resources and opportunities, inhibition of

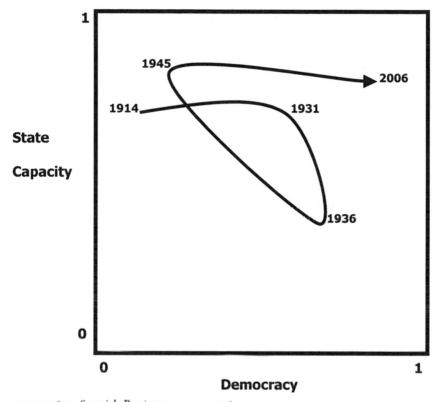

FIGURE 6-3. Spanish Regimes, 1914–2006

autonomous and/or arbitrary coercive power within and outside the state

- Reduction of influence by autonomous power clusters, including those of rulers, over public politics
- Subjection of state to public politics plus facilitation of popular influence over public politics
- Increase in the breadth, equality, and protection of mutually binding consultation in citizen-state relations, which equals democratization

The first cycle left important political residues in the form of popular political organization (both public and clandestine) as well as accumulated experience with democratic institutions. But Franco's victory in the Civil War temporarily reestablished autonomous power clusters: both the army and Franco's own ruling clique. Franco's authoritarian rule then decisively subordinated the army to civilian control.

Less deliberately but no less decisively, the state's management of economic expansion and increased international involvement after 1960 subjected Franco's state to public politics and facilitated popular influence over public politics. Without denying the astute leadership of Adolfo Suarez and King Juan Carlos, we can see that Spain's changing power configurations were becoming favorable to democracy well before 1981. Although the new constitution that took effect in 1979 formalized the subordination of the military to the Basic Law and to the king, it merely ratified the decline in military independence that Franco had already managed during the later decades of his rule. The failed military coup of 1981 simply demonstrated to the world what Franco's regime had accomplished: the army that had for two centuries set the rhythms of Spanish politics no longer enjoyed the autonomy and power to reverse the regime's direction.

Power, Trust, and Inequality

Despite earlier chapters' stress on trust networks and categorical inequality, I have written this chapter as though changes in power configurations and their consequences occurred independently of alterations in trust and inequality. Yet they clearly interacted. In fact, in earlier analyses of trust networks I looked at the same period of Spanish history to propose a conjectural sequence of this kind (Tilly 2005: 149):

1931–1933: Substantial integration of workers' and peasants' trust networks into national public politics through the mediation of unions and political organizations, combined with partial exclusion of the military

1933–1935: Confrontations between partially integrated workers, peasants, and regionalists on one side and national authorities on the other

1936: New mobilizations of workers, peasants, and regionalists; counter-mobilization of military

1936–1939: Incremental (and violent) exclusion of worker, peasant, and regionalist trust networks from national politics

1939–1960: Return to the prevailing patronage, particularistic ties, and evasive conformity of the 1920s, now coupled with authoritarian integration of the military and the Catholic Church into Franco's system of rule

1960–1975: Undermining of old local trust networks by economic expansion, relaxation of repression, and expansion of trust networks within workers' organizations

1976–1978: Democratization resting on and facilitating integration of popular trust networks into national public politics and partial extrusion from the regime of trust networks based in the church and the military

This chronology describes a set of complementary processes with regard to connections between public politics and the routine forms of organization – especially trust networks – within which Spaniards pursued their daily lives. Looking at this chronology in conjunction with changes in relations between major power configurations and public politics makes the period from 1939 to 1960 much more interesting. During that period, after all, republican workers' and peasants' trust networks did not simply dissolve. Their members somehow worked out accommodations with an alien system of rule, mostly through evasive conformity in public combined with clandestine collaboration inside those networks.

As for categorical inequality, its insulation from public politics appears to have occurred before the Second Republic burst onto the scene. To be sure, Spanish women did not get voting rights until 1931 – that is, under the Second Republic. But on the whole, despite the country's remarkable social inequalities, Spanish regimes avoided inscribing differences by class, religion, ethnicity, language, or nobility directly into public politics from the 1890 enactment of manhood suffrage onward. That necessary insulation of public politics from categorical inequality prepared the way for Spain's ultimate democratization and prevailed throughout the period in which trust networks and power configurations were changing turbulently.

As South Africa's drama has already shown us, Spain did not follow the only possible sequence with regard to trust networks, categorical inequality, and power configurations. On the contrary, in South Africa the crucial transformations of the three arrived late and more or less simultaneously, thereby contributing to the intensity of struggle during the 1980s and 1990s. Even as power devolved into African hands, the South African regime faced the serious problem of dissolving or integrating largely autonomous armed forces on both sides.

The United States followed yet another sequence. Its Civil War largely subdued any autonomous centers of coercive power, and (as we have seen)

major integration of trust networks into public politics had occurred by the early 20th century. But categorical inequality by gender and (especially) race continued to scar American public politics long after then.

We still face the problem of analyzing sequences and interactions among the three large sets of changes in the course of democratization and de-democratization. Trajectories in both directions vary according to sequences and interactions among changes in trust networks, categorical inequality, and autonomous power centers. Up to this point, furthermore, we have received intermittent signals of two other influences on those trajectories. First, the existing level of state capacity when a regime begins the process of democratization or de-democratization affects how the process works; consider how differently democratization looked in low-capacity Switzerland and high-capacity France. Second, the shocks of domestic confrontation, conquest, colonization, and revolution accelerate the same processes that take place in more incremental democratization and de-democratization, but that acceleration produces a more intense interaction among their effects. Again, South Africa's revolution demonstrates how intense such an interaction can be, and how drastic its effects on the quality of public politics.

These problems set the agenda for the next chapter. Let us look carefully at the variable paths of regimes through democratization and de-democratization.

7

Alternative Paths

In a democratic theoretician's ideal world, democratization and de-democratization would move along the same straight line, but in opposite directions. As our many encounters with historical experience have shown us, we do not live in an ideal world. The vivid histories of South Africa, Spain, and other regimes follow irregular trajectories fueled by unceasing political struggle. An already undemocratic South Africa de-democratized ferociously after 1948, only to undergo a democratic explosion after 1985; the second transition by no means simply reversed the first. In Spain, we witness sharp changes of direction after World War I, with the peaceful revolution of 1931, with Franco's victory in the civil war, and with the relaxation of Franco's regime starting in the 1960s. History abhors straight lines. Nevertheless it will help discipline our inquiry if we idealize for a moment. Figure 7-1 sketches three stylized trajectories from fairly low-capacity undemocratic regimes to higher-capacity democratic regimes.

Remember the meaning of state capacity: the extent to which interventions of state agents in existing non-state resources, activities, and interpersonal connections alter existing distributions of those resources, activities, and interpersonal connections as well as relations among those distributions. In a *strong state* trajectory, state capacity increases well before significant democratization occurs. As a result, the state enters democratic territory already in possession of means to enforce decisions arrived at through broad, equal, protected, and mutually binding citizen-state interaction. In this idealized scenario, rulers or other political actors eliminate autonomous domestic rivals to the state, subordinate the state's own military, and establish substantial control over resources, activities,

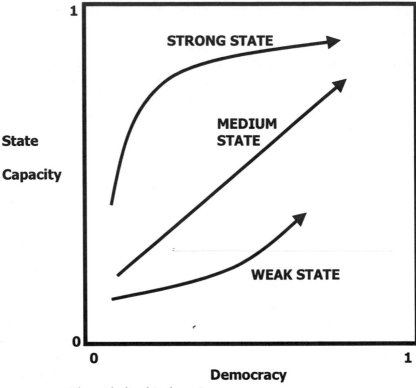

FIGURE 7-1. Three Idealized Paths to Democracy

and populations within the state's territory before serious democratization begins.

According to this book's arguments, the process of state strengthening starts the processes of subjecting the state to public politics and increasing popular control over public politics. Insulation of public politics from categorical inequality and integration of trust networks into public politics then proceed. Together, according to the scenario, the three processes interact to democratize the regime. Early in the trajectory, the risk of revolution and mass rebellion rises as both magnates and ordinary people resist state expansion. But over the long run, we might expect levels of political violence to fall dramatically as relatively peaceful forms of popular politics become available and a strong state monitors the varieties of claim making that are likely to generate violence.

De-democratization, continues the theory, can occur at any point in this idealized trajectory. It results from reversal of one or more of the three basic processes: withdrawal of major trust networks from public politics, inscription of new categorical inequalities into public politics, and/or formation of autonomous power centers that threaten both the influence of public politics on the state and popular control over public politics. Shocks such as conquest, colonization, revolution, and intense domestic confrontation (e.g., civil war) accelerate movement of the basic processes in one direction or the other but still operate through the same mechanisms as more incremental democratization and de-democratization.

In a strong state trajectory, the theory implies that political struggle centers on control over the instruments of state power rather than, say, local disputes or rivalries among lineages. In typical scenarios, ordinary people defend those elements of the state that protect them and guarantee mutually binding consultation, while powerful elites seek either to shield themselves from state control or to divert some portion of the state to their own ends. At any point along the trajectory, the state's strength elevates the stakes of political struggle. Earlier chapters have described segments of this idealized trajectory – by no means all of them arriving at democracy – in Kazakhstan, France, Russia, Belarus, China, Algeria, and India. We might also try to force the South African experience into the strong state trajectory. We would then have to treat the period from the mid-1980s onward as an enormously accelerated democratization phase in the presence of an already formidable state. This perspective does lend insight into South Africa's travails since 1985; the state's extensive capacity, however challenged by African resistance, gave the ANC means of rule that remain the envy of its neighboring regimes.

A stylized *medium state* trajectory moves up and down the diagonal of the capacity-democracy space, with each increment or decrement of state capacity matched by a similar change in degree of democracy. In this idealized case, the state is in the process of building capacity as it enters democratic territory. Accordingly, suppressing autonomous power centers, establishing control over the state by public politics, and expanding popular influence over public politics loom larger and longer in the democratization process than in the strong state path. With rising state capacity, the stakes of political struggle increase incrementally with democratization. We might therefore expect a regime moving along the medium trajectory to be somewhat less at risk to revolution but more at risk to intense domestic confrontation short of revolution than strong state regimes (Goodwin 2001, 2005; Tilly 1993, 2006, chapters 6–8). As compared to strong states, we might also expect medium states to exhibit a higher proportion of political struggles in which the state itself is only peripherally involved, especially early in the trajectory.

Along that diagonal trajectory, de-democratization still results from reversal of one or more of the basic processes: disconnection of trust networks, re-inscription of categorical inequalities, and/or formation of autonomous power centers that jeopardize popular influence over public politics and hence the state. We might conjecture that de-democratization occurs over most of the trajectory more frequently than in strong state regimes because not until late in the process 1) does the state have the capacity to restrain potential defectors from democratic consultation and 2) are the stakes of membership so high that they keep political partici-pants from defecting. Of regimes we have looked at in detail, the United States, Argentina, and Spain broadly resemble the medium state pattern.

Weak states have often existed in history, but until recently they have rarely democratized at all. In a world full of conquest, they have most commonly disappeared into the territories of powerful predators. Since World War II, however, protection by great powers and international insti-tutions have combined with the decline of interstate warfare to increase the survival rate – indeed, the new production – of weak states that had been colonies or satellites of great powers (Creveld 1999; Kaldor 1999; Migdal 1988; Tilly 2006, chapter 6). In recent decades, therefore, an increasing number of regimes have been following weak state trajectories toward democracy. Here we see the opposite of the strong state path: con-siderable democratization that precedes any substantial increase in state capacity.

The implications are obvious, at least in theory: a weak state suffers from significant obstacles to continued democratization beyond some threshold. Those obstacles exist because a weak state fails to suppress or subordinate autonomous power centers, allows citizens to insulate their trust networks from public politics, and tolerates or even encourages the insertion of categorical inequalities into public politics. As compared with strong and medium states, weak states endure a high proportion of conflicts, often violent, in which the state is no more than peripherally involved. As we will see later, they also host the great bulk of the world's many civil wars (Collier and Sambanis 2005, Eriksson and Wallensteen 2004, Fearon and Laitin 2003).

Along weak state trajectories, de-democratization occurs even more frequently than in strong and medium states; incentives to withdraw trust networks, activate categorical inequalities, and establish centers of power that escape the constraints of public politics increase as the capacity of the state to contain those processes declines. Of regimes we have exam-ined closely, Jamaica, Switzerland, and the Dutch Republic before French conquest most closely resemble the weak state model – but Switzerland and the Netherlands eventually moved toward significant strengthening of central state authority and therefore moved onto the medium state track toward democracy. Whether Jamaica will follow suit remains to be seen.

In any case, we should treat the three trajectories as what they are: stylized simplifications of a complex reality. Think back to the trajectories toward democracy of France or Spain, and you will immediately remember deviations from the idealized paths: multiple revolutions and reactions in France, annihilation of a fledgling republic by Franco's military power in Spain. From the three trajectories we should retain chiefly a more fundamental lesson: at each stage of democratization and de-democratization, the past and present capacity of the state strongly affects how those processes occur and what impact they have on social life at large.

Using the distinctions among strong state, medium state, and weak state trajectories as a heuristic, this chapter examines how state capacity interacts with our three basic processes: integration of trust networks into public politics, insulation of public politics from categorical inequality, and (especially) dissolution of autonomous power centers, with its consequences for control of public politics and the state. The surprising experience of Venezuela leads to more general reflection concerning the impact of variable state capacity on democratization and de-democratization. An analysis of the pernicious propensity of weak states for civil war fortifies that general reflection and leads to a discussion of other shocks that sometimes accelerate democratization and de-democratization: conquest, colonization, revolution, and domestic confrontation. Ireland's troubled advance into democratization illustrates all those shocks. Thinking about Ireland's relative success (especially outside of the North) leads us to a final review of what ordinary people actually gain when democratization occurs. The chapter as a whole demonstrates the importance of significant state capacity to successful democratization, but also shows how high capacity tempts rulers into baffling popular will.

Venezuela, Oil, and Switched Trajectories

The history of Venezuela since 1900 documents the influence of changes in state capacity. It shows us a regime that had long existed in the low-capacity undemocratic (hence highly violent) quadrant of the capacity-democracy space but then switched over to what could have been a strong state path to democracy. The state's control over oil revenues made the difference. It also blocked full democratization and eventually drove the regime's trajectory toward high-capacity undemocracy.

Venezuela became a country independent of the Spanish Empire in several stages: as a rebellious province (1810), as part of Simón Bolívar's Gran Colombia (1819), then as a separate republic at Bolívar's death (1830). Until the early 20th century, Venezuela staged a familiar, dreary Latin American drama of military dictators, caudillos, coups, and occasional civilian rule. Large landlords never succeeded in establishing the armed entente that they achieved in major regions of Argentina and Brazil (Centeno 2002: 156). In 1908, however, a coup led by General Juan Vicente Gómez introduced a new era. Gómez ruled Venezuela for 27 years, until his death in 1935. He built up a national army whose officers came largely from his own region of the Andes (Rouquié 1987: 195). He consolidated his rule by distributing large tracts of land to loyal clients (Collier and Collier 1991: 114). He escaped the constant turnover of earlier Venezuelan regimes.

Gómez lasted longer than his predecessors, at least in part, because Venezuela opened its oil fields in 1918 and soon became one of the world's major producers. Oil shifted the Venezuelan economy's pivot from coffee to energy and, eventually, energy-backed manufacturing as well. As we might expect, it also fortified the dictator's evasion of popular consent for his rule. During his entire tenure, Gómez blocked the formation of any mass popular organizations.

Nevertheless, the move away from an agrarian economy expanded the number of workers and students, who supplied the ranks of a militant if relatively powerless opposition. At Gómez' death in 1935, Venezuelan elites banded together to create an elected presidency restricted to a single five-year term and simultaneously acted to ban left activists as Communists. The first elected president – another general from the Andes, Eleazar López Contreras – used a portion of the country's oil revenues to fund welfare programs that would buy popular support and shut out leftists.

The pattern continued long after 1935. True, from that point on those who took power in Venezuela – whether by election or by force – always declared they did so to forward democracy. Venezuela institutionalized general adult suffrage in 1947 and never quite rescinded it. The moderately social democratic party Acción Democrática, furthermore, did supply a vehicle for popular mobilization and support for organized labor (Collier and Collier 1991: 251–270). But oil revenues provided rulers with the means of avoiding mutually binding consultation of citizens. The military junta that governed Venezuela from 1948 to 1958 notably declared that it had seized power to reverse the threat to democracy posed by the previous populist-military government. It received support from the church, from heavily taxed foreign companies, and from traditional elites (Rouquié 1987: 196).

But, remarks Fernando Coronil, the junta's leaders:

were not politicians and in the following years acquired only limited political experience. They gained control of the state during a period of rapid expansion of the oil economy and were not compelled by economic and political conditions to seek support from other social groups. As a consequence of their sense of self-sufficiency, they grew distant even from the armed forces, their original base of support. They sought to avoid politics and to concentrate on visible achievements. (Coronil 1997: 131)

Those "visible achievements" consisted of public works and welfare programs financed by oil revenues. As Albert Hirschman remarked from close observation, the concentration of entrepreneurial and reform activity within Venezuela's state facilitated coordination between the two sorts of activity and made it easy to enlist the private sector in state-led programs (Hirschman 1979: 95–96). But it also removed citizens at large from debates about economic development and welfare.

Increasingly, the ruling junta (led from 1954 onward by Colonel Marcos Pérez Jiménez, long a power behind the scenes) expanded those revenues by selling oil concessions to foreign companies, especially in the United States. In tune with American Cold War policy, Venezuela also justified itself increasingly as a U.S. ally and a bulwark against communism. Lulled by success, Pérez Jiménez radically narrowed the base of his domestic power, alienating a substantial share of military officers. In 1958 a military coup, this time backed by significant popular support, drove the junta from power. The *golpistas* and their civilian allies quickly called for democratic elections, which brought civilian Rómulo Betancourt to the presidency. Betancourt's accession led many observers to think that Venezuela had finally entered the track to democracy.

Felipe Agüero argues that the transition to partial democracy only occurred because the military had lost its previous unity:

Although it included representatives of the civil opposition, a mainly military junta joined efforts with political parties for the adoption of a provisional government and the setting of a calendar for elections and a transfer of power. On this basis, the contrast between a splintered military institution and a unified civic front with strong support by popular mobilization is the best explanation of the transition's success. The civic front presented a stronger and more credible alternative than the military factions opposed to democratization offered. (Agüero 1990: 349)

In fact, the military never strayed far from its seats of power. After 1958, nevertheless, Venezuela lived mostly under civilian rule. The military intervened directly in national politics only one more time: in 1992, a failed pair of coups brought a future president, Lieutenant Colonel Hugo Chávez Frías, into public view. (More on Chávez later.) Power alternated uneasily between two elite political parties, one moderately social democratic, the other moderately Christian democratic. Venezuela became an active organizer of the Organization of Petroleum Exporting States, the cartel OPEC. It used oil revenues to launch an ambitious, and ultimately ill-fated, campaign to make Venezuela a major automobile producer.

After OPEC septupled oil's price in 1973, President Carlos Andres Pérez expanded the public works programs of earlier regimes. He also nationalized the oil industry (1975) while borrowing internationally against future oil revenues; that foreign debt, including pressure from the International Monetary Fund (IMF) would bedevil Venezuelan governments for two decades. Although a few Venezuelans grew very rich, for the population at large the standard of living declined dramatically from the 1970s onward.

During his second presidential term (1988–1993), Pérez paid the price. Pérez had campaigned for the presidency on a program of public works and price containment, but after election he quickly changed direction under pressure from domestic and international financiers. In 1989, Pérez announced an austerity plan including cutbacks in governmental expenditure and price increases in public services. Implementation of the plan soon incited widespread popular resistance.

Caracas' violence of February to March 1989, for example, began with confrontations between commuters on one side and drivers of public transportation who were charging the new prices on the other. It soon spiraled into sacking and looting of downtown stores. In Caracas, 300 people died and more than 2,000 were wounded as the army moved in to clear the streets. During the first two weeks of March, sixteen Venezuelan cities exploded in similar events. The confrontations gained fame as El Caracazo (the Events of Caracas) or El Sacudón (the Shock). They opened a decade of struggle and regime change (López Maya 1999; López Maya, Smilde, and Stephany 2002).

Enter Chávez

Contention did not come only from the streets: during the early 1980s, a group of nationalist army officers organized a secret network called the Revolutionary Bolivarian Movement. Paratroop officer Hugo Chávez became their leader. In 1992, the Bolivarians almost seized power in a military coup whose failure sent Chávez to prison. He was still in jail when the group tried a second time in November. They captured a TV station and broadcast a video in which Chávez announced the government's fall. For that attempt, Chávez spent another two years in prison.

In 1993, while Chávez languished behind bars, the Venezuelan congress impeached president Pérez for corruption and removed him from office. But Pérez' successor, Rafael Caldera, soon faced a collapse of the country's banks, a surge of violent crime, rumors of new military coups, and charges of corruption. As Chávez left prison and entered politics, popular demand for political housecleaning swelled. By the 1998 presidential elections, the only serious opposition to former coup manager Chávez came from a former beauty queen. She dropped out of the running as the Chávez campaign gained widespread support.

Chávez billed himself as a populist and won by a large majority. The following year, according to Freedom House:

Hugo Chávez, the coupist paratrooper-turned-politician who was elected president in a December 1998 landslide, spent most of 1999 dismantling Venezuela's political system of checks and balances, ostensibly to destroy a discredited two-party system that for four decades presided over several oil booms but has left four out of five Venezuelans impoverished. Early in the year, Congressional power was gutted, the judiciary was placed under executive branch tutelage, and Chávez' army colleagues were given a far bigger say in the day-to-day running of the country. A constituent assembly dominated by Chávez followers drafted a new constitution that would make censorship of the press easier, allow a newly strengthened chief executive the right to dissolve Congress, and make it possible for Chávez to retain power until 2013. Congress and the Supreme Court were dismissed after Venezuelans approved the new constitution in a national referendum December 15. (Karatnycky 2000: 522)

As Chávez came to power in 1999, street confrontations between his supporters and his opponents accelerated. The new president's state visit to Fidel Castro's officially socialist Cuba later the same year dramatized his plan to transform the government and its place in the world at large. He began squeezing the state oil company, Petróleos de Venezuela, for more of its revenues and chipped away at its fabled autonomy. Chávez also revived an old, popular Venezuelan claim to a large chunk of western Guyana. Venezuela moved into a new stage of struggle over the country's future.

Over the next seven years, Chávez used his control over oil revenues to consolidate his power, to cramp his opposition, to sponsor populism

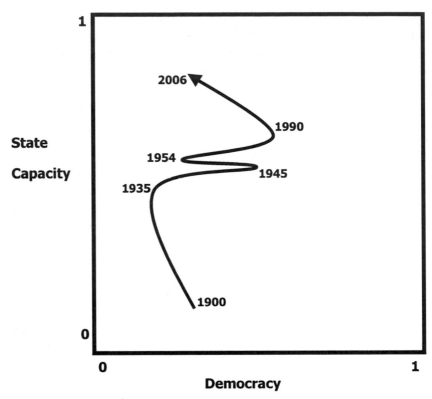

FIGURE 7-2. Venezuelan Regimes, 1900–2006

elsewhere in Latin America, and even to hold off an increasingly hostile United States. He survived a U.S.-backed coup in 2002, concerted resistance from the national oil company in 2002 to 2003, a general strike during the same period, and a U.S.-supported recall referendum in 2004. Step by step he responded with tightened repression. A Chávez-dominated legislature packed the Supreme Court, broadened prohibitions on insulting or showing disrespect for the president, and stepped up surveillance of mass media. Meanwhile, the courts prosecuted increasing numbers of regime opponents. Although he still enjoyed substantial support among Venezuela's numerous poor, like Russia's Putin and Algeria's Bouteflika, Chávez was relying on his country's oil-generated wealth to avoid popular consent.

That was not happening, of course, for the first time. Figure 7-2 traces Venezuela's zigzag trajectory since 1900. Venezuela entered the 20th century after seven decades as a low-capacity undemocratic regime, a weak

state repeatedly taken over by military officers. Under the Gómez dictatorship, the 1918 opening of Venezuelan oil fields started a spectacular augmentation of state capacity. Those new means of top-down control permitted Gómez to de-democratize an already undemocratic regime.
After Gómez' death in 1935, the Venezuelan oligarchy managed modest
democratization while continuing to draw on oil wealth to build up state
capacity.

The 1948 coup quickly de-democratized the regime, bringing it almost
back to its undemocratic condition at Gómez' death. Then a succession
of interventionist governments continued to build state capacity while
promoting another modest phase of democratization. Despite identifying
himself as a fierce self-described populist, Chávez continued one trend and
reversed the other: at the expense of democracy, he formed the highest-
capacity state Venezuela had ever produced. Throughout the entire period
from 1900 to 2006, Venezuela only barely edged into democratic territory.
But, fed by oil, it grew into an impressively high-capacity state.

The Freedom House ratings shown in Figure 7-3 neglect state capacity
as usual but provide substantiation and detail for our account of democratization and (especially) de-democratization over the years from 1972
onward. According to Freedom House, political rights actually increased
during Carlos Andres Pérez' first presidential term. From 1976 to 1986,
an optimistic Freedom House awarded Venezuela the top score of 1 on
political rights and a very high 2 on civil liberties. That put Venezuela in
the company of such democratic stalwarts as France and Ireland (Freedom
House 2002).

Then the irregular downslide began, reaching a low point of 4,4 in 1999
before a slight recovery and then another rapid decline back to 4,4 in 2006.
In short, from what began to look like a democratizing country during
the burst of oil wealth in the 1970s, Venezuela has regressed irregularly
toward fewer political rights and civil liberties – in our terms, it has de-
democratized. At the same time, Venezuelan state capacity has continued
to climb. A high-capacity undemocratic regime has emerged.

We lack the information on Venezuelan trust networks that would
allow us to assess their impact on democratization and de-democratization. It is at least plausible that the oil-financed welfare programs of
the 1970s and 1980s produced partial integration of popular trust networks into public politics before the economically painful 1990s and
(especially) the arrival of Hugo Chávez caused significant withdrawal of
trust networks among the middle classes and organized labor. At the same
time, Chávez' populist policies may well have produced unprecedented

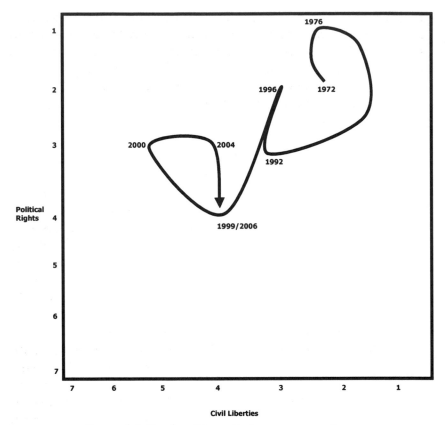

FIGURE 7-3. Venezuela's Freedom House Ratings, 1972–2006
Source: Compiled from Freedom House 2002, 2005, 2006

integration of indigenous and marginal people's trust networks into Venezuelan public politics. Enthusiasts of Chávez' Bolivarian Revolution (e.g., Figueroa 2006) regularly portray his regime as more democratic than its Venezuelan predecessors precisely because of Chávez' outreach to previously excluded poor and indigenous populations. But by the standards of breadth, equality, protection, and binding consultation, his regime de-democratized.

What about categorical inequality? Quite early, populist dictatorships buffered the inscription of Venezuela's extensive inequality into public politics. They thus promoted relatively broad and equal political participation without much protection or mutually binding consultation. That process did not reverse itself significantly. Of our three major processes, changes in autonomous power centers fluctuated most extensively.

For almost a century, empowered military officers, protecting their autonomy by means of oil income, have regularly driven cycles of de-democratization. Their abrupt switches of direction clearly drove Venezuela's phases of democratization and de-democratization. Chávez' own creation of an autonomous power center in the name of Bolivarian democracy actually de-democratized his regime.

If the Entire World Were Venezuela

The entire world is not Venezuela. But if it were, we would have some promising regularities to ponder. Most notably, Venezuela's historical experience confirms an idea that earlier cases foreshadowed: democratization and de-democratization work differently depending on changes in state capacity. More exactly, to the extent that an undemocratic state builds up citizen consent by bargaining with citizens over the means of rule, subsequent democratization proceeds farther and faster. It proceeds farther and faster because bargaining over the means of rule subordinates autonomous power centers, extends popular influence over public politics, and expands control of public politics over the state.

Bargaining over the means of rule commonly occurs, for example, in taxation and military conscription (Levi 1988, 1997; Tilly 1992, 2005b). It activates a number of the autonomy-containing mechanisms we reviewed in Chapter 6: central co-optation of previously autonomous political intermediaries, brokerage of cross-category political alliances, imposition of uniform governmental structures, and so on. To the extent that it supports military forces, bargaining over the means of rule has the ironic effect of making the military itself subject to popular consent and dependent on the civilian administrations that collect and distribute the wherewithal of military activity.

In a tour de force of historical analysis, Miguel Centeno has shown (in my terms, not his) that Western European states, on average, pursued the sequence war-extraction-bargaining-consent–state infrastructure much farther and faster than their Latin American counterparts:

While wars did provide an opportunity for greater state cohesion in some circumstances, for example, Chile in the 1830s, these openings were never used to create the institutional infrastructure needed for further development of state capacity. A critical question is why the wars of independence produced anarchy as opposed to a coherent military authoritarianism. I believe that the answer lies in the relatively limited level of military organization and violence involved in the wars of independence. This is not to deny the destruction that these caused. However, although the wars *weakened* the colonial order, they did not kill it. The armed effort was small enough so as to not require the militarization of society throughout the continent. Certainly in comparison with the equivalent wars in European history, such as the Thirty Years War, the independence conflicts left a much more limited institutional legacy. Postindependence wars also produced ambiguous results. (Centeno 2002: 26–27)

As a result, Centeno demonstrates, Latin American states generally ended up with weaker central structures, less effective intervention in routine social life, and more autonomous power centers than prevailed in modern Western Europe. Obviously, as the experience of Venezuela has taught us, if rulers build up state strength through direct control of valuable and externally salable resources, they undermine or avoid the effects of bargaining for the means of rule. In the cases of colonial administrations and client state, support from an external power similarly undermines or avoids the effects of bargaining.

Along a strong state trajectory, when an early buildup of state power combines with elimination of autonomous power centers, integration of trust networks into public politics becomes more likely. It occurs, when it does, both because the elimination of autonomous power centers shakes non-state protection of trust networks (e.g., in patron-client systems) and because the state and major political actors such as trade unions create new trust networks (e.g., welfare systems) that connect directly with public politics (Lindert 2004, Tilly 2005b). Integration of trust networks then promotes democratization, especially by committing political actors (including the state) to protected, mutually binding consultation.

No consistent relationship exists, however, between state strength and insulation of public politics from categorical inequality. As South African history underscores, some strong states inscribe categorical inequality directly into their systems of control. States on the medium path, such as the United States, sometimes build in racial, religious, or ethnic distinctions. Along the weak state path, racial, religious, and ethnic entrepreneurs repeatedly organize their parts of public politics around categorical distinctions and integrate them into political exclusion when they come to power. Nevertheless, over the longer run, all democratizing regimes move toward some variety of broad, equal citizenship, thereby reducing the role of categorical inequality in public politics.

In regimes with strong, relatively democratic states, de-democratization occurs chiefly through three processes: external conquest, defection from the democratic compact of elite political actors who have previously accepted it, and economic crisis so acute that it undercuts the state's capacity to sustain itself and deliver on its commitments. Nazi Germany inflicted the first fate on France and the Netherlands near the start of World War II, and elites defected with catastrophic results in Brazil, Uruguay, Chile, and Argentina during the 1960s and 1970s while economic crises ushered in authoritarian regimes in many European countries after World War I (Bermeo 2003). Although Venezuela never qualified as strong or relatively democratic, its multiple periods of de-democratization typically combined economic crisis with defection of elites from partially democratic compacts.

Regimes built on weak states behave differently. Anarchists' dreams to the contrary notwithstanding, they have less chance than strong state regimes of ever making their way into democratic territory. If they do so, they arrive with less capacity to check defections, protect minorities, and enforce decisions arrived at through mutual consultation. Yet some very weak states do govern democratic regimes, most often by relying on the protection of – or the stalemate created by association with – powerful neighbors. In 2003, salient examples included Andorra, Bahamas, Barbados, Cape Verde, Greek Cyprus, Dominica, Kiribati, Liechtenstein, Luxembourg, Malta, Marshall Islands, Micronesia, Nauru, Palau, San Marino, Slovenia, and Tuvalu, all of which qualified for 1,1 in Freedom House ratings that year (Piano and Puddington 2004). These regimes fell into two categories: older states that had survived in the geographic interstices left by formation of much larger states, and colonies that passed into formal sovereignty with protection from their former colonial masters.

Along a weak state path to democracy, the three basic democratizing processes – integration of trust networks, insulation of categorical inequalities, and elimination of autonomous power centers – all typically occur slowly and incompletely. Except where a weak state has expressly come into being under control of a single ethnic group, enclaves of distrust; division in public politics by ethnicity, language, race, or religion; and struggles among strongmen regularly challenge whatever democratic agreements have emerged.

In regimes with weak states (as in those with strong states), external conquest, elite defections from democratic compacts, and acute economic crisis promote de-democratization. In addition, the bids of domestic rivals to seize governmental power more frequently cause de-democratization in weak state regimes. Weak states Sierra Leone, Liberia, and Ivory Coast never reached great democratic heights; the highest ratings any of them received from Freedom House between 1972 and 2006 were Sierra Leone's 3,5 (political rights, civil liberties) in 1998 and 4,3 in 2005 (Freedom

House 2002, 2005, 2006). Yet in all three of them civil wars erupted and further de-democratized their regimes at different points between 1990 and 2004. Weak states like Sierra Leone, Liberia, and Ivory Coast have a destructive propensity to civil war.

Weak States and Civil War

Why should that be? Civil war occurs when two or more distinct military organizations, at least one of them attached to the previously existing government, battle one another for control of major governmental means within a single regime (Ghobarah, Huth, and Russett 2003; Henderson 1999; Hironaka 2005; Kaldor 1999; Licklider 1993; Walter and Snyder 1999). In 2003 alone, Scandinavia's professional conflict spotters identified civil wars during which 25 or more people died in Afghanistan, Algeria, Burma/Myanmar, Burundi, Chechnya, Colombia, Iraq, Israel/Palestine, Kashmir, Liberia, Nepal, the Philippines, Sri Lanka, Sudan, Turkey/Kurdistan, and Uganda (Eriksson and Wallensteen 2004: 632–635).

Civil war has not always been so prominent in the world's collective violence. Over the years since World War II, a remarkable change in the world's armed conflicts, including civil wars, has occurred. For two centuries up to that war, most large-scale lethal conflicts had pitted states against one another. During the first half of the 20th century, massive interstate wars produced most of the world's political deaths, although deliberate efforts of state authorities to eliminate, displace, or control subordinate populations also accounted for a significant number of fatalities (Chesnais 1976, 1981; Rummel 1994; Tilly et al. 1995).

During the immediate postwar period, furthermore, European colonial powers faced resistance and insurrection in many of their colonies. Colonial wars surged for several years before subsiding during the 1970s. As the Cold War prevailed between the 1960s and 1980s, great powers – especially the United States, the USSR, and the former colonial masters – frequently intervened in postcolonial civil wars such as those that rent Angola between 1975 and 2003 (Dunér 1985). But increasingly, civil wars without direct military intervention by third parties became the main sites of large-scale killing conflict (Kaldor 1999; Tilly 2003, chapter 3).

During the 20th century's second half, civil war, guerrilla war, separatist struggles, and conflicts between ethnically or religiously divided populations increasingly dominated the landscape of bloodletting (Creveld 1989, 1991; Holsti 1991, 1996; Kaldor 1999; Luard 1987; Mueller

2004). Between 1950 and 2000, civil wars killing half a million people or more occurred in Afghanistan, Angola, Cambodia, Indonesia, Mozambique, Nigeria, Rwanda, and Sudan (Echeverry, Salazar, and Navas 2001: 116). Over the century as a whole, the proportion of war deaths suffered by civilians rose startlingly: 5 percent in World War I, 50 percent in World War II, and up to 90 percent in wars of the 1990s (Chesterman 2001: 2). War burrowed inside regimes.

At first, decolonization and the Cold War combined to implicate the major western powers heavily in new states' domestic conflicts. For the French and the Americans, Indochina provides the most pungent memories of that time. But the Netherlands faced similar crises in Indonesia (1945–1949), as did Great Britain in Malaya (1948–1960). Most former European colonies began their independence as nominal democracies and then rapidly moved to either single-party oligarchies or military rule, or both at once. Military coups multiplied during the 1960s, as segments of national armed forces bid for their shares of state power.

Coups became less common and less effective from the 1970s onward (Tilly et al. 1995). With backing from great powers, existing rulers began to consolidate their holds on the governmental apparatus, to use it for their own benefit, and to exclude their rivals from power. In the process, dissident specialists in violence (often backed by international rivals of the power that patronized the existing rulers) turned increasingly to armed rebellion; they sought either to seize national power or to carve out autonomous territories of their own. Civil war became more and more prevalent.

Scandinavian specialists in the study of armed conflict divide armed conflicts since World War II into these categories (Strand, Wilhelmsen, and Gleditsch 2004: 11):

Extrasystemic: Occurs between a state and a non-state group outside its own territory, the most typical cases being colonial wars
Interstate: Occurs between two or more states
Internal: Occurs between the government of a state and internal opposition groups without intervention from other states – civil war, in short
Internationalized internal: Occurs between the government of a state and internal opposition groups, with military intervention from other states

Scandinavian data show colonial wars declining and then disappearing after 1975, interstate wars fluctuating but never predominating, and internationalized civil wars reaching their maximum during the 1980s and then declining after 2000. In terms of sheer frequency of conflict, the big news comes from civil wars without foreign intervention. These internal armed conflicts climbed irregularly but dramatically from the 1950s to the 1990s, only to decline significantly in frequency from the mid-1990s onward. Soviet and Yugoslav disintegration contributed to the surge of the early 1990s (Beissinger 1998, 2001; Kaldor 1999).

The number of civil wars expanded much more rapidly than the number of independent states, which rose from about 100 in 1960 to more than 160 during the early 21st century. An early peak arrived in 1975, when substantial civil wars were going on in Angola, Burma, Cambodia, Ethiopia, Indonesia, Iran, Iraq, Lebanon, Morocco, Mozambique, Pakistan, the Philippines, Vietnam, and Zimbabwe. But civil wars continued to multiply until they peaked in 1992, when a full 28 internal military conflicts were raging across the world. The number of civil wars fell off during the later 1990s, but internecine killing continued at much higher levels than had prevailed during the 1960s.

During the later 1990s, despite such sore spots as Chechnya and Kosovo, most post-socialist regimes settled into more stable, less violent forms of rule. Partial democratization of previously divided regimes – South Africa is a case in point – also contributed to civil war's decline from 1994 onward (Piano and Puddington 2004). Despite continuing civil wars in Afghanistan, Algeria, Burma/Myanmar, Burundi, Chechnya, Colombia, Iraq, Israel/Palestine, Kashmir, Liberia, Nepal, the Philippines, Sri Lanka, Sudan, Turkey/Kurdistan, and Uganda, the scope of civil war has been shrinking.

Over the longer period since World War II, civil wars have concentrated in two kinds of regimes: 1) relatively high-capacity regimes, however democratic or undemocratic, containing significant zones that escape central control (of recent cases, Chechnya, Israel/Palestine, Kashmir, Peru, the Philippines, Turkey, and possibly Colombia) and 2) low-capacity undemocratic regimes (the rest). Weak states prevailed.

Why should that be? These two types of regime have in common a fundamental principle we have encountered before. Controlling their own government gives rulers advantages denied to subjects of the government who lack that control. Even weak governments give rulers power over resources, activities, and populations – not to mention prestige and deference – that ordinary citizens don't enjoy. In poor countries, control over governments and access to their benefits become even more valuable relative to lack of control and access – fewer alternative sources of support exist.

In poor countries, for example, service in the military typically looks much more attractive relative to other available livelihoods than it does in rich countries. Low-paying governmental jobs, with their opportunities for patronage, perquisites, and bribes, likewise often become more enticing than work in existing private sectors. Those facts alone help explain the survival of visibly corrupt and incompetent governments in many poor countries; they offer their clients little, but little is better than nothing.

Of course capacity and democracy make a difference. By definition, high-capacity governments exert more extensive control over resources, activities, and populations. High-capacity governments also generally limit independent access to coercive force and smash any group that starts to acquire lethal arms. Not quite by definition, democratic regimes not only greatly expand the ruling class and promote turnover in its membership, but they also impose greater costs and constraints on rulers' disposition of government-controlled resources.

Hence a paradox: where the returns from gaining governmental power are lower, violent attempts to seize power occur more frequently. Armed struggle for control of an existing government becomes more attractive in low-capacity undemocratic regimes and in regions of higher-capacity regimes that operate like low-capacity undemocratic regimes: semi-colonial outposts, porous frontiers, areas of inaccessible terrain, and so on. Since their populations often define themselves (or become defined) as ethnically distinct, civil wars based in such territories often acquire the false reputation of being ethnically motivated.

Other Shocks

Civil war brings a shock to any regime and generally reverses all three of the master democratizing processes; it breaks ties between public politics and trust networks, writes categorical inequalities into public politics, and establishes dangerously autonomous centers of coercive power. Other shocks, however, actually forward democratization in some circumstances. In particular, conquest, colonization, revolution, and domestic confrontation sometimes accelerate operation of the three basic processes. As the allied victories over Italy, Germany, and Japan in World War II illustrate, military conquest can forcibly eliminate autonomous power centers, buffer public politics from categorical inequality, and encourage integration of trust networks into public politics. Settler colonies such as Australia and New Zealand decimated the indigenous population but often built up partially democratic regimes along the medium state path. Except for exclusion of indigenous people and women – huge exceptions, to be sure – they early installed rough equality into public politics while restricting autonomous power centers and partially integrating trust networks into public politics.

Ireland's turbulent experience shows how both domestic confrontation and revolution can promote democratization by accelerating the same basic process that occurs in slower transformations. It also demonstrates, however, that conquest and colonization can operate in the other direction, de-democratizing regimes that are already relatively undemocratic. Over many centuries, Ireland's interaction with Great Britain repeatedly visited conquest, colonization, revolution, and domestic confrontation on Ireland's people.

From the 16th to the 20th centuries, Ireland experienced a series of civil wars ending in a revolutionary transfer of power. British control over Ireland fluctuated greatly from phases of fierce civil war to rounds of military occupation to periods of rule at a distance. During the 17th century, for example, Oliver Cromwell invaded and subdued Ireland in 1650, and then Holland's William of Orange, who became king of England and Ireland, conquered the land again between 1688 and 1692. Each of these conquests increased British presence and dominance in Ireland, including major dispossessions of Irish Catholic landowners in favor of Protestants. But each conquest also led to a period of accommodation in which British-backed rulers tried to rule in the face of extensive passive resistance and some active rebellion. Considering Ireland alone, then, we can reasonably place the regime on a weak state path over most of the time from the 16th century to 20th-century independence. At that point, semi-sovereign Ireland shifted to a medium state trajectory, and it democratized rapidly.

Ireland's democratization occurred following centuries of struggle. After assimilation of earlier Anglo-Norman conquerors and colonists from the 12th century onward, Ireland settled into several centuries of competition among indigenous chiefs and kings. Beginning with Henry VIII, however, Tudor invasions generated a new round of armed resistance. Thus began almost five centuries during which some group of Irish power holders always aligned with Great Britain and multiple other power holders always aligned against Great Britain. Between the 1690s and the 1780s, even propertied Catholics lacked any rights to participate in Irish public politics. From the 1780s to the 1820s, they still suffered serious political disabilities. Since the 16th century, Ireland, especially Northern Ireland, has rarely moved far from virulent, violent rivalries. The island has repeatedly careened into civil war.

Not until the 19th century, however, did Ireland become a democratizing country. From the viewpoint of democratization, we might single out 1801, 1829, 1869, 1884, and 1919 to 1923 as crucial dates. In 1801, dissolution of the exclusively Protestant Irish Parliament and absorption of 100 Irish Protestants into its United Kingdom counterpart actually de-democratized an already oligarchic regime; it shattered the unequal accommodations that Ireland's Catholic elites had established with their Protestant rulers. Even elite networks of kinship and religion lost connection with the Irish system of rule. The United Kingdom's passage of Catholic Emancipation in 1829 (which followed similar political concessions to non-Anglican Protestants by a year) reversed that segregation. It gave Ireland's wealthier Catholics formal representation and rights to hold most public offices in the United Kingdom.

During the 19th century, demands for Irish autonomy or independence nevertheless swelled. Conflict between tenants and landlords exacerbated and public shows of force on either side repeatedly generated street violence in Northern Ireland (Tilly 2003: 111–127). A campaign for home rule brought disestablishment of the previously official Church of Ireland in 1869. Despite the eventual backing of Prime Minister William Gladstone, however, the home rule campaign failed to pass the UK Parliament. Irish Protestants rallied against such measures to the theme of "Home rule is Rome rule" (McCracken 2001: 262).

The franchise act of 1884, simultaneous with Great Britain's Third Reform Act, awarded the vote to most of the adult male Irish population and thus greatly expanded the rural Catholic electorate. By that time, however, each major party had attached itself to a single religious segment. Catholic-based parties had committed themselves decisively to Irish autonomy or independence. At that point, autonomous power centers clearly existed, Protestant and (especially) Catholic trust networks remained segregated from public politics, and the Protestant-Catholic division cut directly across public politics.

After multiple anti-British risings over the previous 60 years, the question of whether the Irish should be required to do military service on behalf of the United Kingdom split Ireland profoundly during World War I. In 1919, wartime divisions broke into civil war. The treaty of 1922 established a largely autonomous and overwhelmingly Catholic Irish Free State with dominion status parallel to that of Canada and Australia. Meanwhile, a Protestant-majority Northern Ireland remained closely attached to the United Kingdom but divided even more sharply along religious lines than before.

In the rest of Ireland, direct-action segments of the Irish Republican Army continued to attack Protestants and suspected British collaborators for another year (Hart 1998). Militantly republican forces lost both the Irish Free State's general election of 1922 and the civil war that followed it. The peace settlement with Great Britain and termination of the civil war within Ireland changed the regime fundamentally. Outside of the North, Protestant-Catholic divisions subsided within public politics and Catholic trust networks became major vehicles of political patronage and mobilization, while the once mightily autonomous centers of coercive power began to integrate themselves into the Irish national regime.

Yet republican militants survived and eventually got the full independence from Great Britain for which they had fought. Since the 1920s, the IRA has repeatedly made armed incursions into Northern Ireland (for surveys, see Keogh 2001, White 1993). Stable democracy has by no means arrived in the North. But the Irish Free State gained virtual independence (under its Irish name *Eire*) in 1937 and became the fully independent Irish Republic in 1949. Those increasingly autonomous southern regimes worked more or less democratically from the peace settlement of 1922 onward. Both state capacity and democracy increased after then, with the necessary exception of the North. Outside of two strife-filled years in the early 1990s, Freedom House awarded Ireland its highest possible rating on political rights and civil liberties – 1,1 – for every year from 1976 onward.

Figure 7-4 schematizes Ireland's trajectory over the long period from 1600 to 2006. The double-headed arrow at the end represents the split between North and South, with the northern government de-democratizing from the early 1990s while the southern state continued its move into high-capacity democratic territory. It describes a long first cycle of troubled movement within the low-capacity undemocratic quadrant of the capacity-democracy space. Then comes the 19th century's partial democratization and the interval of rebellion and civil war during and after World War I, followed by decisive movement into the high-capacity democratic quadrant.

To be sure, the first phase of democratization incorporated a fierce struggle against British hegemony. Remember the Fenians, or Irish

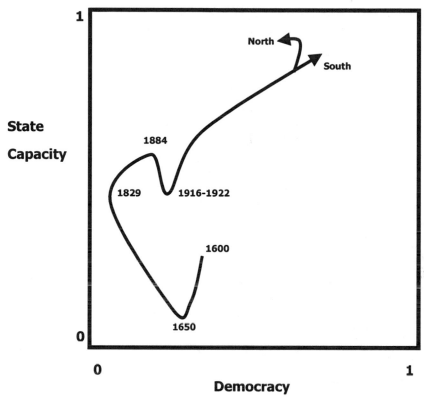

FIGURE 7-4. Irish Regimes, 1600–2006

Republican Brotherhood (IRB), who had such a strong following among Ohio's Irish workers during the 1866 congressional campaign? They had organized formally in 1858 and soon became the most visible among a number of Irish nationalist groups. Their armed risings, most notably in 1867, harassed UK rulers and collaborating landlords as they drew increasingly on support from Irish emigrants in England, the United States, and elsewhere. Eventually armed rebellion made Ireland ungovernable from Westminster or Dublin.

According to the sketch of Figure 7-4, Ireland shifted onto a medium state track during the early 19th century. From that point on, the regime became susceptible to both democratization and de-democratization as never before. Great Britain's grudging concessions to Irish self-rule opened the medium state path to democratization. Except for continuing struggle in the largely Protestant North, a fractious but apparently durable democratic regime took shape.

State Capacity and Democracy

We arrive at a mixed verdict on state capacity and democracy. As anarchists, libertarians, and many conservatives fear, a state with extremely high capacity permits rulers to block or undermine democratization. Worse yet, if the resources supporting state activity flow in without bargaining (however unequal) between rulers and citizens for those resources, tyranny becomes all the more feasible and attractive to rulers. That can happen, as we have seen, either because the state receives its resources from lesser tyrants who extract them from their own subjects or because rulers control the production and distribution of salable resources such as oil. Venezuela amply illustrates the second possibility.

But very low state capacity also has its perils: civil war on one side, fragmented rule by petty tyrants on the other. Ireland before the 19th century provides a telling contrast with oil-rich Venezuela. Despite intermittent British attempts to cow Irish rebels and very effective transfer of Irish land into the hands of English and Scottish Protestant elites, most of the time Great Britain's lieutenants general left the practical work of rule to largely autonomous great landlords, both Protestant and Catholic. During the 19th century, the armature of resistance to British rule became a counter-government that eventually provided the framework for an independent Irish regime.

Between extremely high capacity and extremely low capacity, then, we discover the zone of feasibility for effective democratization. Strong state, medium state, and weak state trajectories toward democracy all pass through that intermediate zone, each in its own sequence. But in all three the basic processes remain the same: integration of trust networks into public politics, shielding of public politics from categorical inequality, and checking of autonomous power centers in ways that enhance popular influence over public politics and the control of public politics over actions of the state.

The lesson goes far beyond Venezuela and Ireland. The many histories this book has detailed make the case that democratization benefits citizens. Let me state the case as a series of half-proven conjectures:

- Well-being of subjects, on average, increases under democratizing regimes partly because political insulation from inequality, integration of trust networks, and suppression of autonomous power centers are goods in themselves and partly because the popular political voice that results from those processes is a good in itself. On average, people who experience equitable treatment from their governments and/or have direct say in governmental operations gain more satisfaction from politics and display greater willingness to bear burdens for the common good.

- To the degree that democratizing regimes act to reduce categorical inequalities, to insulate public politics from those inequalities, and/or to blunt the effects of those inequalities on basic living conditions such as housing, medical care, and food, they increase the likelihood of their own survival as democratic regimes. Populist democrats would like this argument to be true, and there are at least fragments of evidence to encourage them.
- To the degree that democratizing regimes act to reduce categorical inequalities, to insulate public politics from those inequalities, and/or to blunt the effects of those inequalities on basic living conditions such as housing, medical care, and food, they also increase the overall well-being of their subject populations. This attractive principle is an article of faith among populist development specialists but for precisely that reason needs much more careful empirical scrutiny.
- Such interventions take two overlapping forms: 1) exercise of collective control over value-producing resources and the networks that operate them and 2) redistribution of value produced by means of those resources. Regimes qualify as social democratic to the extent that they engage and coordinate both strategies of intervention.
- Up to a relatively high point, rising governmental capacity increases the likelihood and impact of beneficent interventions. Low governmental capacity reduces the efficacy of both regulatory and redistributive efforts. But at very high levels of governmental capacity, runs the reasoning, the opportunity and incentive for governmental agents and other beneficiaries of existing categorical inequality to ally in diverting state power to their own advantage rise irresistibly.

If these conjectures are even roughly correct, we have been tracing not just an interesting set of political transformations, but a path to the enhancement of human capability and welfare.

8

Democracy's Pasts and Futures

The World Bank has discovered democracy. Or at least it has discovered that democracy may promote economic growth. The Bank once spearheaded the Washington Consensus, the belief that integration of poor economies into world markets would rapidly solve their economic and social problems. The Consensus asked for fiscal discipline, public investment in infrastructure, and trade liberalization, but came no closer to democracy than by demanding legal security for property rights. In recent years, however, the Bank has moved increasingly to the view vigorously advocated by institutional economists: that effective markets require extensive social and political infrastructures (see, e.g., North 2005). Titles of the World Bank's influential annual *World Development Report* have undergone an interesting evolution. As listed in Box 8-1, they shift from a strong emphasis on markets, investment, and development to a rising concern with the institutional causes and consequences of economic growth. The state appears in a title as early as 1997, but causes, consequences, and institutions take on ever greater prominence after then. Even poverty makes an appearance in 2000 to 2001.

The 2006 development report, titled *Equity and Development*, introduces a direct concern with democratization. True, Bank President Paul Wolfowitz' foreword to the volume avoids the words democracy and democratization. Instead, it emphasizes two principles:

The first is *equal opportunity:* a person's life achievements should be determined primarily by his or her talents and efforts, rather than by predetermined circumstances such as race, gender, social and family background, or country of birth. The second principle is the *avoidance of deprivation in outcomes* particularly in health, education, and consumption levels. (World Bank 2006: xi)

BOX 8-1. Titles of the World Bank's Development Reports, 1991–2006

1991:	The Challenge of Development
1992:	Development and the Environment
1993:	Investing in Health
1994:	Infrastructure for Development
1995:	Workers in an Integrating World
1996:	From Plan to Market
1997:	The State in a Changing World
1998:	Knowledge for Development
1999:	Entering the 21st Century
2000/2001:	Attacking Poverty
2002:	Building Institutions for Markets
2003:	Sustainable Development in a Dynamic World
2004:	Making Services Work for Poor People
2005:	A Better Investment Climate for Everyone
2006:	Equity and Development

Thus Wolfowitz is advocating breadth and equality of opportunities for well-being, if not specifying the broad, equal, protected, mutually binding consultation that for this book's purposes constitutes democracy. Nevertheless, the 2006 report's text includes explicit descriptions and endorsements of democratization and democracy in Kerala (India), Porto Alegre (Brazil), and Spain. In the case of Spain, it concedes that Franco's economic stabilization and liberalization plan of 1959 stimulated economic growth, but generally argues a close correspondence among democratization, economic expansion, redistribution, and equity:

Following Franco's death in 1975, King Juan Carlos became the Spanish head of state. He immediately launched a process of political change. Employing the legal mechanisms put in place by the very technocratic generation that had reformed the economy in the early 1960s, as well as pointing to wide popular support for democracy, he secured the consent of the old Francoist *Cortes* to establish a truly democratic parliament elected through direct, competitive elections. (World Bank 2006: 106)

The World Bank summary truncates a complex history but gets it mostly right. Chapter 6 showed how earlier changes in relations between public politics and trust networks, categorical inequality, and autonomous power centers cleared the way for the dramatic reforms of 1975 to 1981. The World Bank account of Spain neglects those earlier transformations. On the other hand, it goes farther than Chapter 6 in its claims of the benefits of democratization. It even endorses democratization as a basis for healthy economic development, including equity. After a long period in which many world leaders thought economic development could and should precede any moves toward democracy, international potentates are coming around to the view that democracy provides a desirable complement – or even a prerequisite – for life-sustaining economic growth.

This book's earlier chapters have not looked seriously at democratization's impact on economic development. They have, however, looked seriously at processes that cause democratization and de-democratization. The argument as a whole began with careful setting out of conceptual tools for description and explanation of democracy, democratization, and de-democratization. These tools at hand, it took up the impact of three fundamental processes: first, integration of interpersonal trust networks into public politics; second, insulation of public politics from categorical inequality; and third, reduction of autonomous coercive power centers, with the consequences of increasing influence of ordinary people over public politics and rising control of public politics over state performance.

Each of the three processes occupied a single chapter. Together, they made the book's central arguments:

1. Integration of trust networks, insulation of public politics from categorical inequality, and reduction of autonomous power centers combine to cause democratization, which does not occur in their absence.
2. Reversal of any or all of these processes de-democratizes regimes.

A further chapter (Chapter 7) used the experiences of Venezuela, Ireland, and a few other regimes to illustrate how the three main democratizing processes generate alternative regime trajectories, which vary as a function of state strength at various stages of democratization and de-democratization. This less ambitious final chapter begins with a brief reminder of how external influences and shocks (whether internal or external) affect the pace and character of democratization across the world. It moves on to a more extensive review of tentative answers to the major questions concerning democratization and de-democratization posed throughout the book. It closes with a rapid discussion of how to derive predictions for democracy's possible futures from the book's teachings.

Change and Variation in Regimes

For our purposes, a regime is democratic to the extent that political relations between the state and its citizens feature broad, equal, protected, and
mutually binding consultation. Accordingly, democratization consists of a
regime's movement toward that sort of consultation, de-democratization
a regime's movement away from it. Over the previous seven chapters, we
have witnessed plenty of movement in both directions. Indeed, the histories and contemporary observations in those chapters teach two related
and fundamental lessons: first, that even established democracies such as
India fluctuate constantly between more or less democracy; and second,
that in the contemporary world as in the past, de-democratization occurs
almost as frequently as democratization. Democracy always remains at
risk to narrowing of participation, new forms of political inequality,
declines in protection, and escapes from mutually binding consultation.

Nevertheless, since the 18th century, substantial democratization of
one regime or another has gone from a rare occurrence to a frequent one.
Over that long run its appearances have accelerated, especially since World
War II. Instead of a continuous upward curve, furthermore, democratization has arrived mostly in spurts. The wholesale decolonization of the
1960s and the democratic transformation of about half the Soviet Union's
successor states after the USSR disintegrated provide the most impressive
postwar examples. Both bursts also preceded frequent instances of de-
democratization, for two reasons, one profound, the other banal.

First, the profound reason: regardless of their personal propensities to
autocracy, new rulers of former European colonies and post-Soviet states
had little choice but to launch their regimes with a fanfare of democratic
forms. Otherwise they risked domestic overturn or international rejection. Belarus' autocratic Lukashenka, after all, first came to power as
a popularly elected democratic reformer. Second, the banal reason: the
more democratic regimes that exist, the more regimes run the risk of de-
democratization. Freedom House counted 44 of the world's 151 countries
(29 percent) as Free (that is, more than just formal electoral democracies)
in 1973, but by 2003 had raised the number to 88 out of 192 (46 percent)
(Piano and Puddington 2004: 5). The number of regimes at risk to serious
de-democratization doubled between 1973 and 2003.

Multiplication of democracies, whether partial or fairly extensive,
served as a demonstration for regimes and for external promoters of
democratization such as the United Nations and the National Endowment for Democracy (NED), which receives substantial support from the

U.S. government. Leaders of decolonization knew which forms of rule would bring them UN support, and more recent democracy-promoters created standards for the types of regimes they would certify and reward. The NED Web site declares that:

The Endowment is guided by the belief that freedom is a universal human aspiration that can be realized through the development of democratic institutions, procedures, and values. Governed by an independent, nonpartisan board of directors, the NED makes hundreds of grants each year to support prodemocracy groups in Africa, Asia, Central and Eastern Europe, Eurasia, Latin America, and the Middle East. (NED 2006)

In Venezuela, for example, NED reports that it has been making grants since 1993 (the year of president Carlos Andres Pérez' impeachment for corruption and the year after Hugo Chávez' two attempted coups) to support organizations promoting freedom of the press, human rights, civic education, and independent trade unions, all threatened by Chávez' oil-fed autocracy. In 2003, it also awarded $53,400 to the Venezuela non-governmental organization Súmate, to support monitoring of the failed referendum on Chávez' rule. (Indeed, by 2006 Chávez' government was prosecuting Súmate for its receipt of U.S. funds to support the NGO's involvement in Venezuelan elections.) Like other democracy-promoting agencies, NED intervenes directly in democratization with clear ideas about what will make it work.

Yet demonstration effects and external support have always faced serious limits. They can affect the procedures, organizational forms, and constitutional formulas of democratic consultation, but they cannot produce the social transformations on which democratization finally depends. They cannot in themselves integrate trust networks into public politics, insulate public politics from categorical inequality, or reduce the influence of autonomous power centers over public politics and the state. The nominally democratic forms of Kazakhstan, Belarus, or Venezuela did not deliver broad, equal, protected, mutually binding consultation between citizens and states. Formally democratic institutions do not suffice to produce or sustain democracy.

Looking closely at Uzbekistan, Kyrgyzstan, and Tadjikistan, Kathleen Collins inserts a strong note of caution into any analysis of external effects. As of 1993, she points out that Kyrgyzstan had become a favorite western model for post-Soviet democratization:

Kyrgyz legislators and judges flew to Washington, D.C. for training in democratic principles, the rule of law, and market economics. Where civil society had been nearly nonexistent, nongovernmental organizations suddenly proliferated, defending human rights, supporting women in business, developing a free press, and even creating a Silk Road Internet. Kyrgyz youth watched *Dynasty*, listened to Bruce Springsteen, wore American flag tee shirts, and even studied at Georgetown, Indiana University, and Notre Dame. These changes were foreign not only to communism but also to the region's Asian and Islamic culture. The globalization of capitalism and democracy seemed at its apex. (Collins 2006: 4)

However, manipulated competitive elections followed, ex-Soviet administrators remained in power, and (as in Kazakhstan) clan politics eventually undermined any serious claims to democracy. In these cases, clan boundaries transected public politics, as the trust networks of excluded clans lost their fragile connections with public politics.

In Central Asia and elsewhere, state capacity also matters and responds very little to demonstration effects. Regimes on strong state tracks implement top-down changes more effectively but also give rulers the means and incentives to resist unwanted assaults on their power. Weak state trajectories toward democracy face the opposite problems: little central capacity to initiate change and plenty of competition from power holders outside the state. This book opened with a comparison between strong state Kazakhstan and weak state Jamaica, the first run by a self-seeking family despite its formally democratic constitution, the second beset by competition from drug merchants and petty warlords.

The major shocks we have encountered in the course of this book – conquest, colonization, revolutions, domestic confrontation, and the special version of domestic confrontation called civil war – did not in themselves cause democratization and de-democratization. But they regularly accelerated the processes that produce democratization and de-democratization: integration of trust networks, buffering of categorical inequality, dissolution of autonomous power centers, and their de-democratizing reversals. The book's analyses of France, Spain, and Venezuela identified shocks in abundance. These analyses made the case for those shocks accelerating the basic democratizing processes or their reversals in each episode.

Payoffs

Chapter 3 listed a number of payoff questions concerning democratization and de-democratization whose answers would significantly advance our understanding. Let us return to those questions for a brief review of the sorts of answers this book suggests.

1. In what ways did the truncated democratic institutions of city-states, warrior bands, peasant communities, merchant oligarchies, religious sects, and revolutionary movements provide models for more extensive forms of democracy? Given their availability, why did they never become direct templates for democracy at a national scale?

Consider the vivid images of small-scale democratic consultation we have encountered from before the 19th century: Swiss mountaineers gathering in town squares for voice votes on public affairs, Dutch merchants filling councils to run municipal affairs, religious communities installing radical equality among their members. These forms often survived at the local level. But none of them became direct models for national states. Procedures and organizational forms such as elections, referenda, and legislative bodies did become part of the state apparatus in many regimes. Yet the main forms of democratic national states actually emerged from the very processes by which these states acquired their means of rule – how they produced military forces, how they collected taxes, how they beat down their domestic rivals, and how they negotiated with power holders they could not beat down.

Perhaps the most dramatic example comes from a case we have not much considered: Great Britain. There, the revenue-granting power of Parliament (for centuries the exclusive representative of great magnates) expanded its centrality in British politics as Britain engaged in ever more expensive wars during the 18th century (Brewer 1989, Stone 1994, Tilly 1995). As Parliament took power away from the British crown, unrepresented Britons increasingly addressed claims both to individual members and to Parliament as a whole, parliamentary elections became occasions for expression of popular preferences by the disfranchised, and dissident members of Parliament sought greater non-parliamentary support for their favored programs (Tilly 1997).

In a parallel way, France's fiscal crises of the late 18th century required royal consultation with provincial estates, sovereign courts, and the relatively ineffectual assemblies improvised by the crown during the 1780s. This consultation locked the regime into negotiation with national semi-representative institutions. The French Revolution appropriated that model rather than the oligarchic forms long prevalent in French municipalities. Similarly, the American Revolution of the 1760s to 1780s and the Dutch revolutions of the 1780s and 1790s locked in national forms of negotiation between legislatures and executives as means of rule. Relatively broad, equal, protected, and mutually binding consultation at national scales resulted from national dynamics of struggle. But only in tendentious retrospect can we imagine that self-conscious democratizers put these institutions into place.

2. *Why did Western Europe lead the way toward democratization, followed closely by the Americas?*

It would take another book – one much more explicitly comparative at the national and continental scales than this one – to pursue definitive answers to this pressing historical question. Nevertheless, the connectedness of Atlantic polities and economies during the early phase of world democratization identifies two large, related, and plausible sets of causes. First, political and economic interdependence within the Atlantic region promoted widespread adoption of state approaches to rule that in the long run increased the susceptibility of regimes to both democratization and de-democratization. They did not adopt democratic forms as such, but rather established forms of negotiation with citizens and rival power holders already operating elsewhere. For example, overseas creditors insisted on fiscal systems that would sustain the borrowing state's credit and stabilize the environment for investments.

International influences did not end there. Latin American regimes, for example, regularly adopted policing systems on a Spanish or (originally) French model, with urban police forces (the French *Sûreté*) who were typically under at least partial control of civilian ministries and forces patrolling highways and rural areas (the French *Gendarmerie*) who were almost always subordinated to the national military. Clearly fiscal discipline, uniform policing, and other state resemblances promoted by international interdependence did not spread democratic institutions directly from one regime to another. But they did increase the similarity of political conditions across connected regimes.

More precisely, that interdependence promoted a series of strong effects:

- Imposing uniform systems of taxation and administration
- Creating nominally representative national legislatures to authorize state demands on citizens
- Subordinating military forces to national policies including the conduct of international wars
- Nationalizing systems of social provision and redistribution

In short, interdependent and roughly similar courses of state transformation helped trigger the basic democracy-promoting processes: integration of trust networks, buffering of categorical inequality, and checking of autonomous coercive power centers. Overall, citizen-state bargaining over the means of rule increased those regimes' susceptibility to both democratization and de-democratization.

Second, the 18th century's so-called democratic revolutions created models of state solutions to the knotty problems of governing regimes in which participation of citizens in public politics – whether democratic or not – becomes essential to state activity in general. National citizen armies; generalized systems of policing; nominally representative legislatures; toleration (or even promotion) of associations claiming to speak for citizens; formation of a national press (however controlled); and creation of agencies (at first, chiefly within legislatures) devoted to monitoring citizens' claims via petitions, delegations, letters, and public statements combined not by any means to guarantee democracy but to render regimes more susceptible to both democratization and de-democratization.

3. How did (and do) such countries as France move from absolute immunity against national democratic institutions to frequent alternations between democratization and de-democratization?

To the extent that my answers to questions 1 and 2 are valid, they also reply to the third question. France, as Chapter 2 documented, made a rapid, critical transition with the revolution of 1789 to 1799. Before then, little susceptibility to either democratization or de-democratization existed. After then, frequent, dramatic oscillations between the two occurred. To put it differently from my previous formulations, expanding state activity drew more citizens into state-coordinated efforts, which enlarged public politics. Inevitably, state-coordinated activities favored some organized interests over others – for example, merchants over landlords – which almost as inevitably incited conflicts among them and drew those conflicts into public politics, thus further enlarging public politics.

Enlargement of public politics then made regimes more susceptible to broadening, equalizing, protecting, and rendering more definitive whatever mutually binding consultation was occurring – as well as to reversals of each of these changes. Reversals could still occur to the extent that elites shielded their trust networks from complete integration into public politics, acquired control over their own segments of the state, and/or retained bases of coercive power lying outside of public politics. From Gómez' coup of 1905 to the years just before Chávez' arrival in power,

Venezuela's repeated cycles of de-democratization resulted from one or more of these reversals.

Conversely, to the extent that elites came to depend on the state and public politics for their own programs of self-reproduction and self-aggrandizement, their capacity to precipitate de-democratization through withdrawal from public politics declined. Even South Africa's white elites found themselves locking into the ANC-dominated regime after 1995. Thus, regime by regime, both democratization and de-democratization became possible as never before.

4. *Why, in general, did (and do) surges of de-democratization occur more rapidly than surges of democratization?*

In simplest terms, de-democratization occurs chiefly as a consequence of withdrawal by privileged, powerful political actors from whatever mutually binding consultation exists, whereas democratization depends on integrating large numbers of ordinary people into consultation. In more complex terms, privileged, powerful elites such as large landlords, industrialists, financiers, and professionals have much greater means and incentives than ordinary people to escape or subvert democratic compacts when those compacts turn to their disadvantage. Once they have integrated their lives and life chances into democratic regimes, ordinary people can only with great difficulty detach their trust networks from public politics, much less insert categorical inequalities into public politics or create newly autonomous centers of coercive power. The already rich and powerful can much more easily withdraw their trust networks, install inequalities, and create autonomous power centers. Although the authoritarian de-democratizing movements that multiplied in Europe after World War I, for example, did draw substantial popular support, more generally they aligned privileged elites against organized workers and political parties claiming to represent workers at large.

Again, until the Argentine military (bought off with amnesties and golden parachutes) finally accepted definitive subordination to civilian control during the 1980s, dissident officers could usually find allies among landlords, industrialists, and financiers when they used force to break the semi-democratic accommodations that Argentine elites had made with the bulk of the national population. For all of his later populism and patronage, after all, Colonel Perón became president in 1946 because the army supported his candidacy.

5. *How do we explain the asymmetrical patterns of support for and involvement in democratization and de-democratization?*

Here we must finally unpack the omnibus terms *elites* and *ordinary people*. By *elites*, let us simply mean connected networks of people that exercise control over substantial resources, including other people's labor power. Under the heading of *ordinary people*, let us mean no more than connected networks of people – workers, peasants, local communities, and so on – who *lack* control of substantial resources including other people's labor power. Broadly speaking, elites find democratization costly so long as they belong to current ruling classes. In no regime larger than a city-state do all elites, thus defined, belong to the ruling coalition. Those who do belong make bargains with the state that secure their resources and labor power. So long as they are not seeking to run the state alone, they therefore fare better in undemocratic regimes. There, they need not compete for their own survival with other elites, much less with organized segments of subordinate classes.

In undemocratic regimes, excluded elites do have incentives to form coalitions with ordinary people and thereby to support broadening, equalization, and protection of mutually binding consultation – democratization. Within already democratic regimes, another version of the same logic applies. Included elites must negotiate protection and survival of their control over resources including labor power. That puts them in competition with the state and with other elites. They must negotiate not only with the state but also with other elites and with organized segments of subordinate classes.

Ordinary people, in contrast, acquire strong investments in state-backed rights and benefits, however meager, that would and do dissolve with de-democratization. They acquire rights to organize, to receive compensation for hardship, to collect pensions, and much more. Just remember how much Franco's military victory cost Spanish workers while benefiting large landlords, Catholic elites, military leaders, and the old bourgeoisie.

6. Why does democratization typically occur in waves, rather than in each regime separately at its own peculiar pace?

The obvious answer is mostly wrong: that democracy is a fad, fashion, or organizational model that diffuses among receptive settings like musical styles and public policies. As the histories explored in this volume indicate, two other factors deserve much more attention: background social processes that promote democratization in the long run and external agencies that place pressure on regimes to democratize.

Background social processes that shape possibilities for democratization and de-democratization interact internationally. Consider some of the specific mechanisms that feed our three main democratizing processes – integration of trust networks, insulation of categorical inequality, and dissolution of autonomous coercive power centers:

Integration of Trust Networks into Public Politics

- Disintegration of existing segregated trust networks (e.g., decay of patrons' ability to provide their clients with goods and protection promotes withdrawal of clients from patron-client ties)
- Expansion of population categories lacking access to effective trust networks for their major long-term risky enterprises (e.g., growth of number of landless wage-workers in agrarian regions increases population without effective patronage and/or relations of mutual aid)
- Appearance of new long-term risky opportunities and threats that existing trust networks cannot handle (e.g., substantial increases in war, famine, disease, and/or banditry visibly overwhelm protective capacity of patrons, diasporas, and local solidarities)
- Creation of external guarantees for governmental commitments (e.g., conquest of shattered government by an occupying force committed to rebuilding provides backing for governmental protection from predators)
- Increase of governmental resources for risk reduction and/or compensation of loss (e.g., creation of government-backed disaster insurance draws citizens into collaboration with government agents and/or established political actors)

Insulation of Public Politics from Categorical Inequality

- Equalization of assets and/or well-being across categories within the population at large (e.g., booming demand for the products of peasant agriculture expands middle peasants)
- Reduction or state containment of privately controlled armed force (e.g., disbanding of magnates' personal armies weakens noble control over commoners, thereby diminishing nobles' capacity to translate noble-commoner differences directly into public politics)
- Adoption of procedural devices that insulate public politics from categorical inequalities (e.g., secret ballots; payment of officeholders; and free, equal access of candidates to media forward the formation of cross-category coalitions)

- Wholesale increases of political participation, rights, or obligations that cut across social categories (e.g., state annexation of socially heterogeneous territories promotes categorically mixed politics)

  Dissolution of Autonomous Coercive Power Centers, with Consequent Increases of Popular Influence over Public Politics and Control of State Actions by Public Politics
- Expansion of state activities for which sustaining resources are only available through negotiation with citizens (e.g., a war-making state creates a mass national army through military conscription)
- Imposition of uniform governmental structures and practices through the state's jurisdiction (e.g., creation of uniform nationwide taxes increases likelihood of equity, visibility, and conformity)

In most cases, each of these operates through international interaction among regimes. Many of those interactions occur simultaneously through economic, political, and cultural flows among regimes. Remember, for example, how the United States channeled military and economic aid to Franco's Spain (much to the chagrin of many American democrats), with some of these very consequences, but without immediate democratization.

Furthermore, powerful external parties certify, promote, and sometimes even impose democratization on susceptible regimes. The most extreme examples we have encountered in this book are western powers' more or less simultaneous and forceful impositions of democratic arrangements in Germany, Italy, and Japan at the end of World War II. Related and somewhat later interventions in South Korea and Taiwan resembled those direct campaigns to rebuild state capacity and create semi-democratic institutions while stepping up economic aid and trade. The first three interventions converted undemocratic regimes into relatively democratic regimes.

In South Korea and Taiwan, democratization took longer but still stemmed in part from authoritative external intervention in such forms as military occupation. In terms of the sheer number of regimes involved, however, authoritative external certification, promotion, and imposition occurred much more widely in the course of Europe's decolonization across Asia, Africa, and Latin America; European state socialism's demise; and the European Union's deliberate screening of regimes for membership in that elect international compact.

7. *What explains the spread of democratization and de-democratization during the 19th and (especially) 20th centuries from its Western
European starting points to the rest of the world?*

The rough chronology of democratization sketched in Chapter 2 ran
like this:

1850–1899: Western Europe and Latin America exclusively (North
           America had already established partly democratic arrange-
           ments before then)

1900–1959: Western Europe and the Americas plus Australia, New
           Zealand, and Japan

1950–1979: Southern Europe, Latin America, plus a number of Asia-
           Pacific regimes as well as Egypt, Morocco, and Zambia

1979–2005: Latin America, Eastern Europe, Asia-Pacific, and half a
           dozen African regimes

However rough, that visible geographic shift of focus requires explanation.

The logic of waves, as it happens, also explains the spread of democratization and de-democratization beyond its initial territory. Integration of
new economies and polities into a western-dominated system produced
social transformations that then started the integration of trust networks
into public politics, insulation of public politics from categorical inequality, and dissolution of autonomous coercive power centers. Western
regimes also figured in a second crucial way by accepting and even promoting decolonization after the initial bloody struggles that followed World
War II in such colonial regions as Indonesia and Vietnam. Finally, the
collapse of most state socialist regimes, the end of the Cold War, and the
expansion of the European Union all contributed to the integration of
previously untouchable regimes into western spheres of influence.

8. *Why (with the partial exceptions of Egypt and Japan) did democratization only start to occur in Asia and Africa well after World War II?*

The fact that decolonization only accelerated in the 1960s provides part
of the answer. Since by no means did all colonies democratize (and since
many de-democratized after initial partial democratization), we must also
take into account the deep differences in social organization separating
much of Asia and Africa from the western harbingers of democracy. Trust

networks, categorical inequality, and autonomous power centers operate very differently across those two continents. By comparison, the social organization of the countries in the Americas and Europe is very similar. As a consequence, economic, political, and cultural interaction had more similar impacts on democracy-promoting processes within those regions.

9. *How can we account for the dramatically different experiences of post-socialist states with democratization and de-democratization?*

Everywhere, former socialist managers had great advantages when it came to taking over successor regimes. Nevertheless, their freedom of action depended on three major factors: 1) the extent to which rival centers of power – especially those based on competing ethnic, religious, or regional identities – emerged as socialist regimes disintegrated, 2) the influence of adjacent powers, and 3) the resources locally available for sustaining state activity. Baltic political leaders who defined themselves against Russian influence gained effective support from their Nordic neighbors, as Slovenia immediately received encouragement and aid from Austria and Germany. Kazakhstan's energy resources gave its post-socialist rulers the means of consolidating their power, whereas Belarus' energy reliance on Russia made Belarus a strong sphere of Russian influence. But in much of Central Asia, clans that Soviet rule had subordinated grabbed their pieces of political power and effectively blocked anything like integration of trust networks, buffering of public politics from categorical inequality, and dissolution of autonomous power centers.

10. *Under what conditions, to what extent, and how does the growth of state capacity promote a regime's availability for democratization and de-democratization?*

In general, as we have seen repeatedly, higher capacity means greater susceptibility to democratization and de-democratization. But that generalization depends crucially on control over the resources that sustain state activity. Where rulers must bargain extensively with citizens for resources, paths to democratization open up. Where they either draw their resources from powerful and partly autonomous intermediaries or control resources they can exchange for the means of rule – money, armed force, labor power, information – higher capacity actually blocks democratization. International sale of such resources as oil often promotes de-democratization. When international prices run high, oil-supported rulers can bypass citizen consent. When they decline radically, rulers lose leverage, but their elite domestic rivals frequently bid for power, thus starting new cycles of de-democratization.

Is there then no hope for democratization in energy-rich regimes such as Kazakhstan, Algeria, and Venezuela? In such regimes, we might reasonably expect modest moves toward democracy to occur in either of two circumstances. First, government repression could unite the opposition instead of fragmenting it into rival claimants for control of the state. Coalitions of this sort could do little to integrate trust networks into public politics, but they could buffer public politics from categorical inequality and reduce the influence of autonomous coercive power centers. Second, a decline in the international value of energy supplies could force previously mighty rulers to bargain with their citizens for the means of state survival.

In Venezuela, for example, we might imagine a scenario in which a price-strapped President Chávez has to choose between 1) cutting back radically on his populist programs and 2) striking participatory deals with the already connected trade unions, oil executives, and business people who have formed the nucleus of his strident opposition. Choosing option 2 would push the regime back in the direction of democracy. In an energy-price crisis, Kazakhstan and Algeria would present much more serious obstacles to democratization; in either case, current purchasers and investors could have both interests and means to shore up the existing regimes in hopes of saving or even expanding their investments.

11. *To what extent and how do an undemocratic regime's interactions with democratic regimes promote democratization in that regime?*

As the long coexistence of partial democracies with undemocratic regimes – including their own colonies – indicates, no simple diffusion of democratic forms occurs from regime to regime. Yet three effects do combine to promote democratization. First, where political interaction between a relatively democratic colonial regime and its colony integrates the colony's elites and public politics into those of the dominant regime (pre-independence India is an obvious example), some democratization of colonial politics occurs. Second, economic, political, and cultural interaction with democratic regimes transforms social structure in undemocratic regimes by affecting the organization of trust networks, categorical inequality, and autonomous power centers. Third, powerful democratic regimes intervene directly to promote, finance, certify, or even compel partial democratization in moments of undemocratic regimes' vulnerability. Instead of returning to the obvious examples of Japan, Germany, and Italy after World War II, recall how French revolutionary conquests promoted partial democratization in Switzerland and the Dutch Republic.

12. *How do the forms and sources of a state's sustaining resources (e.g., agriculture, minerals, or trade) affect its regime's susceptibility to democratization and de-democratization?*

This question has recurred throughout the book. The crucial problem concerns the extent to which rulers must bargain with citizens for state-sustaining resources. Two rather different sets of circumstances undercut bargaining. First, where rulers rely heavily on coercion-wielding intermediaries such as great landlords, lineage heads, or heads of private armies, they essentially borrow the intermediaries' coercive power at the cost of significant limits on their own freedom of action and the ever-present possibilities of defection or rebellion. Second, where they themselves control the production and/or distribution of directly usable or externally salable resources – not just oil or diamonds, but also spices, slaves, and similar commodities – they regularly escape bargaining with citizens and thereby block openings to democratization. Note that the forms of sustaining resources themselves make a difference: an agricultural tribute system of the kind that long sustained Chinese empires entails more two-way negotiation with large numbers of people than does the collection of instant revenue from goods passing across borders, which in turn still produces a much more extensive apparatus of surveillance and collection than does the sale of precious minerals.

13. *Do any necessary or sufficient conditions exist for democratization and de-democratization, or (on the contrary) do favorable conditions vary significantly by era, region, and type of regime?*

To state the book's recurrent theme one more time: No necessary *conditions* for democratization and de-democratization exist. But necessary *processes* do exist. Transformations of relations between public politics and trust networks, categorical inequality, and autonomous power centers underlie the susceptibility of regimes across the world to democratization and de-democratization, and have done so for more than the two centuries the book has surveyed. If, of course, some stickler wants to insist that partial integration of trust networks into public politics, partial segregation of public politics from categorical inequality, and partial dissolution or neutralization of autonomous power centers really do qualify as necessary conditions for democratization, I will readily concede the point. The necessary conditions, in that interpretation, consist of partly achieved processes.

I do not claim to have answered all thirteen payoff questions definitively in this one short book. I do claim, however, that the book's analyses provide a fresh way to think about all of them. More than anything else, these analyses call for a shift of attention away from the moments when one regime or another crosses the threshold from authoritarianism to democracy. If the book's arguments are valid, every instance of substantial democratization results from previous political processes that do not in themselves constitute democratization: integration of trust networks into public politics, insulation of public politics from categorical inequality, and checking of autonomous coercive power centers in ways that increase public politics' influence over state performance as they enhance popular power over public politics.

These claims, furthermore, entail an additional risky claim: that the fundamental processes driving democratization and de-democratization have not changed over time. Of course the specific forms of democratic institutions such as legislatures and the relative impacts of specific alterations such as international certification of democracy have mutated across the long history we have surveyed. But from start to finish, runs my claim, the same basic transformations of trust networks, categorical inequality, and autonomous coercive power centers have converged in all substantial moves of regimes toward democracy. Behind those transformations, furthermore, extensive bargaining of rulers with citizens over the means of state activity has always and everywhere moved their regimes from relatively stable undemocracy (whether low- or high-capacity) into the zone in which both democratization and de-democratization become possible. Within that zone, regimes fluctuate incessantly in both directions.

Futures

What does this analysis of past democratization and de-democratization imply for the future(s) of democracy? Let us distinguish between two ways of anticipating any future: extrapolation and if-then prediction. Extrapolation extends past trends into the future on the assumption that the causes of those trends will keep operating in pretty much the same fashion as the years roll on. On the extrapolation front, evidence in previous chapters mainly suggests that net democratization will continue until no more than a hard core of democracy-resisting regimes remains; that de-democratization will persist with slowly diminishing frequency; and that both will occur, when they do, in bursts and in accelerated response to shocks.

Extrapolations run the risk that past causal patterns will shift in the future. If-then predictions provide less crisp scenarios for coming years, but map out alternative futures. In any case, this book's analyses offer only weak bases for extrapolation, while lending themselves well to if-then prediction. For example, our encounters with oil-supported states indicate that increases in the extent of direct ruler control over sustaining resources predict the non-development of democracy, whereas reliance of the state on resources that require bargaining with citizens (e.g., military conscription and broad-based taxation), everything else equal, promotes democratization. A comparison between the trajectories of Russia and Spain makes the point dramatically.

If-then predictions follow from every major argument in this book. The largest contingent predictions obviously concern the effects of changes in relations between public politics and 1) trust networks, 2) categorical inequality, and 3) autonomous power centers. We can invert the book's major arguments to clarify the sorts of if-then predictions they call for. Three conditions block democratization and promote de-democratization wherever they appear: disconnection between trust networks and public politics, inscription of categorical inequality into public politics, and existence of autonomous power centers wielding substantial coercive means. If-then predictions of democratization based on the theories in this book therefore always involve the presence or absence of processes that remove one or more of these deleterious conditions from public politics. Fortification of these conditions, in contrast, predicts de-democratization.

If, for example, the rise of religious fundamentalism across the world encourages people to withdraw religiously bonded networks from public politics, that momentous change should promote widespread de-democratization in regions of religious zealotry. If, on the other hand, a decline occurs in the feasibility and attractiveness of civil war as a means of bidding for state power, that decline should reduce the presence of autonomous power centers in weak states and thereby contribute to democratization.

Again, if rich states dismantle the redistributive and equalizing arrangements that have grown up within democratic capitalism and rich people disconnect their trust networks from public politics by such means as gated communities and private schooling, we should expect those measures to de-democratize their regimes. Such changes would reinsert categorical inequalities into public politics, reduce the influence of ordinary people over public politics, and possibly produce newly autonomous coercive centers of power as well. A decline of relatively broad, equal, binding, and protected consultation – de-democratization – would be the unhappy outcome.

Such if-then predictions have high stakes. If this book's arguments are correct, those of us who hope to see democracy's benefits spread across the undemocratic world will not waste our time focusing on preaching democratic virtues, designing constitutions, forming non-governmental organizations, and identifying pockets of democratic sentiment within undemocratic regimes. We will, in contrast, spend a great deal of effort promoting the integration of trust networks into public politics, helping to shield public politics from categorical inequality, and working against the autonomy of coercive power centers. (To be sure, this effort could then involve us in preaching democratic virtues, designing constitutions, forming non-governmental organizations, and identifying pockets of democratic sentiment, but only in the service of these larger transformations.) The democratizing experiences of South Africa, Spain, and some post-socialist regimes show that such changes always pass through struggle but remain susceptible to external influence. Hopeful democrats need not sit on their hands, waiting.

References

Acemoglu, Daron and James A. Robinson (2006): *Economic Origins of Dictatorship and Democracy.* Cambridge: Cambridge University Press.

Adams, Julia (2005): *The Familial State: Ruling Families and Merchant Capitalism in Early Modern Europe.* Ithaca, NY: Cornell University Press.

Addi, Lahouari (2006): "En Algérie, du Conflit Armé à la Violence Sociale," *Le Monde Diplomatique* April 2006: 6–7.

Agüero, Felipe (1990): "Los Militares y la Democracia en Venezuela," in Louis W. Goodman, Johanna S. R. Mendelson, and Juan Rial, eds., *Los Militares y la Democracia. El Futuro de las Relaciones Cívico-Militares en América Latina.* Montevideo, Uruguay: PEITHO.

Alapuro, Risto (1988): *State and Revolution in Finland.* Berkeley: University of California Press.

Alapuro, Risto and Markku Lonkila (2004): "Russians' and Estonians' Networks in a Tallinn Factory," in Risto Alapuro, Ilkka Liikanen, and Markku Lonkila, eds., *Beyond Post-Soviet Transition: Micro Perspectives on Challenge and Survival in Russia and Estonia.* Saarijärvi, Finland: Kikimora Publications.

Alexander, Gerard (2002): *The Sources of Democratic Consolidation.* Ithaca, NY: Cornell University Press.

Amnesty International (2001): "Jamaica. Police Killings: Appeals against Impunity," http://web.amnesty.org/library/print/ENAMR380122001, viewed 5 April 2005.

Anderson, Eugene N. and Pauline R. Anderson (1967): *Political Institutions and Social Change in Continental Europe in the Nineteenth Century.* Berkeley: University of California Press.

Anderson, Grace M. (1974): *Networks of Contact: The Portuguese and Toronto.* Waterloo, ON: Wilfrid Laurier University Publications.

Andrews, George Reid and Herrick Chapman (1995): eds., *The Social Construction of Democracy, 1870–1990.* New York: New York University Press.

Andrey, Georges (1986): "La Quête d'un État National," in Jean-Claude Fayez, ed., *Nouvelle Histoire de la Suisse et des Suisses*. Lausanne, Switzerland: Payot.

Anthony, Denise and Christine Horne (2003): "Gender and Cooperation: Explaining Loan Repayment in Micro-Credit Groups," *Social Psychology Quarterly* 66: 293–302.

AR Algeria (2004): "Algeria," *The Annual Register. A Record of World Events 1988*: 221–223.

AR Russia (1997): "Russia," *The Annual Register. A Record of World Events 1997*: 135–140.

(2004): "Russia," *The Annual Register. A Record of World Events 2004*: 105–110.

AR South Africa (1989): "South Africa," *The Annual Register. A Record of World Events 1989*: 292–296.

AR USSR (1988): "Union of Soviet Socialist Republics," *The Annual Register. A Record of World Events 1988*: 103–114.

Arblaster, Anthony (1987): *Democracy*. Minncapolis: University of Minnesota Press.

Ardant, Gabriel (1971, 1972): *Histoire de l'Impôt*. Paris: Fayard. 2 vols.

Ashforth, Adam (1990): *The Politics of Official Discourse in Twentieth-Century South Africa*. Oxford: Clarendon Press.

(2005): *Witchcraft, Violence, and Democracy in South Africa*. Chicago: University of Chicago Press.

Auyero, Javier (1997): "Evita como *Performance*. Mediación y Resolución de Problemas entre los Pobres Urbanos del Gran Buenos Aires," in Javier Auyero, ed., *¿Favores por Votes? Estudios Sobre Clientelismo Politico Contemporáneo*. Buenos Aires: Editorial Losada.

(2001): *Poor People's Politics: Peronist Survival Networks and the Legacy of Evita*. Durham, NC: Duke University Press.

(2002): *La Protesta. Retratos de la Beligerencia Popular en la Argentina Democratica*. Buenos Aires: Libros del Rojas.

(2003): *Contentious Lives. Two Argentine Women, Two Protests, and the Quest for Recognition*. Durham, NC: Duke University Press.

Avert (2006): "South Africa: HIV/AIDS Statistics," www.avert.org/safricastats.htm, viewed 18 April 2006.

Baily, Samuel L. (1999): *Immigrants in the Land of Promise: Italians in Buenos Aires and New York City, 1870–1914*. Ithaca, NY: Cornell University Press.

Ballbé, Manuel (1985): *Orden Público y Militarismo en la España Constitucional (1812–1983)*. Madrid: Alianza. 2nd ed.

Barber, Benjamin (1974): *The Death of Communal Liberty: The History of Freedom in a Swiss Mountain Canton*. Princeton, NJ: Princton University Press.

Bates, Robert H. et al. (1998): *Analytical Narratives*. Princeton, NJ: Princeton University Press.

Bax, Mart (1976): *Harpstrings and Confessions: Machine-Style Politics in the Irish Republic*. Amsterdam: Van Gorcum.

Bayat, Asef (1997): *Street Politics: Poor People's Movements in Iran*. New York: Columbia University Press.

Bayon, Denis (1999): *Les S. E. L., "Systèmes d'Échanges Locaux". Pour un Vrai Débat.* Levallois-Perret, France: Yves Michel.

Bearman, Peter S. (1993): *Relations into Rhetorics. Local Elite Social Structure in Norfolk, England, 1540–1640.* New Brunswick, NJ: Rutgers University Press.

Beissinger, Mark (1998): "Nationalist Violence and the State. Political Authority and Contentious Repertoires in the Former USSR," *Comparative Politics* 30: 401–433.

  (2001): *Nationalist Mobilization and the Collapse of the Soviet State.* Cambridge: Cambridge University Press.

Bensel, Richard Franklin (2004): *The American Ballot Box in the Mid-Nineteenth Century.* Cambridge: Cambridge University Press.

Bermeo, Nancy (2000): "Civil Society after Democracy: Some Conclusions," in Nancy Bermeo and Philip Nord, eds., *Civil Society before Democracy: Lessons from Nineteenth-Century Europe.* Lanham, MD: Rowman and Littlefield.

  (2003): *Ordinary People in Extraordinary Times. The Citizenry and the Breakdown of Democracy.* Princeton, NJ: Princeton University Press.

Bernstein, Thomas P. and Xiaobo Lü (2002): *Taxation without Representation in Contemporary Rural China.* Cambridge: Cambridge University Press.

Besley, Timothy (1995): "Nonmarket Institutions for Credit and Risk Sharing in Low-Income Countries," *Journal of Economic Perspectives* 9: 169–188.

Biggart, Nicole Woolsey (2001): "Banking on Each Other: The Situational Logic of Rotating Savings and Credit Associations," *Advances in Qualitative Organization Research* 3: 129–153.

Biggart, Nicole Woolsey and Richard P. Castanias (2001): "Collateralized Social Relations: The Social in Economic Calculation," *American Journal of Economics and Sociology* 60: 471–500.

Blickle, Peter (1997): ed., *Resistance, Representation, and Community.* Oxford: Clarendon Press.

Boix, Carles (2003): *Democracy and Redistribution.* Cambridge: Cambridge University Press.

Bollen, Kenneth A. and Pamela Paxton (2000): "Subjective Measures of Liberal Democracy," *Comparative Political Studies* 33: 58–86.

Bozzoli, Belinda (2004): *Theatres of Struggle and the End of Apartheid.* Edinburgh: Edinburgh University Press for the International African Institute, London.

te Brake, Wayne (1989): *Regents and Rebels: The Revolutionary World of the 18th Century Dutch City.* Oxford: Blackwell.

  (1990): "How Much in How Little? Dutch Revolution in Comparative Perspective," *Tijdschrift voor Sociale Geschiedenis* 16: 349–363.

  (1998): *Shaping History: Ordinary People in European Politics 1500–1700.* Berkeley: University of California Press.

Brass, Paul R. (1994): *The New Cambridge History of India. IV.1. The Politics of India since Independence.* Cambridge: Cambridge University Press. 2nd ed.

  (2003): *The Production of Hindu-Muslim Violence in Contemporary India.* Seattle: University of Washington Press.

Bratton, Michael and Nicolas van de Walle (1997): *Democratic Experiments in Africa: Regime Transitions in Comparative Perspective*. Cambridge: Cambridge University Press.

Braun, Rudolf (1960): *Industrialisierung und Volksleben*. Zurich, Switzerland: Rentsch.

(1965): *Sozialer und Kultureller Wandel in Einem Ländlichen Industriegebiet*. Zurich, Switzerland: Rentsch.

Brewer, John (1980): "The Wilkites and the Law, 1763–74: A Study of Radical Notions of Governance," in John Brewer and John Styles, eds., *An Ungovernable People: The English and their Law in the Seventeenth and Eighteenth Centuries*. New Brunswick, NJ: Rutgers University Press.

(1989): *The Sinews of Power. War, Money and the English State, 1688–1783*. New York: Knopf.

Buchan, Nancy R., Rachel T. A. Croson, and Robyn M. Dawes (2002): "Swift Neighbors and Persistent Strangers: A Cross-Cultural Investigation of Trust and Reciprocity in Social Exchange," *American Journal of Sociology* 108: 168–206.

Bunce, Val (2001): "Democratization and Economic Reform," *Annual Review of Political Science* 4: 43–66.

Burns, John F. (1998): "In the Final Stage of India's Election, a Fearful City Votes," *New York Times* 1 March, Y6.

Burt, Ronald S. and Marc Knez (1995): "Kinds of Third-Party Effects on Trust," *Rationality and Society* 7: 255–292.

Caramani, Daniele (2000): *The Societies of Europe: Elections in Western Europe since 1815. Electoral Results by Constituencies*. London: Macmillan.

(2003): *The Formation of National Electorates and Party Systems in Europe*. Cambridge: Cambridge University Press.

Casanova, Julián, Ángela Cenarro, Julita Cifuentes, Pilar Maluenda, and Pilar Salomón (1992): *El Pasado Oculto. Fascismo y Violencia en Aragón (1936–39)*. Madrid: Siglo Veintiuno de España.

Castrén, Anna-Maija and Markku Lonkila (2004): "Friendship in Finland and Russia from a Micro Perspective," in Anna-Maija Castrén, Markku Lonkila, and Matti Peltonen, eds., *Between Sociology and History: Essays on Microhistory, Collective Action, and Nation-Building*. Helsinki, Finland: SKS/Finnish Literature Society.

Centeno, Miguel Angel (2002): *Blood and Debt: War and the Nation-State in Latin America*. University Park: Pennsylvania State University Press.

Cerruti, Simona, Robert Descimon, and Maarten Prak (1995): eds., "Cittadinanze," *Quaderni Storici* 30: 281–514.

Chesnais, Jean-Claude (1976): *Les Morts Violentes en France depuis 1826. Comparaisons Internationales*. Paris: Presses Universitaires de France.

(1981): *Histoire de la Violence en Occident de 1800 à Nos Jours*. Paris: Robert Laffont.

Chesterman, Simon (2001): ed., *Civilians in War*. Boulder, CO: Lynne Rienner.

Clark, Janine A. (2004): "Islamist Women in Yemen: Informal Nodes of Activism," in Quintan Wictorowicz, ed., *Islamic Activism: A Social Movement Theory Approach*. Bloomington: Indiana University Press.

Cleary, Matthew R. and Susan C. Stokes (2006): *Democracy and the Culture of Skepticism: Political Trust in Argentina and Mexico*. New York: Russell Sage Foundation.

Cohen, Lizabeth (2003): *A Consumer's Republic: The Politics of Mass Consumption in Postwar America*. New York: Knopf.

Collier, David and Steven Levitsky (1997): "Democracy with Adjectives: Conceptual Innovation in Comparative Research," *World Politics* 49: 430–451.

Collier, Paul and Nicholas Sambanis (2005): eds., *Understanding Civil War*. Washington, DC: World Bank. 2 vols.

Collier, Ruth Berins (1999): *Paths toward Democracy: The Working Class and Elites in Western Europe and South America*. New York: Cambridge University Press.

Collier, Ruth Berins and David Collier (1991): *Shaping the Political Arena: Critical Junctures, the Labor Movement, and Regime Dynamics in Latin America*. Princeton, NJ: Princeton University Press.

Collins, Kathleen (2006): *Class Politics and Regime Transition in Central Asia*. Cambridge: Cambridge University Press.

Conzen, Kathleen Neils (1976): *Immigrant Milwaukee, 1836–1860: Accommodation and Community in a Frontier City*. Cambridge, MA: Harvard University Press.

Cook, Karen S. (2001): ed., *Trust in Society*. New York: Russell Sage Foundation.

Cordero-Guzmán, Héctor R., Robert C. Smith, and Ramón Grosfoguel (2001): eds., *Migration, Transnationalization, and Race in a Changing New York*. Philadelphia: Temple University Press.

Coronil, Fernando (1997): *The Magical State: Nature, Money, and Modernity in Venezuela*. Chicago: University of Chicago Press.

van Creveld, Martin (1989): *Technology and War from 2000 B.C. to the Present*. New York: Free Press.

(1991): *The Transformation of War*. New York: Free Press.

(1999): *The Rise and Decline of the State*. Cambridge: Cambridge University Press.

Cruz, Consuelo (2005): *Political Culture and Institutional Development in Costa Rica and Nicaragua: World Making in the Tropics*. Cambridge: Cambridge University Press.

Cruz, Rafael (1987): *El Partido Comunista de España en la II Republica*. Madrid: Alianza.

(1997): "'Sofía Loren, Sí; Montini, No'. Transformación y Crisis del Conflicto Anticlerical," *Ayer* 27: 181–217.

(2006): *En el Nombre del Pueblo. República, Rebelión y Guerra en la España de 1936*. Madrid: Siglo.

Curtin, Philip D. (1984): *Cross-Cultural Trade in World History*. Cambridge: Cambridge University Press.

Dahl, Robert A. (1998): *On Democracy*. New Haven, CT: Yale University Press.

(2005): "What Political Institutions Does Large-Scale Democracy Require?" *Political Science Quarterly* 120: 187–197.

Darr, Asaf (2003): "Gifting Practices and Interorganizational Relations: Constructing Obligation Networks in the Electronics Sector," *Sociological Forum* 18: 31–51.

Daunton, Martin (2001): *Trusting Leviathan: The Politics of Taxation in Britain, 1799–1914*. Cambridge: Cambridge University Press.

Davenport, Rodney and Christopher Saunders (2000): *South Africa: A Modern History*. New York: St. Martin's. 5th ed.

Davids, Karel and Jan Lucassen (1995): eds., *A Miracle Mirrored: The Dutch Republic in European Perspective*. Cambridge: Cambridge University Press.

Diamond, Larry (1999): *Developing Democracy. Toward Consolidation*. Baltimore: Johns Hopkins University Press.

Diamond, Larry et al. (2004): "The Quality of Democracy," *Journal of Democracy* 15: 20–109.

Diamandouros, P. Nikiforos (1997): "Southern Europe: A Third Wave Success Story," in Larry Diamond, Marc F. Plattner, Yun-han Chu, and Hung-mao Tien, eds., *Consolidating the Third Wave Democracies. Regional Challenges*. Baltimore: Johns Hopkins University Press.

Diani, Mario (1995): *Green Networks: A Structural Analysis of the Italian Environmental Movement*. Edinburgh: Edinburgh University Press.

Di Palma, Giuseppe (1990): *To Craft Democracies: An Essay on Democratic Transitions*. Berkeley: University of California Press.

DiMaggio, Paul (2001): ed., *The Twenty-First Century Firm: Changing Economic Organization in International Perspective*. Princeton, NJ: Princeton University Press.

DiMaggio, Paul and Hugh Louch (1998): "Socially Embedded Consumer Transactions: For What Kinds of Purchases Do People Most Often Use Networks?" *American Sociological Review* 63: 619–637.

Dunér, Bertil (1985): *Military Intervention in Civil Wars: The 1970s*. Aldershot, UK: Gower.

Ebbinghaus, Bernhard (1995): "The Siamese Twins: Citizenship Rights, Cleavage Formation, and Party-Union Relations in Western Europe," in Charles Tilly, ed., *Citizenship, Identity and Social History*. Cambridge: Cambridge University Press.

Echeverry, Juan Carlos, Natalia Salazar, and Verónica Navas (2001): "El Conflicto Colombiano en el Contexto Internacional," in Astrid Martínez, ed., *Economía, Crimen y Conflicto*. Bogotá: Universidad Nacional de Colombia.

Economist (2006): "The Net Closes In," 4 March: 40.

Elster, Jon (1999): *Alchemists of the Mind: Rationality and the Emotions*. Cambridge: Cambridge University Press.

Elster, Jon, Claus Offe, and Ulrich K. Preuss (1998): *Institutional Design in Post-Communist Societies. Rebuilding the Ship at Sea*. Cambridge: Cambridge University Press.

Engelstad, Fredrik and Øyvind Østerud (2004): eds., *Power and Democracy: Critical Interventions*. Aldershot, UK: Ashgate.

Eriksson, Mikael and Peter Wallensteen (2004): "Armed Conflict, 1989–2003," *Journal of Peace Research* 41: 625–636.

Evans, Ivan (1990): "The Native Affairs Department and the Reserves in the 1940s and 1950s," in Robin Cohen, Yvonne G. Muthien, and Abebe Zegeye, eds., *Repression and Resistance: Insider Accounts of Apartheid*. London: Hans Zell.

Fearon, James D. and David D. Laitin (2003): "Ethnicity, Insurgency, and Civil War," *American Political Science Review* 97: 75–90.

Feige, Edgar (1997): "Underground Activity and Institutional Change: Productive, Protective, and Predatory Behavior in Transition Economies," in Joan Nelson, Charles Tilly, and Lee Walker, eds., *Transforming Post-Communist Political Economies*. Washington, DC: National Academy Press.

Fernandez, Roberto and Doug McAdam (1988): "Social Networks and Social Movements: Multiorganizational Fields and Recruitment to Mississippi Freedom Summer," *Sociological Forum* 3: 357–382.

Figueroa, Victor M. (2006): "The Bolivarian Government of Hugo Chávez: Democratic Alternative for Latin America?" *Critical Sociology* 32: 187–212.

Finer, S. E. (1997): *The History of Government from the Earliest Times*. Oxford: Oxford University Press. 3 vols.

Fish, M. Steven (2001): "The Dynamics of Democratic Erosion," in Richard D. Anderson, Jr. et al., *Postcommunism and the Theory of Democracy*. Princeton, NJ: Princeton University Press.

(2005): *Democracy Derailed in Russia: The Failure of Open Politics*. Cambridge: Cambridge University Press.

Fontaine, Laurence (1993): *Histoire du Colportage en Europe XVe-XIXe Siècle*. Paris: Albin Michel.

Forte, Riccardo (2003): *Fuerzas Armadas, Cultura Política y Seguridad Interna. Origines y Fortalecimiento del Poder Militar en Argentina (1853–1943)*. Mexico City: Biblioteca de Signos.

Fredrickson, George M. (1981): *White Supremacy: A Comparative Study in American and South African History*. Oxford: Oxford University Press.

Freedom House (2002): "Freedom in the World 2002: The Democracy Gap," www.freedomhouse.org/research/survey2002.htm, viewed 29 March 2002.

(2005): "Table of Independent Countries 2005," www.freedomhouse.org/template.cfm?/page=211&year+2005, viewed 14 March 2006.

(2006): "Freedom in the World 2006: Selected Data from Freedom House's Annual Global Survey of Political Rights and Civil Liberties," www.freedomhouse.org/template.cfm?page=5, viewed 11 March 2006.

Freedom House Jamaica (2005): "Freedom in the World – Jamaica," www.freedomhouse.org/template.cfm?page=22&country=2956&year=2004&view=mof, viewed 27 February 2006.

Freedom House Kazakhstan (2005): "Freedom in the World – Kazakhstan," www.freedomhouse.org/template.cfm?page=22&country=6764&year=2005&view=mof, viewed 27 February 2006.

Gambetta, Diego (1993): *The Sicilian Mafia: The Business of Private Protection*. Cambridge, MA: Harvard University Press.

Ganguly, Sumit (1999): "Explaining India's Transition to Democracy," in Lisa Anderson, ed., *Transitions to Democracy*. New York: Columbia University Press.

Gastil, Raymond Duncan (1991): "The Comparative Survey of Freedom: Experiences and Suggestions," in Alex Inkeles, ed., *On Measuring Democracy: Its Consequences and Concomitants*. New Brunswick, NJ: Transaction.

Geddes, Barbara (1999): "What Do We Know about Democratization after Twenty Years?" *Annual Review of Political Science* 2: 115–144.

Genieys, William (1997): *Les Élites Espagnoles Face à l'État. Changements de Régimes Politiques et Dynamiques Centre-Périphéries*. Paris: L'Harmattan.

Gentles, Ian (1992): *The New Model Army in England, Ireland and Scotland, 1645–1653*. Oxford: Blackwell.

(2001): "The *Agreements of the People* and their Political Contexts, 1647–1649," in Michael Mendle, ed., *The Putney Debates of 1647: The Army, the Levellers, and the English State*. Cambridge: Cambridge University Press.

Ghobarah, Hazem Adam, Paul Huth, and Bruce Russett (2003): "Civil Wars Kill and Maim People – Long after the Shooting Stops," *American Political Science Review* 97: 189–202.

Glete, Jan (2002): *War and the State in Early Modern Europe: Spain, the Dutch Republic, and Sweden as Fiscal-Military States, 1500–1660*. London: Routledge.

González Calleja, Eduardo (1999): *El Máuser y el Sufragio. Orden Público, Subversion y Violencia Política en la Crisis de la Restauración (1917–1931)*. Madrid: Consejo Superior de Investigaciones Científicas.

Goodin, Robert E., Bruce Headey, Ruud Muffels, and Henk-Jan Dirven (1999): *The Real Worlds of Welfare Capitalism*. Cambridge: Cambridge University Press.

Goodwin, Jeff (2001): *No Other Way Out: States and Revolutionary Movements, 1945–1991*. Cambridge: Cambridge University Press.

(2005): "Revolutions and Revolutionary Movements," in Thomas Janoski, Robert R. Alford, Alexander M. Hicks, and Mildred A. Schwartz, eds., *Handbook of Political Sociology: States, Civil Societies, and Globalization*. Cambridge: Cambridge University Press.

Gould, Roger V. (1995): *Insurgent Identities: Class, Community, and Protest in Paris from 1848 to the Commune*. Chicago: University of Chicago Press.

(1999): "Collective Violence and Group Solidarity: Evidence from a Feuding Society," *American Sociological Review* 64: 356–380.

(2003): *Collision of Wills: How Ambiguity about Social Rank Breeds Conflict*. Chicago: University of Chicago Press.

Granovetter, Mark (1995): "The Economic Sociology of Firms and Entrepreneurs," in Alejandro Portes, ed., *The Economic Sociology of Immigration: Essays on Networks, Ethnicity, and Entrepreneurship*. New York: Russell Sage Foundation.

Griffen, Clyde and Sally Griffen (1978): *Natives and Newcomers: The Ordering of Opportunity in Mid-Nineteenth-Century Poughkeepsie*. Cambridge, MA: Harvard University Press.

Grimson, Alejandro (1999): *Relatos de la Diferencia y la Igualdad. Los Bolivianos en Buenos Aires*. Buenos Aires: Editorial Universitaria de Buenos Aires.

Grimsted, David (1998): *American Mobbing, 1828–1861: Toward Civil War.* New York: Oxford University Press.

Gruner, Erich (1968): *Die Arbeiter in der Schweiz im 19. Jahrhundert.* Bern, Switzerland: Francke.

Gschwind, Franz (1977): *Bevölkerungsentwicklung und Wirtschaftsstruktur der Landschaft Basel im 18. Jahrhundert.* Liestal, Switzerland: Kantonale Drucksachen- und Materialzentrale.

Guinnane, Timothy W. (2005): "Trust: A Concept Too Many," *Jahrbuch für Wirtschaftsgeschichte* 2005, Part I: 77–92.

Guiso, Luigi, Paola Sapienza, and Luigi Zingales (2004): "The Role of Social Capital in Financial Development," *American Economic Review* 94: 526–556.

Gurr, Ted Robert, Keith Jaggers, and Will H. Moore (1990): "The Transformation of the Western State: The Growth of Democracy, Autocracy, and State Power since 1800," *Studies in Comparative International Development* 25: 73–108.

Haber, Stephen, Armando Razo, and Noel Maurer (2003): *The Politics of Property Rights: Political Instability, Credible Commitments, and Economic Growth in Mexico, 1876–1929.* Cambridge: Cambridge University Press.

't Hart, Marjolein (1993): *The Making of a Bourgeois State: War, Politics and Finance during the Dutch Revolt.* Manchester, UK: Manchester University Press.

Hart, Peter (1998): *The I.R.A. & Its Enemies: Violence and Community in Cork, 1916–1923.* Oxford: Clarendon Press.

Havik, Philip J. (1998): "Female Entrepreneurship in a Changing Environment: Gender, Kinship and Trade in the Guinea Bissau Region," in Carla Risseeuw and Kamala Ganesh, eds., *Negotiation and Social Space: A Gendered Analysis of Changing Kin and Security Networks in South Asia and Sub-Saharan Africa.* Walnut Creek, CA: AltaMira Press.

Head, Randolph C. (1995): *Early Modern Democracy in the Grisons. Social Order and Political Language in a Swiss Mountain Canton, 1470–1620.* Cambridge: Cambridge University Press.

Heimer, Carol A. (1985): *Reactive Risk and Rational Action: Managing Moral Hazard in Insurance Contracts.* Berkeley: University of California Press.

Held, David (1996): *Models of Democracy.* Stanford, CA: Stanford University Press. 2nd ed.

Henderson, Errol A. (1999): "Civil Wars," in Lester Kurtz, ed., *Encyclopedia of Violence, Peace, and Conflict.* San Diego, CA: Academic Press. Vol. I, 279–287.

Herzog, Don (1989): *Happy Slaves: A Critique of Consent Theory.* Chicago: University of Chicago Press.

Hironaka, Ann (2005): *Neverending Wars: The International Community, Weak States, and the Perpetuation of Civil War.* Cambridge, MA: Harvard University Press.

Hirschman, Albert O. (1970): *Exit, Voice, and Loyalty: Responses to Decline in Firms, Organizations, and States.* Cambridge, MA: Harvard University Press.

(1979): "The Turn to Authoritarianism in Latin America and the Search for its Economic Determinants," in David Collier, ed., *The New Authoritarianism in Latin America*. Princeton, NJ: Princeton University Press.

Hoffman, Philip T., Gilles Postel-Vinay, and Jean-Laurent Rosenthal (2000): *Priceless Markets: The Political Economy of Credit in Paris*. Chicago: University of Chicago Press.

Hoffmann, Stefan-Ludwig (2003): "Democracy and Associations in the Long Nineteenth Century: Toward a Transnational Perspective," *Journal of Modern History* 75: 269–299.

Holsti, Kalevi J. (1991): *Peace and War: Armed Conflicts and International Order 1648–1989*. Cambridge: Cambridge University Press.

 (1996): *The State, War, and the State of War*. Cambridge: Cambridge University Press.

Human Rights Watch (2004): "Letter Urging Jamaican Government to Protect Rights Defenders and Address Violence and Abuse Based on Sexual Orientation and HIV Status," www.hrw.org/english/docs/2004/ll/30/jamaic9750.txt. htm, viewed 5 April 2005.

 (2005): *World Report 2005. Events of 2004*. New York: Human Rights Watch.

 (2006): "Overview of Human Rights Issues in Russia," www.hrw.org/english/ docs/2006/01/18/russia2218.htm, viewed 30 April 2006.

Huntington, Samuel P. (1991): *The Third Wave. Democratization in the Late Twentieth Century*. Norman: University of Oklahoma Press.

Inkeles, Alex (1991): ed., *On Measuring Democracy: Its Consequences and Concomitants*. New Brunswick, NJ: Transaction.

Jamaica Constitution (2006): "Jamaica Constitution of 1962 with Reforms through 1999," www.georgetown.edu/pdba/Constitutions/Jamaica/jam62. html, viewed 27 January 2006.

Johnson, R. W. (2004): *South Africa: The First Man, the Last Nation*. London: Weidenfeld & Nicolson.

Joris, Elisabeth (1994): "Auswirkungen der Industrialisierung auf Alltag und Lebenszusammenhänge von Frauen im Zürcher Oberland (1820–1940)," in Joseba Agirreazkuenaga and Mikel Urquijo, eds., *Historias Regionales – Historia Nacional: La Confederación Helvetica*. Bilbao, Spain: Servicio Editorial, Universidad del País Vasco.

Joris, Elisabeth and Heidi Witzig (1992): *Brave Frauen, Aufmüpfige Weiber. Wie Sich die Industrialisierung auf Alltag und Lebenszusammenhänge von Frauen Auswirkte (1820–1940)*. Zurich, Switzerland: Chronos.

Jung, Courtney (2000): *Then I Was Black: South African Political Identities in Transition*. New Haven, CT: Yale University Press.

Jung, Courtney and Ian Shapiro (1995): "South Africa's Negotiated Transition: Democracy, Opposition, and the New Constitutional Order," *Politics & Society* 23: 269–308.

Kaldor, Mary (1999): *New & Old Wars: Organized Violence in a Global Era*. Cambridge: Polity.

Karatnycky, Adrian (2000): ed., *Freedom in the World: The Annual Survey of Political Rights & Civil Liberties 1999–2000*. New York: Freedom House.

Karatnycky, Adrian and Peter Ackerman (2005): "How Freedom Is Won: From Civic Resistance to Durable Democracy," www.freedomhouse.org/ 65.110.85.181/uploads/special_report/29.pdf, viewed 12 March 2006.

Kaufman, Jason (2002): *For the Common Good? American Civic Life and the Golden Age of Fraternity*. Oxford: Oxford University Press.

Kazakh Constitution (2006): "Republic of Kazakstan Constitution," www. geocities.com/CapitolHill/Lobby/2171/kzconst.html, viewed 20 January 2006.

Keogh, Dermot (2001): "Ireland at the Turn of the Century: 1994–2001," in T. W. Moody and F. X. Martin, eds., *The Course of Irish History*. Lanham, MD: Roberts Rinehart. 4th ed.

Kettering, Sharon (1993): "Brokerage at the Court of Louis XIV," *The Historical Journal* 36: 69–87.

Keyssar, Alexander (2000): *The Right to Vote: The Contested History of Democracy in the United States*. New York: Basic Books.

Khazanov, Anatoly M. (1995): *After the USSR: Ethnicity, Nationalism, and Politics in the Commonwealth of Independent States*. Madison: University of Wisconsin Press.

Kohli, Atul (1990): *Democracy and Discontent: India's Growing Crisis of Governability*. Cambridge: Cambridge University Press.

(1994): "Centralization and Powerlessness: India's Democracy in a Comparative Perspective," in Joel S. Migdal, Atul Kohli, and Vivienne Shue, eds., *State Power and Social Forces: Domination and Transformation in the Third World*. Cambridge: Cambridge University Press.

Kozub, Robert M. (2003): "Evolution of Taxation in England, 1700–1850: A Period of War and Industrialization," *Journal of European Economic History* 32: 363–390.

Kurzman, Charles (1998): "Waves of Democratization," *Studies in Comparative International Development* 33: 42–64.

Lafargue, Jérôme (1996): *Contestations Démocratiques en Afrique*. Paris: Karthala and IFRA.

Landa, Janet Tai (1994): *Trust, Ethnicity, and Identity: Beyond the New Institutional Economics of Ethnic Trading Networks, Contract Law, and Gift-Exchange*. Ann Arbor: University of Michigan Press.

Laurie, Bruce (1973): "Fire Companies and Gangs in Southwark: The 1840s," in Allen F. Davis and Mark H. Haller, eds., *The Peoples of Philadelphia: A History of Ethnic Groups and Lower-Class Life, 1790–1940*. Philadelphia: Temple University Press.

Ledeneva, Alena (1998): *Russia's Economy of Favours: Blat, Networking, and Informal Exchange*. Cambridge: Cambridge University Press.

(2004): "Genealogy of *Krugovaya Poruka*: Forced Trust as a Feature of Russian Political Culture," *Proceedings of the British Academy* 123: 85–108.

Levi, Margaret (1988): *Of Rule and Revenue*. Berkeley: University of California Press.

(1997): *Consent, Dissent, and Patriotism*. Cambridge: Cambridge University Press.

Levi, Margaret and Laura Stoker (2000): "Political Trust and Trustworthiness," *Annual Review of Political Science* 3: 475–508.

Licklider, Roy (1993): ed., *Stopping the Killing: How Civil Wars End*. New York: NYU Press.

Light, Ivan and Edna Bonacich (1988): *Immigrant Entrepreneurs: Koreans in Los Angeles, 1965–1982*. Berkeley: University of California Press.

Lijphart, Arend (1999): *Patterns of Democracy: Government Forms and Performance in Thirty-Six Countries*. New Haven, CT: Yale University Press. Rev. ed.

Lindert, Peter H. (2004): *Growing Public: Social Spending and Economic Growth since the Eighteenth Century*. Cambridge: Cambridge University Press. 2 vols.

Linz, Juan J. and Alfred Stepan (1996): *Problems of Democratic Transition and Consolidation: Southern Europe, South America, and Post-Communist Europe*. Baltimore: Johns Hopkins University Press.

Lodge, Tom (1996): "South Africa: Democracy and Development in a Post-Apartheid Society," in Adrian Leftwich, ed., *Democracy and Development: Theory and Practice*. London: Polity Press.

Lonkila, Markku (1999a): *Social Networks in Post-Soviet Russia*. Helsinki, Finland: Kikimora.

(1999b): "Post-Soviet Russia: A Society of Networks?" in Markku Kangaspuro, ed., *Russia: More Different than Most*. Helsinki, Finland: Kikimora.

López Maya, Margarita (1999): "La Protesta Popular Venezolana entre 1989 y 1993 (en el Umbral del Neoliberalismo)," in Margarita López Maya, ed., *Lucha Popular, Democracia, Neoliberalismo: Protesta Popular en América Latina en los Años de Ajuste*. Caracas, Venezuela: Nueva Sociedad.

López Maya, Margarita, David Smilde, and Keta Staphany (2002): *Protesta y Cultura en Venezuela. Los Marcos de Acción Colectiva en 1999*. Caracas, Venezuela: FACES-UCV, CENDES, FONACIT.

López-Alves, Fernando (2003): *La Formación del Estado y la Democracia en América Latina*. Bogotá, Colombia: Grupo Editorial Norma.

Luard, Evan (1987): *War in International Society*. New Haven, CT: Yale University Press.

Luebke, David Martin (1997): *His Majesty's Rebels: Communities, Factions, and Rural Revolt in the Black Forest, 1725–1745*. Ithaca, NY: Cornell University Press.

Lundqvist, Sven (1977): *Folkrörelserna i det Svenska Samhället, 1850–1920*. Stockholm: Almqvist & Wiksell.

MacCulloch, Diarmaid (2003): *Reformation: Europe's House Divided 1490–1700*. London: Allen Lane.

Machiavelli, Niccolò (1940): *The Prince and the Discourses*. New York: Modern Library.

MacLean, Lauren Morris (2004): "Empire of the Young: The Legacies of State Agricultural Policy on Local Capitalism and Social Support Networks in Ghana and Côte d'Ivoire," *Comparative Studies in Society and History* 46: 469–496.

Malefakis, Edward E. (1970): *Agrarian Reform and Peasant Revolution in Spain.* New Haven, CT: Yale University Press.

Manor, James (2004): "'Towel over Armpit': Small-Time Political 'Fixers' in India's States," in Ashutosh Varshney, ed., *India and the Politics of Developing Countries: Essays in Memory of Myron Weiner.* New Delhi: Sage Publications.

Maravall, José María and Julián Santamaria (1986): "Political Change in Spain and the Prospects for Democracy," in Guillermo O'Donnell, Philippe C. Schmitter, and Laurence Whitehead, eds., *Transitions from Authoritarian Rule: Southern Europe.* Baltimore: Johns Hopkins University Press.

Markoff, John (1996a): *The Abolition of Feudalism: Peasants, Lords, and Legislators in the French Revolution.* University Park: Pennsylvania State University Press.

(1996b): *Waves of Democracy: Social Movements and Political Change.* Thousand Oaks, CA: Pine Forge.

(2005): "Transitions to Democracy," in Thomas Janoski, Robert R. Alford, Alexander M. Hicks, and Mildred A. Schwartz, eds., *Handbook of Political Sociology: States, Civil Societies, and Globalization.* Cambridge: Cambridge University Press.

Marques, M. Margarida, Rui Santos and Fernanda Araújo (2001): "Ariadne's Thread: Cape Verdean Women in Transnational Webs," *Global Networks* 1: 283–306.

Marx, Anthony W. (1995): "Contested Citizenship: The Dynamics of Racial Identity and Social Movements," *International Review of Social History* 40: 159–183.

Mauro, Frédéric (1990): "Merchant Communities, 1350–1750," in James D. Tracy, ed., *The Rise of Merchant Empires: Long-Distance Trade in the Early Modern World, 1350–1750.* Cambridge: Cambridge University Press.

McCracken, J. L. (2001): "Northern Ireland: 1921–66," in T. W. Moody and F. X. Martin, eds., *The Course of Irish History.* Lanham, MD: Roberts Rinehart. 4th ed.

McFaul, Michael (1997): "Russia's Rough Ride," in Larry Diamond, Marc F. Plattner, Yun-han Chu, and Hung-mao Tien, eds., *Consolidating the Third Wave Democracies: Regional Challenges.* Baltimore: Johns Hopkins University Press.

Meisch, Lynn A. (2002): *Andean Entrepreneurs: Otavalo Merchants and Musicians in the Global Arena.* Austin: University of Texas Press.

Migdal, Joel S. (1988): *Strong Societies and Weak States: State-Society Relations and State Capabilities in the Third World.* Princeton, NJ: Princeton University Press.

Mihalisko, Kathleen J. (1997): "Belarus: Retreat to Authoritarianism," in Karen Dawisha and Bruce Parrott, eds., *Democratic Changes and Authoritarian Reactions in Russia, Ukraine, Belarus, and Moldova.* Cambridge: Cambridge University Press.

Montgomery, David (1993): *Citizen Worker: The Experience of Workers in the United States with Democracy and the Free Market during the Nineteenth Century.* Cambridge: Cambridge University Press.

(1998): ed., "Patronage, Paternalism, and Company Welfare," *International Labor and Working-Class History* 53: 1–163.

Morawska, Ewa (1985): *For Bread with Butter: Life-Worlds of East Central Europeans in Johnstown, Pennsylvania, 1890–1940*. Cambridge: Cambridge University Press.

(1996): *Insecure Prosperity: Small-Town Jews in Industrial America, 1890–1940*. Princeton, NJ: Princeton University Press.

(2003): "Disciplinary Agendas and Analytic Strategies of Research on Immigration and Transnationalism: Challenges of Interdisciplinary Knowledge," *International Migration Review* 37: 611–640.

Morgan, Edmund S. (1988): *Inventing the People: The Rise of Popular Sovereignty in England and America*. New York: Norton.

Morlino, Leonardo (2003): *Democrazie e Democratizzazioni*. Bologna, Italy: Il Mulino.

Moya, Jose C. (1998): *Cousins and Strangers: Spanish Immigrants in Buenos Aires, 1850–1930*. Berkeley: University of California Press.

Mueller, John (2004): *The Remnants of War*. Ithaca, NY: Cornell University Press.

Muldrew, Craig (1993): "Interpreting the Market: The Ethics of Credit and Community Relations in Early Modern England," *Social History* 18: 163–183.

(1998): *The Economy of Obligation*. London: Macmillan.

(2001): "'Hard Food for Midas': Cash and its Social Value in Early Modern England," *Past and Present* 170: 78–120.

Murray, Martin (1987): *South Africa: Time of Agony, Time of Destiny*. London: Verso.

Myers, Steven Lee (2006): "Days before Vote, Belarus Cracks Down on Opposition," *New York Times* 17 March, A3.

Myers, Steven Lee and C. J. Chivers (2006): "Protesters Charge Fraud in Belarus Presidential Election," *New York Times* 20 March, A11.

Nabholz, Hans, Leonhard von Muralt, Richard Feller, and Edgar Bonjour (1938): *Geschichte der Schweiz*. Zurich, Switzerland: Schultheiss and Co. 2 vols.

Narayan, Deepa and Patti Petesch (2002): eds., *Voices of the Poor: From Many Lands*. New York: Oxford University Press and Washington, DC: World Bank.

NED (2006): National Endowment for Democracy website, www.ned.org, viewed 24 May 2006.

Nicolas, Jean (2002): *La Rébellion Française. Mouvements Populaires et Conscience Sociale 1661–1789*. Paris: Seuil.

North, Douglass C. (2005): *Understanding the Process of Economic Change*. Princeton, NJ: Princeton University Press.

O'Donnell, Guillermo (1999): *Counterpoints: Selected Essays on Authoritarianism and Democratization*. Notre Dame, IN: University of Notre Dame Press.

Ogilvie, Sheilagh (2005): "The Use and Abuse of Trust: Social Capital and Its Deployment by Early Modern Guilds," *Jahrbuch für Wirtschaftsgeschichte* 2005, Part I: 15–52.

Ohlemacher, Thomas (1993): *Brücken der Mobilisierung. Soziale Relais und Persönliche Netzwerke in Bürgerinitiativen Gegen Militärischen Tiefflug*. Wiesbaden, Germany: Deutscher Universitäts Verlag.

Öhngren, Bo (1974): *Folk i Rörelse. Samhällsutveckling, Flyttningsmonster och Folkrörelser i Eskilstuna 1870–1900*. Uppsala, Sweden: Almqvist & Wicksell.

Olcott, Martha Brill (2002): *Kazakhstan. Unfulfilled Promise*. Washington, DC: Carnegie Endowment for International Peace.

Olivier, Johan (1991): "State Repression and Collective Action in South Africa, 1970–84," *South African Journal of Sociology* 22: 109–117.

Opp, Karl-Dieter and Christiane Gern (1993): "Dissident Groups, Personal Networks, and Spontaneous Cooperation: The East German Revolution of 1989," *American Sociological Review* 58: 659–680.

Ortega Ortiz, Reynaldo Yunuen (2000): "Comparing Types of Transitions: Spain and Mexico," *Democratization* 7: 65–92.

(2001): ed., *Caminos a la Democracia*. Mexico City: El Colegio de México.

Ostergren, Robert C. (1988): *A Community Transplanted: The Trans-Atlantic Experience of a Swedish Immigrant Settlement in the Upper Middle West, 1835–1915*. Uppsala, Sweden: Acta Universitatis Upsaliensis.

Ostrom, Elinor (1990): *Governing the Commons: The Evolution of Institutions for Collective Action*. Cambridge: Cambridge University Press.

(1998): "A Behavioral Approach to the Rational Choice Theory of Collective Action," *American Political Science Review* 92: 1–22.

Palmer, R. R. (1959, 1964): *The Age of the Democratic Revolution*. Princeton, NJ: Princeton University Press. 2 vols.

Passy, Florence (1998): *L'Action Altruiste. Contraintes et Opportunités de l'Engagement dans les Mouvements Sociaux*. Geneva, Switzerland: Droz.

(2001): "Socialization, Connection, and the Structure/Agency Gap: A Specification of the Impact of Networks on Participation in Social Movements," *Mobilization* 6: 173–192.

Pastor, Reyna, Esther Pascua, Ana Rodríguez-López, and Pablo Sánchez-León (2002): *Beyond the Market: Transactions, Property and Social Networks in Monastic Galicia 1200–1300*. Leiden, Netherlands: Brill.

Paxton, Pamela (1999): "Is Social Capital Declining in the United States? A Multiple Indicator Assessment," *American Journal of Sociology* 108: 88–127.

(2000): "Women's Suffrage in the Measurement of Democracy: Problems of Operationalization," *Studies in Comparative International Development* 35: 92–111.

Payne, Stanley G. (1967): *Politics and the Military in Modern Spain*. Stanford, CA: Stanford University Press.

(2000): *The Franco Regime, 1936–1975*. London: Phoenix Press. Rev. ed.

Piano, Aili and Arch Puddington (2004): *Freedom in the World 2004. The Annual Survey of Political Rights & Civil Liberties*. New York and Washington, DC: Freedom House.

Piipponen, Minna (2004): "Work-Related Ties in the Everyday Life of a Russian Karelian Mill Community," in Risto Alapuro, Ilkka Liikanen, and Markku Lonkila, eds., *Beyond Post-Soviet Transition: Micro Perspectives on Challenge and Survival in Russia and Estonia*. Saarijärvi, Finland: Kikimora.

Portes, Alejandro (1995): ed., *The Economic Sociology of Immigration: Essays on Networks, Ethnicity, and Entrepreneurship*. New York: Russell Sage Foundation.

Postel-Vinay, Gilles (1998): *La Terre et l'Argent. L'Agriculture et le Crédit en France du XVIIIe au Début du Xxe Siècle*. Paris: Albin Michel.

Powell, Walter W. (1990): "Neither Market Nor Hierarchy: Network Forms of Organization," in Barry Staw and Lawrence L. Cummings, eds., *Research in Organizational Behavior*. Greenwich, CT: JAI Press.

Powell, Walter W. and Laurel Smith-Doerr (1994): "Networks and Economic Life," in Neil J. Smelser and Richard Swedberg, eds., *The Handbook of Economic Sociology*. Princeton, NJ: Princeton University Press and New York: Russell Sage Foundation.

Prak, Maarten (1991): "Citizen Radicalism and Democracy in the Dutch Republic: The Patriot Movement of the 1780s," *Theory and Society* 20: 73–102.

(1999): "Burghers into Citizens: Urban and National Citizenship in the Netherlands during the Revolutionary Era (c. 1800)," in Michael P. Hanagan and Charles Tilly, eds., *Expanding Citizenship, Reconfiguring States*. Lanham, MD: Rowman and Littlefield.

Price, Robert M. (1991): *The Apartheid State in Crisis: Political Transformation in South Africa 1975–1990*. New York: Oxford University Press.

Przeworski, Adam, Michael Alvarez, José Antonio Cheibub, and Fernando Limongi (2000): *Democracy and Development: Political Institutions and Well-Being in the World, 1950–1990*. Cambridge: Cambridge University Press.

Putnam, Robert D., Robert Leonardi, and Raffaella Y. Nanetti (1993): *Making Democracy Work: Civic Traditions in Modern Italy*. Princeton, NJ: Princeton University Press.

(2000): *Bowling Alone: The Collapse and Revival of American Community*. New York: Simon & Schuster.

Ray, Raka and Mary Fainsod Katzenstein (2005): "Introduction: In the Beginning, There Was the Nehruvian State," in Raka Ray and Mary Fainsod Katzenstein, eds., *Social Movements in India. Poverty, Power, and Politics*. Lanham, MD: Rowman and Littlefield.

Remak, Joachim (1993): *A Very Civil War: The Swiss Sonderbund War of 1847*. Boulder, CO: Westview.

Rosenband, Leonard N. (1999): "Social Capital in the Early Industrial Revolution," *Journal of Interdisciplinary History* 29: 435–458.

Rotberg, Robert (1999): ed., "Patterns of Social Capital: Stability and Change in Comparative Perspective," Special issue, *Journal of Interdisciplinary History* 29: nos. 3 and 4.

Rouquié, Alain (1987): *The Military and the State in Latin America*. Berkeley: University of California Press.

Rueschemeyer, Dietrich, Evelyne Huber Stephens, and John D. Stephens (1992): *Capitalist Development and Democracy*. Chicago: University of Chicago Press.

Rummel, R. J. (1994): *Death by Government*. New Brunswick, NJ: Transaction.

Sabato, Hilda (2001): *The Many and the Few: Political Participation in Republican Buenos Aires*. Stanford, CA: Stanford University Press.

Sahlins, Peter (2004): *Unnaturally French: Foreign Citizens in the Old Regime and After*. Ithaca, NY: Cornell University Press.

Sauter, Beat Walter (1972): *Herkunft und Entstehung der Tessiner Kantonsverfassung von 1830*. Zurich, Switzerland: Schulthess.

Schama, Simon (1977): *Patriots and Liberators. Revolution in the Netherlands 1780–1813*. London: Collins.

Schatz, Edward (2006): "Access by Accident: Legitimacy Claims and Democracy Promotion in Authoritarian Central Asia," *International Political Science Review* 27: 263–284.

Scherzer, Kenneth A. (1992): *The Unbounded Community: Neighborhood Life and Social Structure in New York City, 1830–1875*. Durham, NC: Duke University Press.

Schmidt, Steffen W., Laura Guasti, Carl H. Landé, and James C. Scott (1977): eds., *Friends, Followers, and Factions: A Reader in Political Clientelism*. Berkeley: University of California Press.

Schmitt, Gary J. (2006): "Natural Gas: The Next Energy Crisis?" *Issues in Science and Technology*, Summer: 59–64.

Schmitter, Philippe C. and Terry Lynn Karl (1991): "What Democracy Is . . . and Is Not," *Journal of Democracy* 2: 77–88.

Schock, Kurt (2005): *Unarmed Insurrections: People Power Movements in Non-democracies*. Minneapolis: University of Minnesota Press.

Science (2006): "Qatar Taps Wells of Knowledge," 312 (7 April): 46–47.

Seekings, Jeremy and Nicoli Nattrass (2005): *Class, Race, and Inequality in South Africa*. New Haven, CT: Yale University Press.

Seip, Jens Arup (1974, 1981): *Utsikt over Norges Historie*. Oslo, Norway: Gylendal Norsk Forlag. 2 vols.

Seligman, Adam (1997): *The Problem of Trust*. Princeton, NJ: Princeton University Press.

Séréni, Jean-Pierre (2006): "Où Va l'Argent des Hydrocarbures," *Le Monde Diplomatique* April 2006: 8.

Shapiro, Susan P. (1987): "The Social Control of Impersonal Trust," *American Journal of Sociology* 93: 623–658.

Sheller, Mimi (2000): *Democracy after Slavery: Black Publics and Peasant Radicalism in Haiti and Jamaica*. London: Macmillan (Warwick University Caribbean Studies).

Shorter, Edward and Charles Tilly (1974): *Strikes in France, 1830–1968*. Cambridge: Cambridge University Press.

Singerman, Diane (1995): *Avenues of Participation: Family, Politics, and Networks in Urban Quarters of Cairo*. Princeton, NJ: Princeton University Press.

(2004): "The Networked World of Islamist Social Movements," in Quintan Wiktorowicz, ed., *Islamic Activism: A Social Movement Theory Approach*. Bloomington: Indiana University Press.

Skocpol, Theda (2003): *Diminished Democracy: From Membership to Management in American Civic Life*. Norman: University of Oklahoma Press.

(2004): "Voice and Inequality: The Transformation of American Civic Democracy," *Perspectives on Politics* 2: 3–20.

Skocpol, Theda and Morris P. Fiorina (1999): eds., *Civic Engagement in American Democracy*. Washington, DC: Brookings Institution and New York: Russell Sage Foundation.

Solnick, Steven L. (1998): *Stealing the State: Control and Collapse in Soviet Institutions*. Cambridge, MA: Harvard University Press.

Sørensen, Georg (1998): *Democracy and Democratization. Processes and Prospects in a Changing World*. Boulder, CO: Westview.

Soto Carmona, Álvaro (1988): *El Trabajo Industrial en la España Contemporanea (1874–1936)*. Barcelona: Anthropos.

Spilerman, Seymour (2000): "Wealth and Stratification Processes," *Annual Review of Sociology* 26: 497–524.

Stark, Oded (1995): *Altruism and Beyond: An Economic Analysis of Transfers and Exchanges within Families and Groups*. Cambridge: Cambridge University Press.

Stenius, Henrik (1987): *Frivilligt, Jämlikt, Samfällt. Föreningsväsendets utveckling I Finland fram till 1900-talets början med speciell hänsyn till massorganisationsprincipens genombrott*. Helsinki, Finland: Svenska Litteratursällskapet I Finland.

Stone, Lawrence (1994): ed., *An Imperial State at War: Britain from 1689 to 1815*. London: Routledge.

Strand, Håvard, Lars Wilhelmsen, and Nils Petter Gleditsch (2004): *Armed Conflict Dataset Codebook*. Oslo, Norway: International Peace Research Institute.

Suny, Ronald Grigor (1993): *The Revenge of the Past: Nationalism, Revolution, and the Collapse of the Soviet Union*. Stanford, CA: Stanford University Press.

Tarrow, Sidney and Doug McAdam (2005): "Scale Shift in Transnational Contention," in Donatella della Porta and Sidney Tarrow, eds. *Transnational Protest and Global Activism*. Lanham, MD: Rowman and Littlefield.

Terreblanche, Sampie (2002): *A History of Inequality in South Africa, 1652–2002*. Pietermaritzburg, South Africa: University of Natal Press and Sandton, South Africa: KMM Review Publishing.

Thompson, Leonard (2000): *A History of South Africa*. New Haven, CT: Yale University Press. 3rd ed.

Thucydides (1934): Joseph Gavorse, ed., *The Complete Writings of Thucydides: The Peloponnesian War*. New York: Modern Library.

Tilly, Charles (1964): *The Vendée*. Cambridge, MA: Harvard University Press.
(1986): *The Contentious French*. Cambridge, MA: Harvard University Press.
(1990): "Transplanted Networks," in Virginia Yans-McLaughlin, ed., *Immigration Reconsidered: History, Sociology, and Politics*. New York: Oxford University Press.
(1992): *Coercion, Capital, and European States, 990–1992*. Oxford: Blackwell. Rev. ed.

(1993): *European Revolutions, 1492–1992.* Oxford: Blackwell.

(1995): *Popular Contention in Great Britain, 1758–1834.* Cambridge, MA: Harvard University Press.

(1997): "Parliamentarization of Popular Contention in Great Britain, 1758–1834," *Theory and Society* 26: 245–273.

(1998): *Durable Inequality.* Berkeley: University of California Press.

(2000): "Chain Migration and Opportunity Hoarding," in Janina W. Dacyl and Charles Westin, eds., *Governance of Cultural Diversity.* Stockholm: Centre for Research in International Migration and Ethnic Relations, University of Stockholm.

(2003): *The Politics of Collective Violence.* Cambridge: Cambridge University Press.

(2004): *Contention and Democracy in Europe, 1650–2000.* Cambridge: Cambridge University Press.

(2005a): "Historical Perspectives on Inequality," in Mary Romero and Eric Margolis, eds., *The Blackwell Companion to Social Inequalities.* Oxford: Blackwell.

(2005b): *Trust and Rule.* Cambridge: Cambridge University Press.

(2006): *Regimes and Repertoires.* Chicago: University of Chicago Press.

Tilly, Charles and Wim P. Blockmans (1994): eds., *Cities and the Rise of States in Europe A. D. 1000 to 1800.* Boulder, CO: Westview.

Tilly, Charles et al. (1995): "State-Incited Violence, 1900–1999," *Political Power and Social Theory* 9: 161–225.

Tishkov, Valery (1997): *Ethnicity, Nationalism and Conflict in and after the Soviet Union: The Mind Aflame.* London: Sage.

Titarenko, Larissa, John D. McCarthy, Clark McPhail, and Boguslaw Augustyn (2001): "The Interaction of State Repression, Protest Form and Protest Sponsor Strength during the Transition from Communism in Minsk, Belarus, 1990–1995," *Mobilization* 6: 129–150.

Tsai, Kellee S. (2002): *Back-Alley Banking: Private Entrepreneurs in China.* Ithaca, NY: Cornell University Press.

UNDP [United Nations Development Programme] (2005): *Human Development Report 2005.* New York: Oxford University Press.

U.S. Department of Commerce, Bureau of the Census (1975): *Historical Statistics of the United States, Colonial Times to 1970.* Washington, DC: U.S. Department of Commerce. 2 vols.

Uslaner, Eric M. (2002): *The Moral Foundations of Trust.* Cambridge: Cambridge University Press.

Vanhanen, Tatu (1997): *Prospects of Democracy: A Study of 172 Countries.* London: Routledge.

Wåhlin, Vagn (1986): "Opposition og statsmagt," in Flemming Mikkelen, ed., *Protest og Oprør. Kollektive aktioner I Danmark 1700–1985.* Aarhus, Denmark: Modtryk.

Walter, Barbara F. and Jack Snyder (1999): eds., *Civil Wars, Insecurity, and Intervention.* New York: Columbia University Press.

Warren, Mark E. (1999): ed., *Democracy and Trust.* Cambridge: Cambridge University Press.

Webber, Carolyn and Aaron Wildavsky (1986): *A History of Taxation and Expenditure in the Western World*. New York: Simon & Schuster.

Weber, Linda R. and Allison I. Carter (2003): *The Social Construction of Trust*. New York: Kluwer/Plenum.

Weiner, Myron (2001): "The Struggle for Equality: Caste in Indian Politics," in Atul Kohli, ed., *The Success of India's Democracy*. Cambridge: Cambridge University Press.

Wells, Charlotte C. (1995): *Law and Citizenship in Early Modern France*. Baltimore: Johns Hopkins University Press.

Westrich, Sal Alexander (1972): *The Ormée of Bordeaux. A Revolution during the Fronde*. Baltimore: Johns Hopkins University Press.

White, Harrison C. (2002): *Markets from Networks: Socioeconomic Models of Production*. Princeton, NJ: Princeton University Press.

White, Robert W. (1993): "On Measuring Political Violence: Northern Ireland, 1969 to 1980," *American Sociological Review* 58: 575–585.

Whitehead, Laurence (2002): *Democratization: Theory and Experience*. Oxford: Oxford University Press.

Wiktorowicz, Quintan (2001): *The Management of Islamic Activism. Salafis, the Muslim Brotherhood, and State Power in Jordan*. Albany: State University of New York Press.

Willerton, John P. (1992): *Patronage and Politics in the USSR*. Cambridge: Cambridge University Press.

Wilson, Richard A. (2001): *The Politics of Truth and Reconciliation in South Africa: Legitimizing the Post-Apartheid State*. Cambridge: Cambridge University Press.

Woloch, Isser (1970): *Jacobin Legacy: The Democratic Movement under the Directory*. Princeton, NJ: Princeton University Press.

(1994): *The New Regime: Transformations of the French Civic Order, 1789–1820s*. New York: Norton.

World Bank (2004 [sic]): *World Development Report 2005: A Better Investment Climate for Everyone*. New York: Oxford University Press and Washington, DC: World Bank.

(2006): *Equity and Development: World Development Report 2006*. Washington, DC: World Bank and New York: Oxford University Press.

Wuthnow, Robert (2004): "Trust as an Aspect of Social Structure," in Jeffrey C. Alexander, Gary T. Marx, and Christine L. Williams, eds., *Self, Social Structure, and Beliefs: Explorations in Sociology*. Berkeley: University of California Press.

Yamagishi, Toshio and Midori Yamagishi (1994): "Trust and Commitment in the United States and Japan," *Motivation and Emotion* 18: 129–166.

Yashar, Deborah J. (1997): *Demanding Democracy: Reform and Reaction in Costa Rica and Guatemala, 1870s–1950s*. Stanford, CA: Stanford University Press.

Zelizer, Viviana A. (2002): "La Construction des Circuits de Commerce: Notes sur l'Importance des Circuits Personnels et Impersonnels," in Jean-Michel Servet and Isabelle Guérin, *Exclusion et Liens Financiers: Rapport du Centre Walras*. Paris: Economica.

(2004): "Circuits within Capitalism," in Victor Nee and Richard Swedberg, eds, *The Economic Sociology of Capitalism*, Princeton, NJ: Princeton University Press.

(2005a): "Culture and Consumption," in Neil J. Smelser and Richard Swedberg, eds., *The Handbook of Economic Sociology*. Princeton, NJ: Princeton University Press and New York: Russell Sage Foundation. 2nd ed.

(2005b): *The Purchase of Intimacy*. Princeton, NJ: Princeton University Press.

Zuern, Elke (2001): "South Africa's Civics in Transition: Agents of Change or Structures of Constraint?" *Politikon* 28: 5–20.

(2002): "Fighting for Democracy: Popular Organizations and Postapartheid Government in South Africa," *African Studies Review* 45: 77–102.

de Zwart, Frank (1994): *The Bureaucratic Merry-Go-Round: Manipulating the Transfer of Indian Civil Servants*. Amsterdam: Amsterdam University Press.

Index

CPSIA information can be obtained
at www.ICGtesting.com
Printed in the USA
LVOW10s2050021216

515536LV00002B/232/P